Green Innovation and Industrial Organization

World Scientific-Economic Growth Centre Contemporary Series in Modern Economy

---

Published:

Vol. 4 *Green Innovation and Industrial Organization*
edited by Joanna Poyago-Theotoky

Vol. 3 *Managing for Sustainability: The Role of Human Resource Management in Advancing SDG Goals*
edited by Chitra Krishnan, Abhishek Behl & Arup Varma

Vol. 2 *The Prosperous Society: From Economics of Scarcity to Economics of Abundance*
by Yoram Kirsh

Vol. 1 *Economic Integration Among D-8 Muslim Countries: Prospects and Challenges*
edited by Ahmed M Khalid, R James Ferguson & M Niaz Asadullah

World Scientific-Economic Growth Centre
Contemporary Series in Modern Economy 4

Series Editor: Euston Quah

Green Innovation and Industrial Organization

Editor

Joanna Poyago-Theotoky
University of Salento, Italy

World Scientific

NEW JERSEY • LONDON • SINGAPORE • BEIJING • SHANGHAI • HONG KONG • TAIPEI • CHENNAI • TOKYO

Published by

World Scientific Publishing Co. Pte. Ltd.

5 Toh Tuck Link, Singapore 596224

USA office: 27 Warren Street, Suite 401-402, Hackensack, NJ 07601

UK office: 57 Shelton Street, Covent Garden, London WC2H 9HE

Library of Congress Cataloging-in-Publication Data
Names: Poyago-Theotoky, Joanna, 1961– editor.
Title: Green innovation and industrial organization /
editor Joanna Poyago-Theotoky, University of Salento, Italy.
Description: Hackensack, NJ : World Scientific Publishing, [2026] |
Series: World Scientific-Economic Growth Centre contemporary series in modern economy ;
volume 4 | Includes bibliographical references and index.
Identifiers: LCCN 2025028349 | ISBN 9789819816026 hardcover |
ISBN 9789819816033 ebook for institutions | ISBN 9789819816040 ebook for individuals
Subjects: LCSH: Industrial management--Environmental aspects. |
Economic development--Environmental aspects. | Environmental economics.
Classification: LCC HD30.255 .G7385 2026 | DDC 658.4/083--dc23/eng/20250911
LC record available at https://lccn.loc.gov/2025028349

British Library Cataloguing-in-Publication Data
A catalogue record for this book is available from the British Library.

For any available supplementary material, please visit
https://www.worldscientific.com/worldscibooks/10.1142/14389#t=suppl

Desk Editors: Eshak Nabi Akbar Ali/Sandhya Venkatesh

Typeset by Stallion Press
Email: enquiries@stallionpress.com

https://doi.org/10.1142/9789819816033_fmatter

Preface

Rapid economic growth in the past few decades has helped many industrialised and developing countries achieve economic development coupled with rapid increases in productivity. However, this has led to dramatic increases in Greenhouse Gas (GHG) emissions as well as other pollutants. Concerns by policy makers over the global increases in GHG emissions and their adverse effects on climate change are well documented. The challenge in addressing the several issues associated with the increased pollution is enormous given the global nature of the problem of climate change. However, a first step must be taken at the level where national governments are targeting polluting emissions via environmental economic policy.

Even though environmental policies can be seen with positive effects on social welfare, there are significant economic costs involved in framing and implementing them. Hence, a regulator needs to understand the balance between additional environmental benefits versus societal costs when formulating an environmental policy. For this reason, it has long been argued that the spread of emissions-reducing technologies will be among the most important determinants of the long-run success of environmental economic policy. However, it has also been understood for some time that each environmental economic policy instruments can have significantly different effects on both the rate and direction of technological change, firm profitability, innovation incentives, as well as social welfare consequences.

Environmental economic policy involves a range of instruments that have been developed to deal with pollutants that would, otherwise, be disposed of in the environment without charge. Economists refer to the latter as "negative externalities", because they are not priced (i.e., "internalised") by markets and, as such, the allocation of resources for consumption and production does not account for environmental damages created as a by-product of economic activity leading to a market failure. Typical examples of environmental economic policies include emissions standards, quotas on production, emission taxes, targeted subsidies, and tradable permits.

"Green" innovation policy can be broadly defined as a mix of innovation and environmental economic policy, targeted at promoting research and development (R&D) in technology specifically designed to reduce a negative externality, such as greenhouse gas emissions. It is well known that firms may not have incentives to invest in "green" innovation, for this reason, patents, licenses and other policy instruments may not be sufficient to incentivise R&D in green technologies. For "green" innovation to be successfully implemented, an external impetus such as an environmental economic policy needs to be put in place alongside the existing patent system, as well as coordination with other areas of policy affecting international markets is required. For this reason the integration of environmental economic policy and innovation policy becomes essential.

This volume presents a collection of contributions that address several distinct issues within the main broad conceptual described above. The distinctive characteristic of the contributions lies in the interplay of environmental policy aspects ("green innovation") and the competitive environment polluting firms operate in, which is mostly characterised by imperfectly competitive ("industrial organisation").

I would like to thank all chapter contributors for their insightful and detailed analysis of specific topics. I also express my sincere appreciation to the publisher for the efficient processing of the manuscript, and especially Sandhya Venkatesh. Finally, I thank Professor Euston Quah, Albert Winsemius Chair Professor of Economics and Director of Economic Growth Centre, Nanyang Technological University, Singapore, for encouraging me to publish this book under the World Scientific-Economic Growth Centre Contemporary Series in Modern Economy.

Joanna A. Poyago-Theotoky
University of Salento, Lecce, Italy

https://doi.org/10.1142/9789819816033_fmatter

About the Editor

Joanna Poyago-Theotoky is a Full Professor of Economic Policy at the Department of Economics, University of Salento, Lecce, Italy. She was a Professor of Economics at La Trobe University, Melbourne and served as the Head of the School of Economics from January 2012 to January 2015. Previously she was Professor of Microeconomics at Loughborough University and has also taught at the Universities of St Andrews, Nottingham and Bristol. She received her PhD in Economics from the University of Bristol, England, UK. Her visiting appointments include the University of Zurich, Switzerland, the University of East Anglia Business School and the Research School of Economics at the Australian National University. Previous scholarly affiliations include: the Centre for Research into Industry, Enterprise, Finance and the Firm (CRIEFF), University of St Andrews, the Social Innovation and Entrepreneurship Research Centre (SIERC), Massey University, New Zealand, the Rimini Centre for Economics Analysis (RCEA). At present, she is also a Non-Resident Research Fellow at the Centre for Development Economics and Sustainability at Monash University, Australia and Affiliated Professor at the Alliance of Excellence for Research and Innovation on Aephoria (AE4RIA), in Athens, Greece. Professor Poyago-Theotoky's research interests lie in the subject field of industrial organization, especially innovation, R&D cooperation and research joint ventures, with a focus on technology and environmental policies. She is an Associate Editor of *Economic Modelling* and an Editorial Board Member of *Managerial and Decision Economics*.

https://doi.org/10.1142/9789819816033_fmatter

List of Contributors

Marie-Laure Cabon-Dhersin
Université Rouen Normandie, LERN, Rouen, France

Christos Constantatos
University of Macedonia, Department of Economics, Thessaloniki, Greece

Ana Espinola-Arredondo
Washington State University, School of Economic Sciences, Pullman, USA

Luca Lambertini
University of Bologna, Department of Economics and Alma Climate Centre, Bologna, Italy

Sang-Ho Lee
Chonnam National University, Department of Economics, Gwangju, Korea

Mario Martínez Fernández
University of Valencia, Department of Economic Analysis and ERI-CES, Valencia, Spain

Apostolos Ioannis Martis
University of Macedonia, Department of Economics, Thessaloniki, Greece

Flavio M. Menezes
The University of Queensland, School of Economics, Brisbane, Australia

Rafael Moner-Colonques
University of Valencia, Department of Economic Analysis and ERI-CES, Valencia, Spain

Felix Munoz-Garcia
Washington State University, School of Economic Sciences, Pullman, USA

Jean-Philippe Nicolaï
University of Grenoble, Grenoble INP – Génie Industriel, France

Chul-Hi Park
Gwangju National University of Education, Department of Social Studies Education, Gwangju, Korea

Jorge Pereira
The University of Queensland, School of Economics, Brisbane, Australia

Joanna Poyago-Theotoky
University of Salento, Department of Economic Sciences, Lecce, Italy

Natacha Raffin
ENS Paris Saclay, CEPS, Gif-sur-Yvette, France

Jose J. Sempere-Monerris
University of Valencia, Department of Economic Analysis and ERI-CES, Valencia, Spain, and CORE/LIDAM, UCLouvain, Louvain-la-Neuve, Belgium

https://doi.org/10.1142/9789819816033_fmatter

Contents

https://doi.org/10.1142/9789819816033_0001

Chapter 1

Green Innovation and Industrial Organization: A Guided Tour

Ana Espinola-Arredondo[*,‡], **Felix Munoz-Garcia**[*,§], **and Joanna Poyago-Theotoky**[†,||]

[*] *Washington State University, School of Economic Sciences, Pullman, USA*

[†] *University of Salento, Department of Economic Sciences, Lecce, Italy*

[‡] *anaespinola@wsu.edu*

[§] *fmunoz@wsu.edu*

[||] *joanna.poyago-theotoky@unisalento.it*

We examine the literature on firms' incentives to invest in abatement, also known as green R&D, and how these incentives are affected by environmental regulation. We identify two externalities: the tax-saving and the emission-reduction externality. The analysis highlights how the timing of regulation affects firms' investment decisions, particularly the formation of Environmental Research Cartels (ERCs), as well as the role of spillover effects. We then investigate other extensions in this literature, such as considering that firms sequentially invest in abatement, that firms have asymmetric investment costs, alternative spillover effects, disruptive investments, and endogenous entry.

Keywords: Green R&D, Abatement, Environmental policy, Spillover effects, Cooperative R&D, Environmental research cartels.

1. Introduction

The intersection of environmental policy and industrial organisation is critical in addressing environmental sustainability in concentrated markets. This chapter investigates the incentives for firms to invest in green research and development (R&D), particularly in abatement technologies, and how these incentives are influenced by environmental regulations, the timing of abatement decisions, the timing of regulation, the presence of spillover effects, disruptive R&D, firm asymmetry, and entry decisions, among others. We review several studies in this literature, summarising their main results in a unified, tractable model.

First, we identify two externalities stemming from a larger investment in abatement by one of the firms operating in the industry. On one hand, an increase in abatement reduces the stringency of the emission fee, which applies to all firms (i.e., tax-saving externality (TSE)). This occurs even in the absence of spillover effects across firms. On the other hand, a second externality arises when spillover effects are present. In particular, a larger abatement from a firm's rival reduces this firm's per-unit emissions, thus lowering its tax bill as well (i.e., emission reduction externality (ERE)). While the TSE occurs regardless of whether spillover effects are present or absent, the ERE only arises when they are present, providing firms with stronger incentives to free-ride their rivals' abatement.

Then, we examine how regulatory commitment affects firms' abatement decisions. When regulators act first by setting emission fees before firms decide on their abatement, the likelihood of forming Environmental Research Cartels (ERCs) diminishes. This regulatory preemption influences the strategic interactions between firms and regulators, reducing the incentives for cooperative behaviour between firms when regulation is predetermined. This can also be interpreted as a lack of flexibility, that is, regulation was designed before firms' acquire their abatement technologies.

We also allow for firms to sequentially invest in abatement, which has been observed in industries with a leader, or with more experienced firms. Comparing simultaneous and sequential abatement decisions, we show that they are similar when pollution severity is small or extremely high. When pollution severity is moderate, however, abatement is larger when firms invest sequentially than simultaneously, highlighting the need for adapting regulation to firms' interaction, namely, setting less stringent fees when they compete sequentially.

While the literature assumes firms are symmetric in their abatement costs, we also examine cost asymmetries across firms. This asymmetry entails that, at the first-best outcome, firms should not be taxed equally. In other words, firms should be subject to type-dependent (non-uniform) emission fees, instead of type-independent (uniform) emission fees. We show that type-dependent fees, which vary based on firms' characteristics, are more effective in promoting efficient abatement levels when spillover effects are low. In contrast, when spillover effects are strong, both types of emission fees (uniform or non-uniform) yield similar results.

1.1. *Related literature*

The literature on firms' incentives to invest in cost-reducing R&D provides a foundation for studies considering abatement decisions and environmental regulation. Arrow (1962) posits that competitive markets provide stronger incentives for R&D investment due to greater potential gains. Yi (1999) expands on this work by demonstrating that under Cournot competition, firms' R&D incentives diminish as the number of firms increases.[1] In the context of abatement decisions, Montero (2002) finds that more concentrated markets can lead to higher levels of abatement; while Lambertini *et al.* (2017) show an inverted-U relationship, indicating that aggregate investment initially grows when the market becomes more competitive, but eventually decreases. The difference in their results is partly due to the timing of environmental policy, allowing for the regulator to commit to the emission fee before firms choose their abatement levels or not, as we show in Section 4.

The literature also examines cooperative R&D and its welfare implications. d'Aspremont and Jacquemin (1988) analyse research joint ventures (RJVs) and their impact on cost-reducing R&D investment and market outcomes, finding that RJVs can lead to higher

[1] Delbono and Denicolò (1990), further this analysis by allowing both Cournot and Bertrand competition.

R&D investment and improved welfare compared to non-cooperative scenarios. Kamien *et al.* (1992) and Amir *et al.* (2003) explore conditions under which cooperative R&D is more beneficial than competitive R&D, particularly when spillover effects are significant. In the context of abatement decisions, Poyago-Theotoky (2007) and Ouchida and Goto (2014) investigate firms' abatement under environmental policy, identifying the role of spillovers.

The chapter is organised into several sections. Section 2 presents the model, while Section 3 provides the equilibrium analysis. Section 4 discusses cooperative R&D, and Section 5 examines the role of spillovers and market concentration. We then analyse how the main results are affected by different time structures, sequential investments, firm asymmetry, alternative forms of spillover effects, disruptive investments, endogenous entry, along other extensions considered in this literature.

2. Model

In this section, we present the modelling assumptions common in this literature, focusing on the time structure of the game. Importantly, the regulator setting emission fees (e.g., Environmental Protection Agency in the US) observes firms' abatement decisions, responding by setting an emission fee. This implies that the regulator's decision is time-consistent.

Consider an industry with two firms facing inverse demand function $p(Q) = 1 - Q$, where $Q = q_1 + q_2$ denotes aggregate output, and operating with symmetric marginal cost c, where $1 > c \geq 0$. Firms interact in the following sequential-move game:

(1) In the first stage, every firm i, $i = 1, 2$, independently and simultaneously invests $z_i \geq 0$ in abatement "green" R&D, which reduces firm i's emissions, from $e_i = q_i$ to $e_i = q_i - z_i - \beta z_j$ where $j \neq i$, and $\beta \in [0, 1]$ denote spillovers. When $\beta = 0$, spillovers in abatement are absent and firm i's emissions become $e_i = q_i - z_i$. In contrast, when $\beta > 0$ firm i benefits from a share, β, of its rival's abatement effort; and when $\beta = 1$ every firm fully benefits from every unit of its rival's abatement effort, i.e., $e_i = q_i - z_i - z_j$.

The total cost of investing to obtain a reduction in abatement of z_i is $\frac{\gamma(z_i)^2}{2}$, being increasing and convex in abatement, and where

$\gamma > 0$ denotes firm i's investment efficiency (a lower γ indicates a higher efficiency).

(2) In the second stage, the regulator observes the investment decisions $z = (z_1, z_2)$, and sets an emission fee t per unit of output, implying that every firm i pays $t(q_i - z_i - \beta z_j)$ in emission fees.[2]

(3) In the third stage, every firm i observes the investment decisions and the emission fee, and responds simultaneously and independently choosing its output level q_i (i.e., firms compete à la Cournot).

The regulator considers the following, standard welfare function

$$W = CS + PS + T - ED \tag{1}$$

where $CS = \frac{Q^2}{2}$ denotes consumer surplus, $PS = \pi_1 + \pi_2$ represents producer surplus, $T = t(Q - Z)$ is total tax collection so emission fees are revenue neutral, with $Z = z_1 + z_2$ being the aggregate abatement, and $ED = \frac{d}{2}(Q - Z)^2$ denotes environmental damage. This function, ED, is increasing and convex is net emissions, $Q - Z$, and the parameter d captures the severity of pollution, where $d \geq 1/2$ to avoid corner solutions.

3. Equilibrium Analysis: Non-Cooperative Behaviour

We next solve the game by backward induction, first identifying, as a benchmark, equilibrium behaviour in the absence of spillovers ($\beta = 0$), then when spillover effects are present ($\beta > 0$). We carry out this analysis assuming that firms do not coordinate their investment-abatement decisions. Later on, we examine how equilibrium results would be affected if, instead, firms coordinate their abatement.

3.1. *No spillovers*

Third stage. In the last stage, every firm i chooses its output q_i to solve

$$\max_{q_i \geq 0}(1 - q_i - q_j)q_i - cq_i - t(q_i - z_i) - \frac{\gamma\left(z_i\right)^2}{2} \tag{2}$$

[2]This emission fee is also known as an emission tax.

where the first term denotes total revenues, the second term represents production costs (without considering per-unit taxes), the third term captures taxes on firm's net emissions, and the fourth term is R&D costs.

Differentiating with respect to q_i, yields best response function $q_i(q_j) = \frac{1-c-t}{2} - \frac{1}{2}q_j$, which is decreasing in its rival's output, q_j, indicating that output decisions are strategic substitutes; and shifts downward when emission fees become more stringent (higher t). This function is, however, unaffected by abatement because this investment does not provide firm i with a cost advantage; instead, it only generates less stringent fees, which symmetrically affect both firms.

In a symmetric equilibrium, $q_i = q_j = q$, output becomes $q = \frac{1-c-t}{3}$, which is decreasing in after-tax cost, $c + t$; and equilibrium profit $\pi_i = q^2 + tz_i - \frac{\gamma(z_i)^2}{2}$.

Second stage. Anticipating output q and profit π_i, the regulator sets the emission fee t that solves

$$\max_{t\geq 0} W = \underbrace{\frac{Q^2}{2}}_{CS} + \underbrace{Q^2 + tZ - \frac{\gamma Z^2}{2}}_{PS} + \underbrace{t(Q-Z)}_{T} - \underbrace{\frac{d}{2}(Q-Z)^2}_{ED} \tag{3}$$

where $Q = \frac{2(1-c-t)}{3}$ denotes the equilibrium aggregate output and $Z = z_i + z_j$ represents aggregate abatement. Differentiating with respect to t and solving for t, yields an equilibrium fee

$$t = \frac{(2d-1)(1-c) - 3dZ}{2(1+d)} \tag{4}$$

which becomes more stringent when pollution is more severe (higher d), but less stringent when output is more costly to produce (higher c).

Importantly, this fee decreases in aggregate abatement, Z, implying that when either firm i or j increases its abatement (z_i or z_j), the regulator anticipates less emissions per unit of output, and reduces the severity of the emission fee by

$$\frac{\partial t}{\partial z_i} = \frac{\partial t}{\partial z_j} = -\frac{3d}{3(1+d)} < 0 \tag{5}$$

This effect is symmetric across firms, entailing that firm i can free ride off its rival's investment, z_j. Firms, then, face investing incentives that resemble those of private donors in a public good game.

In this class of games, every donor does not internalise the positive externality that her donation generates on other donors' payoffs. Similarly, in our setting every firm i does not internalise the tax-saving effect that its investment has on its rival's profit. Therefore, firms tend to invest below the amount that they would select if they could coordinate their investment decisions (internalising this externality). We return to this point below in more detail.

Hence, evaluating $q = \frac{1-c-t}{3}$ at the equilibrium fee found in (4), yields $q = \frac{1-c+dZ}{2(1+d)}$, which is increasing in aggregate abatement, Z; with associated profits $\pi_i = q^2 + tz_i - \frac{\gamma(z_i)^2}{2}$.

First stage. Anticipating profit π_i, every firm i chooses its abatement, z_i, to solve

$$\max_{z_i \geq 0} \pi_i = q^2 + tz_i - \frac{\gamma\,(z_i)^2}{2}$$

$$= \frac{(1-c+dZ)^2}{4(1+d)^2} + \frac{(2d-1)(1-c)-3dZ}{2(1+d)} z_i - \frac{\gamma\,(z_i)^2}{2} \quad (6)$$

which, differentiating with respect to z_i and solving, yields best response function

$$z_i(z_j) = \frac{[2d(1+d)-1](1-c)}{d(6+5d)+2\gamma(1+d)^2} - \frac{d(3+2d)}{d(6+5d)+2\gamma(1+d)^2} z_j$$

which is decreasing in its rival's abatement, z_j, indicating that firms deem each other's abatement as strategic substitutes. This result stems from the free-riding incentives described above since firm i decreases its (investment in) abatement, z_i, when its rival increases its own, z_j.

In a symmetric equilibrium, $z_i = z_j = z$, abatement becomes

$$z^{\mathrm{NC}} = \frac{[2d(1+d)-1](1-c)}{d(9+7d)+2\gamma(1+d)^2} \quad (7)$$

where the superscript NC denotes "non-cooperative" (i.e., firms do not coordinate their investment to maximise their joint profits), and satisfies $z^{\mathrm{NC}} > 0$ given that $d > 1/2$ by definition. Inserting z^{NC} into the equilibrium output found above, that is, $q = \frac{1-c+dZ}{2(1+d)}$, yields $q^{\mathrm{NC}} = \frac{[d(7+4d)+2\gamma(1+d)](1-c)}{2d(9+7d)+4\gamma(1+d)^2}$. Similarly, evaluating emission fee $t = \frac{(2d-1)(1-c)-3dZ}{2(1+d)}$ at z^{NC}, we obtain $t^{\mathrm{NC}} = \frac{[d(2d(1+2\gamma)-3-2\gamma)](1-c)}{2d(9+7d)+4\gamma(1+d)^2}$.

3.2. *Abatement spillovers*

We next examine the three-stage game but allowing for abatement spillovers, i.e., $\beta > 0$.

Third stage. Relative to the setting without spillovers analysed in Section 3.1, every firm i now solves

$$\max_{q_i \geq 0} (1 - q_i - q_j)q_i - cq_i - t(q_i - z_i - \beta z_j) - \frac{\gamma (z_i)^2}{2} \tag{8}$$

which coincides with the profit-maximisation problem in (2), except for the third term, as net emissions are now reduced by spillover effects in R&D, βz_j. Therefore, equilibrium output is still $q = \frac{1-c-t}{3}$, implying that Cournot competition is unaffected by the presence of spillovers. Technically, spillovers do not directly affect output decisions, although they impact them indirectly via less stringent fees, as we show next.

Second stage. Anticipating output q and profit π_i, the regulator sets the emission fee t as in the previous section but yields an equilibrium fee

$$t = \frac{(2d-1)(1-c) - 3d(1+\beta)Z}{2(1+d)} \tag{9}$$

which coincides with the fee in (4) when spillover effects are absent, $\beta = 0$, but decreases when spillover effects become stronger (higher β). Intuitively, a given investment level reduces the emissions of both firms to a larger extent, thus requiring less stringent fees to curb pollution. This is confirmed when examining the sensitivity of fee t to a marginal increase in abatement, $\frac{\partial t}{\partial z_i} = \frac{\partial t}{\partial z_j} = -\frac{3d(1+\beta)}{3(1+d)} < 0$, which is increasing in spillover effects, β. Evaluating $q = \frac{1-c-t}{3}$ at the equilibrium emission fee found in (9), we obtain $q = \frac{1-c+d(1+\beta)Z}{2(1+d)}$.

First stage. In this stage, every firm i chooses its abatement level z_i to solve

$$\max_{z_i \geq 0} \pi_i = \frac{[1-c+d(1+\beta)Z]^2}{4(1+d)^2} + \frac{(2d-1)(1-c) - 3d(1+\beta)Z}{2(1+d)} \times (z_i + \beta z_j) - \frac{\gamma (z_i)^2}{2} \tag{10}$$

which, differentiating with respect to z_i, yields best response function

$$z_i(z_j) = \frac{[d(2+\beta+2d)-1](1-c)}{d(1+\beta)\,[6+(5-\beta)d]+2\gamma(1+d)^2} - \frac{d(3+2d)(1+\beta)^2}{d(1+\beta)\,[6+(5-\beta)d]+2\gamma(1+d)^2} z_j \tag{11}$$

which coincides with the best response function in (6) when spillover effects are absent, $\beta = 0$. When spillovers are present, $\beta > 0$, expression (11) shows that abatement levels are still strategic substitutes; as in the absence of spillovers. It is, however, easy to show that the slope of this best response function is increasing in β, implying that spillover effects emphasise every firm's incentives to free ride off its rival's investment. Intuitively, firm j's "green" R&D, z_j, yields two externalities on firm i: (i) it reduces the stringency of emission fee, t (tax-saving effect, TSE); and (ii) it lowers the per-unit emissions that firm i's output generates because of spillovers (emission reduction effect, ERE). While the TSE occurs regardless of whether spillover effects are present or absent, the ERE only arises when $\beta > 0$.

In a symmetric equilibrium, $z_i = z_j = z$, abatement becomes

$$z^{\mathrm{NC}} = \frac{[d(2+\beta+2d)-1](1-c)}{d(1+\beta)\,[9+7d+\beta(3+d)]+2\gamma(1+d)^2} \tag{12}$$

Figure 1 depicts this equilibrium abatement, as a function of β in the horizontal axis evaluated, for illustration purposes, at $c = 1/2$

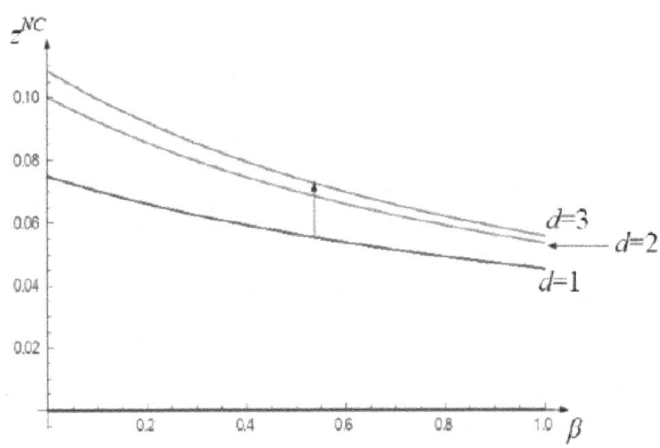

Fig. 1. z^{NC} as a function of β.

and $\gamma = 1/4$. The figure shows that investment z^{NC} monotonically decreases when spillover effects are more intense (higher β).

For completeness, the figure considers three different pollution severities, $d = 1$, $d = 2$, and $d = 3$, illustrating that, because the emission fee becomes more severe, firms have more incentives to invest in abatement, explaining why z^{NC} experiences an upward shift. In contrast, an increase in production cost c entails a downward shift in the equilibrium abatement z^{NC}.

3.3. *Cooperative R&D: Environmental research cartels*

Still allowing for spillovers, let us now identify the investment in abatement that firms choose when coordinating their investment decisions. As described above, every firm's individual investment gives rise to two positive externalities, that firms' joint maximisation problem can internalise. This investment decision is analogous to a research cartel in industries without environmental regulation, and in the literature it is commonly known as "environmental research cartel" (ERC). If, in addition, firms share information from their innovations completely, $\beta = 1$, thus avoiding duplicities in their R&D, the ERC would become a so-called environmental research joint venture (ERJV).

In this context, solving the game again by backward induction, we find that equilibrium behaviour in stages 2–3 are unaffected, but it changes in the first stage, since firms now choose z_i and z_j to maximise their joint profits as follows

$$\max_{z_i, z_j \geq 0} \pi_i + \pi_j \tag{13}$$

where profit π_i was defined in expression (10). Differentiating with respect to z_i and z_j, yields an equilibrium abatement

$$z^{\mathrm{ERC}} = \frac{[(1+d)(2d-1)]\,(1-c)}{4d(3+2d)(1+\beta)^2 + 2\gamma(1+d)^2} \tag{14}$$

which is positive since $d > 1/2$ by assumption. Figure 2 illustrates z^{ERC} using, for comparison purposes, the same parameter values as in Fig. 1. Visually comparing z^{NC} and z^{ERC} in Figs. 1 and 2, suggests

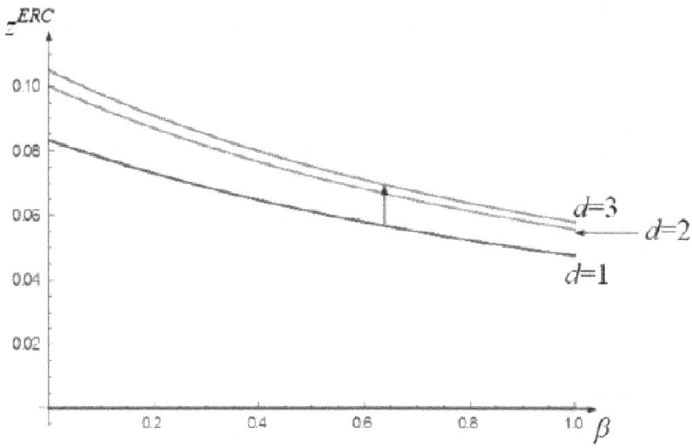

Fig. 2. z^{ERC} as a function of β.

that $z^{\text{ERC}} > z^{\text{NC}}$ under most, but not all, parameter conditions. We next formally compare these abatement levels.

3.4. *"Green" R&D comparisons*

Figure 3 depicts the difference $z^{\text{ERC}} - z^{\text{NC}}$, as a function of β on the horizontal axis, and evaluated at the same parameter values as in Fig. 1. When spillovers are absent, $\beta = 0$, only the TSE is present, illustrated in the vertical intercepts of the figure. In this context, $z^{\text{ERC}} > z^{\text{NC}}$ holds when environmental damages are small (i.e., $d = 1$). When they increase to $d = 2$, both investment levels coincide, $z^{\text{ERC}} = z^{\text{NC}}$; and when these damages further increase to $d = 3$, the investment ranking switches to $z^{\text{ERC}} < z^{\text{NC}}$. Intuitively, when damages are small, fees are less stringent, and aggregate output is high, lying in the *inelastic* portion of the demand curve. In this case, every firm j's abatement, z_j, induces less stringent emission fees, which helps firm i increase its output, lowering the equilibrium price, but by a less-than-proportional amount, ultimately increasing firm i's profit (positive externality).

In contrast, when environmental damages become more severe, emission fees are more stringent, and aggregate output lies in the *elastic* portion of the demand curve. In this setting, every firm's investment, while still lowering emission fees and output, it yields

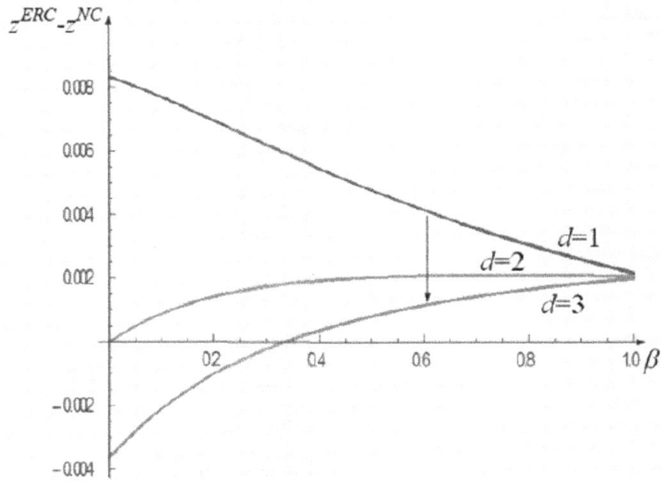

Fig. 3. $z^{\mathrm{ERC}} - z^{\mathrm{NC}}$ as a function of β.

a more-than-proportional decrease in prices, ultimately decreasing its rival's profits (negative externality). This explains why the ERC helps internalise a positive externality when d is relatively, increasing abatement and investment relative to the NC scenario.

When spillovers are present, $\beta > 0$, the ERC seeks to internalise both the TSE, which can be positive or negative as shown above; and that stemming from ERE, which is unambiguously positive. When β is sufficiently high (strong spillovers), the positive externality in ERE dominates that in TSE, regardless of whether the latter is positive or negative (i.e., for all values of d). Graphically, all curves depicting the difference $z^{\mathrm{ERC}} - z^{\mathrm{NC}}$ lie on the positive quadrant of Fig. 3 when β is sufficiently high, i.e., $\beta > 1/3$.

Finally, when firms fully share the results of their innovation in an ERJV, $\beta = 1$, the difference $z^{\mathrm{ERC}} - z^{\mathrm{NC}}$ is unambiguously positive, and unaffected by changes in pollution severity (i.e., different values of d yield the same height, at the right-hand side of the figure).

4. Allowing for Different Time Structures

Lambertini *et al.* (2017) consider a similar setting, but assume that the first and second stages are switched: the regulator chooses the emission fee in the first stage, every firm responds with its own investment in abatement, z_i, in the second stage, and then firms compete à la Cournot (this case is known as "commitment by the regulator"). This timing can help explain industries where firms can easily revise their investments (i.e., scrubs, pipe filters, or other small projects) while regulation cannot be easily adjusted and thus remains fixed during all periods. In contrast, the setting in Poyago-Theotoky (2007) better fits industries where firms' investments are large and difficult to revise, making regulation easier to adjust than investments.

For generality, Lambertini *et al.* (2017) also allow for $n \geq 2$ firms, thus examining how aggregate investment is affected by the number of firms in the industry, potentially recommending entry under certain conditions to boost abatement.

Firm i's net emissions are, then, given by $e_i = q_i - z_i - \beta Z_{-i}$, where $Z_{-i} \equiv \sum_{j \neq i} z_j$ denotes the aggregate abatement efforts from firm i's rivals. For simplicity, we consider that $d = 2$, so environmental damages are $ED = (e_1 + \cdots + e_n)^2$.

Third stage. Every firm i chooses its output q_i to solve

$$\max_{q_i \geq 0} \pi_i(q_i) = (1 - q_i - Q_{-i})q_i - cq_i - t(q_i - z_i - \beta Z_{-i}) - \frac{\gamma}{2} z_i^2 \tag{15}$$

where $Q_{-i} = \sum_{j \neq i} q_j$ denotes the aggregate output from firm i's rivals. Differentiating with respect to q_i, we obtain firm i's best response function $q_i(Q_{-i}) = \frac{1-c-t}{2} - \frac{1}{2}Q_{-i}$. In a symmetric equilibrium, $q_i = q_j = q$, which entails $Q_{-i} = (N-1)q_i$. Therefore, equilibrium output becomes $q_i(t) = \frac{1-c-t}{n+1}$, which is decreasing in the emission fee t that the regulator sets in the first period, the number of firms competing in the industry, n, and the marginal production cost c.[3]

[3]One can also note that aggregate output is $Q(t) = nq_i(t) = \frac{n(1-c-t)}{n+1}$, which increases in the number of firms in the industry, n, decreases in the emission fee t, and in the marginal production cost c. In addition, $Q(t)$ asymptotically approaches $1 - c - t$ when the market becomes perfectly competitive.

Substituting output $q_i(t)$ into the firm i's profit function, we find that

$$\begin{aligned}\pi_i(z_i,t) &= [1-q_i(t)-Q_{-i}(t)]\,q_i(t)-cq_i(t)\\ &\quad -t\,(q_i(t)-z_i-\beta Z_{-i})-\frac{\gamma}{2}z_i^2\\ &= \left(\frac{1-c-t}{n+1}\right)^2+t\,(z_i+\beta Z_{-i})-\frac{\gamma}{2}z_i^2 \qquad (16)\end{aligned}$$

Second stage. Every firm i anticipates the profit that it earns in the third stage, $\pi_i(z_i,t)$, and chooses its abatement effort z_i to solve

$$\max_{z_i\geq 0}\pi_i(z_i,t) \qquad (17)$$

Differentiating with respect to z_i, we obtain $t=\gamma z_i$, where the left side indicates the benefit from a marginal increase in abatement (lower taxes) and the right side measures the cost of this additional abatement. Importantly, this first-order condition is not a function of the abatement efforts from firm i's rivals, Z_{-i}, entailing that abatement decisions are strictly dominant strategies when the regulator chooses emission fees in the first stage, namely, firm i chooses the same abatement level regardless of its rivals' choices.

Solving for z_i in $t=\gamma z_i$ yields the equilibrium abatement effort $z_i(t)=\frac{t}{\gamma}$, which is increasing in the emission fee that regulator sets in the first stage, t. Intuitively, as the emission fee becomes more stringent, firms have stronger incentives to invest in abatement to save on taxes. Of course, if environmental regulation was absent, $t=0$, all firms would choose to invest zero in green R&D. In addition, firm i makes fewer investments in green R&D if innovation investments become more difficult (i.e., γ increases).

In this setting, aggregate abatement becomes $Z(t)=nz_i(t)=\frac{nt}{\gamma}$, which increases in the number of firms, n. As suggested by Lambertini *et al.* (2017) "if taxation were exogenous, we obtain a clear-cut Arrowian result: increased competition (higher n) leads to an increase in aggregate R&D (innovation)." As we show in the first stage of the game, when emission fees are endogenous, the above comparative statics result can be reversed.

Therefore, the emission of every firm i becomes $e_i(t) = q_i(t) - z_i(t) - \beta(n-1)z_i(t)$, which simplifies to $e_i(t) = \frac{1-c-t}{n+1} - \frac{t(1+\beta(n-1))}{\gamma}$, and equilibrium profits become

$$\begin{aligned}\pi_i(t) &= \left(\frac{1-c-t}{n+1}\right)^2 + t\left(\frac{t}{\gamma} + \beta(n-1)\frac{t}{\gamma}\right) - \frac{\gamma}{2}\left(\frac{t}{\gamma}\right)^2 \\ &= \left(\frac{1-c-t}{n+1}\right)^2 + \frac{t^2(1+2\beta(n-1))}{2\gamma} \qquad (18)\end{aligned}$$

First stage. In this stage, the regulator chooses the emission fee that maximises the social welfare defined in expression (1).

$$\begin{aligned}W(t) &= \frac{1}{2}[Q(t)]^2 + n\pi_i(t) - n^2[e_i(t)]^2 \\ &= \frac{n^2}{2}\left(\frac{1-c-t}{n+1}\right)^2 + n\left(\frac{1-c-t}{n+1}\right)^2 \\ &\quad + \frac{Nt^2[1+2\beta(n-1)]}{2\gamma} - n^2\left[\left(\frac{1-c-t}{n+1}\right)^2\right. \\ &\quad \left. - \frac{2t(1-c-t)[1+\beta(N-1)]}{\gamma(n+1)} + \frac{t^2[1+\beta(n-1)]^2}{\gamma^2}\right] \\ &= \frac{2n^2[1+\beta(n-1)](1-c-t)t}{\gamma(n+1)} - \frac{n(n-2)(1-c-t)^2}{2(n+1)^2} \\ &\quad + \frac{n\left[\gamma(1+2\beta(n-1)) - 2n(1+\beta(n-1))^2\right]t^2}{2\gamma^2} \qquad (19)\end{aligned}$$

Differentiating with respect to t, we obtain the optimal emission fee

$$t(n) = \frac{\gamma[2n(n+1)(1+\beta(n-1)) + \gamma(n-2)](1-c)}{4\gamma n(n+1)[1+\beta(n-1)] + \gamma^2(n-2) - A(\gamma)} \qquad (20)$$

where, for compactness, $A(\gamma) \equiv (n+1)^2[\gamma(1+2\beta(n-1)) - 2n(1+\beta(n-1))^2]$. Furthermore, we thereafter consider $c = 0$ and $\gamma = 5$, which helps us focus on the role of the number of firms, n, and spillover effects, β. In this simplified and illustrative context, the equilibrium abatement effort, $z_i(n) = \frac{t(n)}{\gamma}$, is

$$z_i(n) = \frac{2n(n+1)[1+\beta(n-1)] + 5(n-2)}{20n(n+1)[1+\beta(n-1)] + 25(n-2) - A(5)}. \tag{21}$$

4.1. Role of spillovers and market concentration

We next evaluate aggregate abatement $Z(n) = n \times z_i(n)$ in the case of no spillovers, $\beta = 0$, showing that such investment is unambiguously increasing in the number of firms, n. Then, we evaluate $Z(n)$ in the case of positive spillovers, $\beta > 0$, demonstrating that this investment exhibits an inverted U-shape.

No spillovers. Evaluating aggregate abatement $Z(n) = n \times z_i(n)$ at $\beta = 0$, we find that

$$Z(n) = \frac{n(2n^2 + 7n - 10)}{2n^3 + 19n^2 + 37n - 55} \tag{22}$$

Differentiating the above expression with respect to n yields $\frac{\partial Z(n)}{\partial n} = \frac{24n^4+188n^3+119n^2-770n+550}{(2n^3+19n^2+37n-55)^2}$, which is unambiguously positive since $n \geq 2$, implying that aggregate abatement unambiguously increases with the number of firms n. Intuitively, every firm does not benefit from the investment of its rivals, and thus responds increasing its own investment when more firms enter the industry. Figure 4a depicts $Z(n)$ as a function of n when $\beta = 0$.

Note that, in the absence of spillovers, every firm's investment does not generate the type-(i) externality found in previous sections.

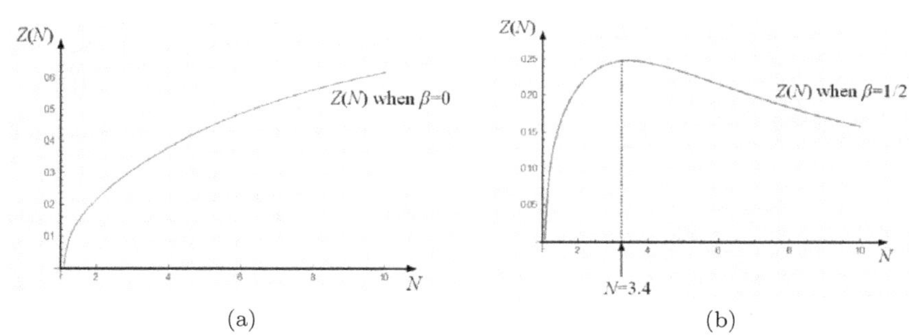

Fig. 4. Aggregate abatement. (a) Aggregate abatement when $\beta = 0$, (b) Aggregate abatement when $\beta = 1/2$.

This is due to the change in the time structure of the game: investments do not affect the stringency of the emission fee in the current setting, since it is set by the regulator in the first stage. In contrast, in Poyago-Theotoky (2007) a more intense investment abatement led to a less stringent fee in the next stage.

Spillovers. Evaluating aggregate abatement $Z(n)$ at $\beta = 1/2$, we obtain

$$Z(n) = \frac{2n^4 + 4n^3 + 12n^2 - 20n}{n^5 + 4n^4 + 16n^3 + 24n^2 + 61n - 100} \tag{23}$$

Differentiating with respect to n yields

$$\frac{\partial Z(n)}{\partial n} = \frac{2\left(-n^8 - 4n^7 - 10n^6 + 40n^5 + 255n^4 + 164n^3 + 6n^2 - 1200n + 1000\right)}{\left(n^5 + 4n^4 + 16n^3 + 24n^2 + 61n - 100\right)^2} \tag{24}$$

Setting this expression equal to zero, we find that $\frac{\partial Z(n)}{\partial n} > 0$ for all $n \in [2, \overline{n}]$, but $\frac{\partial Z(n)}{\partial n} < 0$ when $n > \overline{n} = 3.432$. This explains the inverted U-shape relationship between market competition and green innovation, as depicted in Fig. 4b. Intuitively, when the market is represented by four or fewer firms, increasing the number of firms in the industry (and their output) stimulates green innovation. However, when the market becomes increasingly more competitive, every firm i exhibits stronger incentives to "free ride" on the investments of all other firms, and this, in turn, induces every firm to make fewer investments in green innovation.

Therefore, the positive externality in Poyago-Theotoky (2007), labelled as ERE in Section 3.2, can also be found when $\beta > 0$, implying that an ERC could help internalise this externality. However, because the TSE is absent, the need for an ERC appears to be less urgent than when firms choose their investment levels before the regulator sets the emission fee.

5. Allowing for Sequential Investments

A natural question is how the equilibrium results are affected when firms invest sequentially in abatement, as opposed to simultaneously in Poyago-Theotoky (2007), Strandholm *et al.* (2018), and Ouchida and Goto (2022). Firms' abatement is generally simultaneous in small investment projects (e.g., end-of-pipe scrubs), but sequential otherwise (e.g., installing new machinery, filters, or clean-up after an oil spill). Examples of large investment projects abound, which may take years to complete, allowing a firm to observe its rival's abatement before choosing its own.[4]

Strandholm *et al.* (2023) consider sequential investments, but abstract from spillovers to focus on the role of sequentiality. They show that equilibrium output in the third stage is still $q = \frac{1-c-t}{3}$, and the equilibrium fee in the second stage is also unaffected at $t = \frac{(2d-1)(1-c)-3d(1+\beta)Z}{2(1+d)}$, as our results in Section 3.2. In the first stage, however, the follower (firm 2) exhibits a negatively sloped best response function $z_2(z_1)$, indicating that firms regard each other's investment as strategic substitutes. Anticipating this best response function, the leader chooses its abatement, $z_1^{\text{Seq}} > 0$, which induces the follower to respond with a positive investment in equilibrium, $z_2^{\text{Seq}} > 0$.

Interestingly, Strandholm *et al.* (2023) find that the presence of a "first-mover advantage", where the leader free-rides off the follower's investment by investing less, $z_1^{\text{Seq}} < z_2^{\text{Seq}}$, if and only if its investment cost (as captured by parameter γ) is sufficiently high, i.e., $\gamma > \widehat{\gamma} \equiv \max\{0, \frac{4d-3}{2}\}$ as depicted in Fig. 5. We can rationalise this result by considering that the benefit from investing in abatement stems from a less stringent fee in the next stage. When the leader's cost of investment (as captured by γ) is lower than its benefit, the leader invests more than the follower. When γ increases, however, the leader finds that the cost of abatement exceeds its benefit. In this case, it free-rides off the follower, namely, investing less in abatement, which induces the follower to respond investing more (since investment decisions are strategic substitutes). These incentives are analogous to those in sequential public-good games, where leaders

[4]Consider, for instance, Intel's commitment in May 2020 to invest in reducing greenhouse gas emissions 10% by 2030, the first to make such a commitment in the chipset industry. In the following year, their closest rival, AMD, announced new environmental sustainability goals, including a 50% reduction in absolute greenhouse gas emissions by 2030. Announcements of large investments in abatement are also observed in the steel industry.

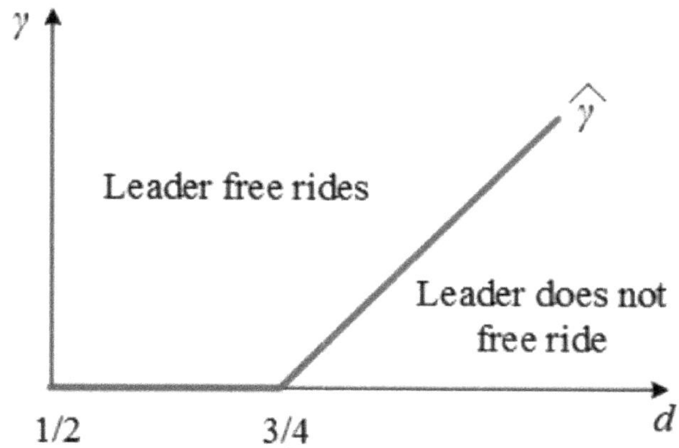

Fig. 5. Leader's free-riding incentives.

contribute less to charities, forcing followers to submit more generous donations.

As illustrated by Fig. 5, this result is affected by the severity of pollution. More severe pollution (higher d) induces more stringent emission fees, which increase the leader's benefit from investing in abatement, ultimately reducing its incentives to free ride (investing less than the follower). In contrast, when pollution is less severe (low d), the benefit from investing in abatement decreases, inducing the leader to free-ride under larger conditions.

Comparing equilibrium investment in sequential and simultaneous settings, they find that $z_i^{\text{Seq}} > z_i^{\text{NC}}$ for every firm $i = \{1, 2\}$, where z_i^{NC} was described in Section 3.2. While this ranking holds unambiguously, its intensity, however, is affected by the parameters. Overall, the difference $z_i^{\text{Seq}} - z_i^{\text{NC}}$ is particularly large when environmental damage is intermediate. Otherwise, firms' investments are similar under both the sequential and simultaneous settings.

Finally, note that the results in Lambertini *et al.* (2017) are unaffected by whether investment decisions happen simultaneously or sequentially. In particular, every firm's abatement level in the second stage, $z_i(t) = \frac{t}{\gamma}$, is not a function of z_j. In other words, every firm finds its investment in abatement to be a strictly dominant strategy. Therefore, the sequentiality in abatement decisions only plays a role when firms' investment occurs before regulation, which may occur when a large green investment project is difficult to adjust after regulation is announced.

6. Allowing for Firm Asymmetry

Previous literature assumed that firms are symmetric in their cost of investing in abatement, $\frac{\gamma(z_i)^2}{2}$, but in certain industries some firms may have more experience in R&D activities, benefiting from lower costs, i.e., $\gamma_i < \gamma_j$ where $j \neq i$. In such a setting, a first-best policy would call for type-dependent (non-uniform) emission fees, (t_i, t_j), setting different fees to each firm in function of their R&D efficiency, γ_i. In a second-best scenario, however, regulators set a type-independent fee (the same, or uniform, fee t on all firms), based on the average R&D efficiency.[5]

Essentially, type-dependent emission fees seek to curb *each firm's* marginal environmental damage from pollution, thus eliminating the TSE externality identified in Section 3.2; while type-independent fees curb *aggregate* environmental damages, not being able to internalise type-(i) externality. To understand this point, recall that under a type-independent policy (single fee t, as in the setting analysed in all previous sections) every firm i's abatement, z_i, reduces the stringency of emission fees to both firms. In contrast, under a type-dependent fee, firm i's investment lowers its specific fee t_i without affecting its rival's fee t_j, which eliminates firms' free-riding incentives in abatement when spillovers are absent. (When spillovers are present, the ERE externality still arises, inducing firms to free-ride off each other's investments.)

Strandholm *et al.* (2021) examine this setting in detail, showing that emission fees are more stringent under uniform than type-dependent policies. This difference in emission fees, nonetheless, diminishes when spillovers increase. Intuitively, when spillovers are small, firms exhibit different marginal environmental damages, yielding distinct emission fees in each regime. However, when spillover

[5]Other papers have looked at the effects of fine-tuned environmental policy, but do not consider investment in clean R&D, see Tietenberg (1974), Henderson (1977), Hochman *et al.* (1977), Hochman and Ofek (1979), and Munoz-Garcia and Akhundjanov (2016).

effects are large, all firms benefit from each other's investment, and thus marginal environmental damages coincide. In this context, the use of either policy regime (type-dependent or -independent) yields the same emission fee, abatement, investment in R&D, and welfare. Therefore, when regulating industries with small spillovers, the use of type-dependent policies becomes more relevant since they promote further investment in R&D and larger welfare.

In contrast, when spillovers are significant both policy regimes yield similar outcomes, such as in clustered industries, where several authors find large spillovers.[6] When firms are located far from other competitors in the same industry, however, spillover effects are generally small, and the above results would indicate that it is precisely in this type of industry where the choice of policy regime matters the most.

Strandholm *et al.* (2021) also evaluate profits under each policy regime, showing that the most efficient firm (that with the lowest γ_i) has incentives to lobby for a type-dependent policy since its investment in R&D entails a more significant reduction in its own emission fee which its rival cannot benefit from. The profit difference across policy regimes, however, diminishes as spillovers increase since, as described above, firms face the same emission fees. In this setting, firms are not critically affected by the policy regime that regulators use to curb externalities. In contrast, when spillovers are small, the profit difference is substantial, leading efficient (inefficient) firms to favour type-dependent (uniform, respectively) policies. This may explain why certain firms, such as Exxon-Mobil, openly favoured policies "that ensure a uniform [...] cost of greenhouse gas emissions across the economy."

Finally, the above article considers an ERC like that in Poyago-Theotoky (2007), showing that investment in abatement under the ERC is larger than under a type-independent regime, a result that is not affected by parameter values; see Fig. 6. In contrast, the ERC investment is larger than that under a type-dependent regime if spillover effects are significant. As described above, when firm j benefits from a large share of firm i's investment in R&D, the

[6]See Jaffe *et al.* (1993), Audretsch and Feldman (1996), Almeida and Kogut (1997), Jaffe *et al.* (2002) and Liu *et al.* (2010).

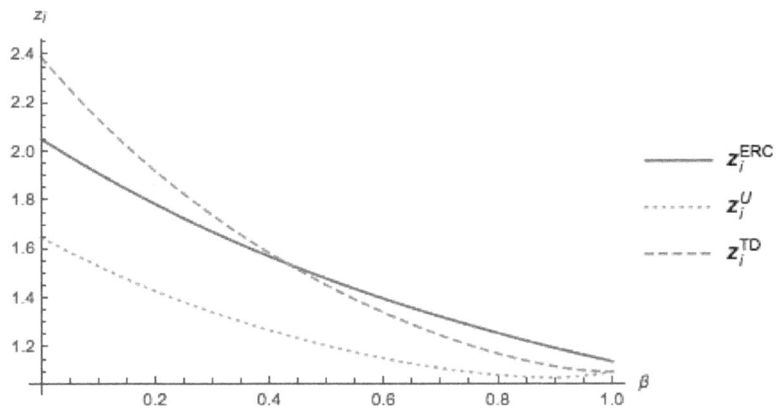

Fig. 6. Investment in R&D under two tax regimes and the ERC.

positive externalities that firm i generates become larger, emphasising firm j's free-riding incentives. Under the ERC, firms internalise these positive effects, thus increasing their investment.

7. Allowing for other Forms of Spillovers

McDonald and Poyago-Theotoky (2017) develop a model where the regulator pre-commits to an emission fee, as in Lambertini *et al.* (2017), and separately examine two forms of R&D spillover:

(1) "input" spillovers, which operate on the expenditure toward pollution reduction, as in Kamien *et al.* (1992), (KMZ model thereafter); and
(2) "output" spillovers, which manifest on as the achieved abatement (i.e., the outcome of the investment), as in d'Aspremont and Jacquemin (1988) (AJ model henceforth).

While the first approach entails that spillovers occur as a consequence of firms using technology developed by other firms, output spillovers imply that firms free-ride of the realised outcome of their rivals' abatement.

When firms do not cooperate in R&D (as in the NC setting in Section 3.2) and spillovers are low, the AJ model shows that there is a negative relationship between the emission fee and spillovers, implying that spillovers and emission fees offset each other. When spillover effects are large, however, there is an incentive for firms to engage in cooperative R&D, either by sharing information or sharing costs. Interestingly, this trade-off does not exist in the KMZ model under non-cooperative R&D regimes; since emissions taxes rise with spillover effects, meaning that input spillovers always create a disincentive to invest when firms operate independently.

By contrast, when firms coordinate their R&D investments (as in Section 3.3), there is always a trade-off between the emission fee and spillovers. Specifically, in the AJ model, firms free-ride off other's abatement effort, as shown in Poyago-Theotoky (2007), whereas in the KMZ model this is not possible. As a consequence, in the KMZ model there always exist decreasing returns to scale in abatement investment. Therefore, the way spillovers operate in each model leads to significant differences in policy implications and implementation. First, regarding the promotion of coordinated investments, both models show a similar outcome: R&D cooperation is more effective in reducing emissions when spillovers are small ($\beta < 0.5$), but R&D competition is more effective in reducing emissions otherwise. This indicates that there is a trade-off between the relative effectiveness of emission fees and cooperative R&D. Second, the scale of investments in abatement is larger in the AJ than the KMZ model, yielding less emissions and less stringent emission fees in equilibrium.

8. Allowing for Disruptive Investments

A recurrent implicit assumption in previous models is that investing in R&D (either in the first or second stage) requires firms to shut down the production process. R&D investments generally disrupt production activities, requiring the participation of workers at all levels, reducing their concentration on production activities, and diverting inputs and equipment to R&D efforts; thus entailing a higher cost of production than when no resources are dedicated to R&D.[7]

---

[7]Capital, for instance, may become more difficult to access, as empirically shown by Czarnitzki *et al.* (2011), or firm productivity may decrease while investing in R&D, as found by Czarnitzki and Thorwarth (2012). Similarly, Rouvinen (2002),

Strandholm *et al.* (2021) relax this assumption, allowing for every firm i to simultaneously choose, in the first period, both its R&D investment, z_i, and output level, x_i. In the second period, observing these decisions, the regulator responds setting a fee t, and then firms compete à la Cournot. As in previous studies, R&D costs are given by $\frac{\gamma(z_i)^2}{2}$.

To account for the possibility of simultaneously dedicating efforts to both R&D and output in the first period, Strandholm *et al.* (2021) consider that this period's cost is $cx_i(1 + \lambda z_i)$, where $\lambda \geq 0$ denotes how much R&D increases the firm's production cost (i.e., "disruption effects" between R&D and output production). When $\lambda = 0$, the firm's output decision is unaffected by its R&D investment today, while when $\lambda > 0$ the firm's investment in R&D increases both its total and marginal production cost.

Strandholm *et al.* (2021) show that three strategy profiles can be sustained in equilibrium where:

(i) firms choose to invest in R&D alone;
(ii) firms produce output but do not invest in R&D[8]; or
(iii) firms carry out both activities simultaneously.

For presentation purposes, let us first focus on a monopoly, which helps isolate incentives to invest in green R&D. Intuitively, when a monopolist invests in R&D during the first period, it induces the regulator to respond by setting a less stringent emission fee. The monopolist then faces lower taxes and, importantly, fully captures the tax-saving effect of its R&D investment, both with and without spillover effects. Under oligopoly, however, every firm has less incentives to invest in R&D since it cannot fully appropriate this tax-saving benefit – a disincentive that is exacerbated when spillover effects are present. As a consequence, more competitive market structures give rise to equilibria where firms choose to focus on production alone without investing in R&D. In contrast, less competitive industries are more likely to sustain equilibria where firms invest in R&D

finds that R&D investments reduce current productivity in most of their model specifications.

[8]This can help explain a recent decision by Global Foundries, a microchip manufacturer, to stop its R&D projects to expand their production scale of existing and older microchip generations; see Cooper (2018).

without producing positive units of output; as the previous literature assumed.

Strandholm *et al.* (2021) also show that disruption effects (as captured by λ) induce firms to reduce their investment in abatement, which ultimately leads the regulator to respond with more stringent emission fees. Evaluating these results in different market structures, they find that, in highly competitive industries firms either engage in both activities (output and R&D) when disruptive effects are small; or only producing output when disruptive effects are large. In this setting, firms are then unlikely to focus on R&D alone. In contrast, when few firms compete, all activity profiles (i)–(iii) can be sustained, including that in which firms focus on R&D alone. A similarly rich pattern arises when R&D generates small (or nil) spillover effects, such as in chemical and pharmaceutical industries which patent most innovations.[9] The findings then suggest that the common assumption in the green R&D literature, where firms only choose R&D in the first period, can naturally emerge in equilibrium, but only when firms interact in highly concentrated industries with small spillover effects. Otherwise, this behaviour is unlikely to be sustained in equilibrium, instead, inducing firms to engage in both activities under broad conditions.

Finally, they also evaluate welfare levels across the three activity profiles, finding that welfare is the highest when firms simultaneously engage in both activities, production and R&D investments, which arises when R&D generates relatively small disruptive effects on production costs. This equilibrium behaviour can be promoted by policies reducing R&D disruption, such as helping firms conduct their R&D projects in government-funded research facilities and labs. In contrast, generous R&D subsidies, which reduce firms' investment costs without affecting its disruptive effects, likely induce large shifts in equilibrium behaviour leading to welfare losses.

In terms of policy implications, these results suggest that, if R&D is disruptive, R&D subsidies may not be welfare improving.

---

[9]For studies considering green R&D investment with spillover effects, see Katsoulacos and Xepapadeas (1995), Montero (2002), Poyago-Theotoky (2007) and Strandholm *et al.* (2018). For empirical studies measuring the extent of spillover effects, see Griliches (1992), Cameron (1998) and Weiser (2005), which report an average private rate of return to R&D around 20–30%, and an estimated spillover of 40–60%.

Policies that, instead, focus on reducing the disruption are preferable, such as government-industry partnership R&D labs; see, for instance, the National Renewable Energy Laboratory's Integrated Bio-refinery Research Facility. The above findings also recommend lowering the fixed cost of entry into industries where R&D activities negatively impact production costs, since reducing concentration – despite its increased pollution – may yield an overall welfare gain. The results also connect with studies showing that, in the presence of market imperfections and second-best environmental policy, reducing the stringency of environmental regulation may actually induce firms to increase their aggregate investment in clean technologies; see, for instance, Gans (2012) and Di Maria and Smulders (2017).

9. Other Extensions

In this section, we briefly review a selection of further extensions to the basic model.

9.1. *Endogenous entry*

While most of the literature considers that the number of firms in a polluting industry is exogenous, $n \geq 2$, Katsoulacos and Xepapadeas (1995) allow for endogenous entry. In their setting, the regulator sets the emission fee in the first stage, firms decide whether or not to enter in the second stage, and then choose output and abatement efforts.

They find that, in equilibrium, the emission fee may exceed marginal environmental damages; a result that did not arise when the market structure is exogenous. Because this finding entails that, in the presence of endogenous entry, environmental policy can lead to an "over-internalisation" of externalities, Katsoulacos and Xepapadeas (1995) explore the use of two policy tools, an entry fee (to curb socially excessive entry) and an emission fee (which lies below the marginal external damages, thus leading to "under-internalisation" of the externality), showing that these policy instruments generate a larger welfare than the over-internalising single emission fee.

9.2. *Subsidies*

Ouchida and Goto (2014) work with a similar setting as that in Poyago-Theotoky (2007), but analyse emissions under subsidies, showing that they can also be welfare improving. As expected, when pollution is not severe (low d), it is socially optimal to subsidise production, i.e., $t < 0$. Intuitively, this occurs because the market failure stemming from pollution is offset by that originating from underproduction in oligopoly, ultimately leading the regulator to provide a per-unit subsidy on output. In this context, when R&D investments are costly (high γ), firms' abatement is low in equilibrium, leading them to pollute more when they are subject to regulation than when they are not (laissez-faire scenario).

While regulation in this setting leads, essentially, to more pollution, its presence can still be welfare improving. In contrast, when R&D investments are inexpensive (low γ), firms choose large abatement levels in equilibrium, which entails their pollution lies below that under no regulation.

9.3. *Different ERC rules*

Ouchida and Goto (2016) study how different government policies around research joint ventures lead to different R&D cartelisation in the ERC, investment levels, and welfare, thus following a similar approach as Kamien *et al.* (1992)) in non-polluting industries. In particular, they assume that, in the first period, the government decides the type of R&D cooperation between firms:

(i) environmental R&D competition, which is analogous to the NC setting in Poyago-Theotoky (2007) allowing for a generic spillover effect $\beta \in [0, 1]$.
(ii) environmental R&D cartelisation, which is equivalent to the ERC considered in Section 3.2, still assuming a generic spillover β.
(iii) environmental ERJV competition, where each firm independently chooses its R&D investment, as in model (i), but setting $\beta = 1$ thus avoiding duplicities in firms' innovations.
(iv) environmental RJV cartelisation, which coincides with the ERC in model (ii) but assuming that $\beta = 1$.

In particular, the government has two choice variables: whether or not to prohibit ERJVs (i.e., whether $\beta \neq 1$ or not) and whether or not to allow R&D coordination. When both are prohibited, model

(i) arises; when the government allows ERJVs ($\beta = 1$) but prohibits R&D coordination, models (i) and (ii) can endogenously arise, depending on which of them firms find most profitable; when, instead, the government prohibits ERJVs ($\beta \neq 1$) but allows R&D coordination, models (iii) and (iv) can emerge in equilibrium, also depending on which one is most profitable; and when the regulator allows both ERJVs and coordination, all four models can occur in equilibrium.

The authors demonstrate that firms have unambiguous incentives to form ERJV cartels. In addition, they show that ERJV cartelisation is not welfare superior under all parameter conditions. Specifically, when pollution severity is low (low d) R&D competition, in model (i), is socially preferred, thus recommending the prohibition of investment coordination and sharing of firms' innovations. When pollution is more severe (or if R&D costs, as captured by γ, is high), however, their article finds that ERJV cartels become socially preferred which is also individually preferred by each firm.

9.4. *To patent or license green innovations?*

Biglaiser and Horowitz (1995) examine a setting where firms choose whether to patent or license the innovation. In particular, firms invest in R&D in the first period, face emission fees in the second period, patent or license technology in the last period, and choose their output levels in the fourth period. They study firms' investment decisions and their incentives to adopt their own discoveries or license them to competing firms.

Denicolo (1999) considers a similar setting, but assuming that only one firm can invest in green R&D, subsequently choosing whether to use its innovation or license it to other companies. This study considers two cases, one where the governments sets emission fees before firms invest in R&D, and another in which it responds to their R&D investment.

9.5. *Product differentiation*

Poyago-Theotoky and Teerasuwannajak (2002) examine how the standard results are affected when products are horizontally differentiated, considering both a "pre-commitment" emission fee (chosen in the first period, before firms responds with their abatement decisions) and a no-commitment fee (chosen in the second period, after firms select their abatement levels). They find that, when products are highly differentiated, the optimal no commitment fee is unambiguously less stringent than the optimal pre-commitment tax. As products become more homogeneous, however, the no commitment fee exceeds the pre-commitment one if R&D is relatively efficient and pollution is severe (low values of γ and high values of d).

They also show that equilibrium abatement levels are higher under the time-consistent regime if products are sufficiently differentiated, but may be lower when the R&D technology is extremely efficient. The welfare ranking holds under similar parameter conditions. However, as products become more and more homogeneous, these results are (partially) reversed and pre-commitment could induce firms to invest more in abatement, yielding higher welfare.

9.6. *Mixed oligopolies*

In a mixed oligopoly (one public firm competing against a number of private firms), the public firm seeks to maximise an objective function that is a linear combination of profits and welfare, where the latter considers the environmental damage from pollution; whereas private firms maximise profits. As a consequence, the presence of a public firm helps internalise the environmental externality, enhancing social welfare. In this context, Barcena-Ruiz and Garzon (2006) demonstrate that privatisation can be detrimental when an emission tax is in place, as it induces firms to abate their emissions, reducing their output, and exacerbating the underproduction typical in oligopoly models. The presence of the public firm can remedy this issue, at least partially, implying that a privatisation is welfare improving only when the number of private firms is sufficiently large. Haruna and Goel (2019) find similar results, showing that the presence of the public firm leads to an overall reduction in output, seeking to reduce total emissions. This lowers, in turn, the stringency of the emission fee, which can become a per-unit subsidy when pollution is not severe. Conversely, Pal and Saha (2014) show that a combination of abatement subsidies and output taxes can achieve first-best outcomes without privatisation. For a detailed review of this literature, see Poyago-Theotoky (2024).

10. Concluding Remarks

Policy design. The findings of this literature have implications for the design and implementation of environmental policies. The timing of regulatory actions and the structure of emission fees play crucial roles at inducing firms' abatement activities. Specifically, allowing the regulator to act first by setting emission fees before firms decide on their abatement investments can reduce the likelihood of ERCs being formed reducing, in consequence, aggregate investments in abatement.

Simultaneous or sequential investments. Our results show that, when firms invest sequentially in abatement, the leader tends to invest less, seeking to free-ride on the follower's investment, especially if the leader's investment costs are high. More severe pollution, nonetheless, attenuates the leader's free-riding incentive. Sequential investments can lead to higher overall abatement levels compared to simultaneous investments, particularly when environmental damage is moderate. This finding highlights the importance of considering the timing of investment decisions in the design of environmental policies.

Spillovers. We show that the effectiveness of emission fees and cooperative R&D varies depending on the type and extent of spillovers. When spillovers are small, cooperative R&D is more effective in reducing emissions, whereas competitive R&D is more effective when spillovers are large.

Disruptive investments. Regarding disruptive R&D investments that affect production costs, we show that three equilibria can be sustained: investing in R&D alone, producing output without R&D, and engaging in both activities simultaneously. Our findings suggest that the common assumption of periods when firms only engage in R&D is valid only in highly concentrated industries with small spillovers. Policies that reduce the disruptive effects of R&D, such as government-industry partnerships, can enhance welfare by promoting simultaneous R&D and production activities.

References

Almeida, P. and Kogut, B. (1997). The exploration of technological diversity and geographic localization in innovation: Start-up firms in the semiconductor industry, *Small Business Economics* **9**, 21–31.

Amir, R., Evstigneev, I. and Wooders, J. (2003). Noncooperative versus cooperative R&D with endogenous spillover rates, *Games and Economic Behavior* **42**(2), 183–207.

Arrow, K. (1962). Economic welfare and the allocation of resources for invention, in *The Rate and Direction of Inventive Activity: Economic and Social Factors*, pp. 609–626, Princeton University Press, Princeton, New Jersey, US.

Audretsch, D. B. and Feldman, M. P. (1996). R&D spillovers and the geography of innovation and production, *The American Economic Review* **86**(3), 630–640.

Barcena-Ruiz, J. and Garzon, B. (2006). Mixed oligopoly and environmental policy, *Spanish Economic Review* **8**, 139–160.

Biglaiser, G. and Horowitz, J. K. (1995). Pollution regulation and incentives for pollution control research, *Journal of Economics and Management Strategy* **3**(4), 663–684.

Cameron, G. (1998). Innovation and growth: A survey of the empirical evidence, *Nuffield College, Working Paper*, pp. 1–34.

Cooper, R. K. (2018). Globalfoundries announces more layoffs, stops 7 nanometer project, https://www.bizjournals.com/albany/news/2018/08/27/more-layoffs-as-globalfoundries-freezes-7-nm.html, accessed: 2025-10-31.

Czarnitzki, D., Hottenrott, H. and Thorwarth, S. (2011). Industrial research versus development investment: The implications of financial constraints, *Cambridge Journal of Economics* **35**(3), 527–544.

Czarnitzki, D. and Thorwarth, S. (2012). Productivity effects of basic research in low-tech and high-tech industries, *Research Policy* **41**(9), 1555–1564.

d'Aspremont, C. and Jacquemin, A. (1988). Cooperative and noncooperative R&D in duopoly with spillovers, *The American Economic Review* **78**(5), 1133–1137.

Delbono, F. and Denicolò, V. (1990). R&D investment in a symmetric and homogeneous oligopoly: Bertrand vs. cournot, *International Journal of Industrial Organization* **8**(2), 297–313.

Denicolo, V. (1999). Pollution-reducing innovations under taxes or permits, *Oxford Economic Papers* **51**, 184–199.

Di Maria, C. and Smulders, S. (2017). A paler shade of green: Environmental policy under induced technical change, *European Economic Review* **19**(C), 151–169.

Gans, J. S. (2012). Innovation and climate change policy, *American Economic Journal: Economic Policy* **4**(4), 125–145.

Griliches, Z. (1992). Introduction to "output measurement in the service sectors", in *Output Measurement in the Service Sectors*, pp. 1–22, University of Chicago Press, Chicago, US.

Haruna, S. and Goel, R. K. (2019). Optimal pollution control in a mixed oligopoly with research spillovers, *Australian Economic Papers* **58**(1), 21–40.

Henderson, J. V. (1977). Externalities in a spatial context, *Journal of Public Economics* **7**, 89–110.

Hochman, E. and Ofek, H. (1979). A theory of the behavior of municipal governments: The case of internalizing pollution externalities, *Journal of Urban Economics* **6**, 416–431.

Hochman, E., Pines, D. and Zilberman, D. (1977). The effects of pollution taxation on the pattern of resource allocation: The downstream diffusion case, *The Quarterly Journal of Economics* **91**, 625–638.

Jaffe, A. B., Newell, R. G. and Stavins, R. N. (2002). Environmental policy and technological change, *Environmental and Resource Economics* **22**, 41–70.

Jaffe, A. B., Trajtenberg, M. and Henderson, R. (1993). Geographic localization of knowledge spillovers as evidenced by patent citations, *The Quarterly Journal of Economics* **108**(3), 577–598.

Kamien, M. I., Muller, E. and Zang, I. (1992). Research joint ventures and R&D cartels, *The American Economic Review* **82**(5), 1293–1306.

Katsoulacos, Y. and Xepapadeas, A. (1995). Environmental policy under oligopoly with endogenous market structure, *The Scandinavian Journal of Economics* **97**(3), 411–420.

Lambertini, L., Poyago-Theotoky, J. and Tampieri, A. (2017). Cournot competition and "green" innovation: An inverted-U relationship, *Energy Economics* **68**, 116–123.

Liu, H.-L., Lin, H.-Y. and Peng, S.-K. (2010). The spillover effects of R&D on manufacturing industry in Taiwan's metropolitan areas, *The Annals of Regional Science* **45**, 519–546.

McDonald, S. and Poyago-Theotoky, J. (2017). Green technology and optimal emissions taxation, *Journal of Public Economic Theory* **19**(2), 362–376.

Montero, J.-P. (2002). Market structure and environmental innovation, *Journal of Applied Economics* **5**, 293–325.

Munoz-Garcia, F. and Akhundjanov, S. B. (2016). Firm preferences for environmental policy: Industry uniform or firm specific? *Strategic Behavior and the Environment* **6**, 135–180.

Ouchida, Y. and Goto, D. (2014). Do emission subsidies reduce emission? in the context of environmental R&D organization, *Economic Modelling* **36**, 511–516.

Ouchida, Y. and Goto, D. (2016). Environmental research joint ventures and time-consistent emission tax: Endogenous choice of R&D formation, *Economic Modelling* **55**, 179–188.

Ouchida, Y. and Goto, D. (2022). Strategic non-use of the government's precommitment ability for emissions taxation: Environmental R&D formation in a Cournot duopoly, *Australian Economic Papers* **61**(1), 181–206.

Pal, R. and Saha, B. (2014). Mixed duopoly and environment, *Journal of Public Economic Theory* **16**(1), 96–118.

Poyago-Theotoky, J. A. (2007). The organization of R&D and environmental policy, *Journal of Economic Behavior & Organization* **62**(1), 63–75.

Poyago-Theotoky, J. (2024). *Mixed Oligopoly and Public Enterprises*, Cambridge University Press, Cambridge, UK.

Poyago-Theotoky, J. and Teerasuwannajak, K. (2002). The timing of environmental policy: A note on the role of product differentiation, *Journal of Regulatory Economics* **21**(3), 305–316.

Rouvinen, P. (2002). R&D—productivity dynamics: Causality, lags, and 'dry holes', *Journal of Applied Economics* **5**(1), 123–156.

Strandholm, J., Espinola-Arredondo, A. and Munoz-Garcia, F. (2018). Regulation, free-riding incentives, and investment in R&D with spillovers, *Resource and Energy Economics* **53**, 133–146.

Strandholm, J., Espinola-Arredondo, A. and Munoz-Garcia, F. (2021). Pollution abatement with disruptive R&D investment, *Resource and Energy Economics* **66**, 101258.

Strandholm, J., Espinola-Arredondo, A. and Munoz-Garcia, F. (2023). Being green first: Simultaneous vs. sequential abatement decisions, *Economics Letters* **227**, 111123.

Tietenberg, T. H. (1974). On taxation and the control of externalities: Comment, *The American Economic Review* **64**(3), 462–466.

Weiser, R. (2005). Research and development, productivity and spillovers: Empirical evidence at the firm level, *Journal of Economic Surveys* **19**(4), 587–621.

Yi, S.-S. (1999). Market structure and incentives to innovate: The case of Cournot oligopoly, *Economics Letters* **65**(3), 379–388.

https://doi.org/10.1142/9789819816033_0002

Chapter 2

On the Optimal Smoothing of R&D for Abatement Technologies in Monopoly

Luca Lambertini

University of Bologna, Department of Economics and Alma Climate Centre, Bologna, Italy

luca.lambertini@unibo.it

The private and collective efficiency of investment smoothing in R&D projects for green technologies is illustrated in a monopoly model where the policy maker adopts a time-consistent emission tax and the firm's reaction includes the parcelisation of abatement efforts in multiple labs. This is also conducive to a validation of the Porter hypothesis in its strong form.

Keywords: Investment smoothing, Jensen's inequality, Green innovation, Emission taxation, Porter hypothesis.

1. Introduction

The integration of green innovation in the debate about the bearings of market competition and its intensity on the environment has taken place in (at least, and with a certain degree of simplification for expositional purposes) two phases.[1] During the first one, the subject was the adoption of green technologies made available to firms (but not costly developed therein), as a reaction to environmental regulation in the form of emission taxation, emission standards or emission trading systems. This approach appears in Downing and White (1986), Malueg (1989), Milliman and Prince (1989), Laffont and Tirole (1996a), Montero (2002b), Requate and Unold (2003) and several others. In the second phase, abatement and backstop technologies became endogenous variables, accompanied by endogenous R&D costs (see Biglaiser and Horowitz (1995), Parry (1995), Denicolo (1999), Laffont and Tirole (1996b), Montero (2002a) and Sunnevåg (2003), *inter alia*). This was complemented by the parallel discussion about the nature and timing of environmental policies, which I will touch upon below.

A relevant aspect of the modelisation of R&D activity is the common assumption whereby, whenever it is endogenous to the model, green innovation is subject to decreasing returns, which implies increasing technical progress goes along with the presence of convex cost curves. While respecting casual observation and intuition, and being in line with the parallel debate about process and product innovation in the theory of industrial organisation (see, e.g., Tirole (1988), Martin (1993)), this evolution left something behind. And it should be added that the feature I'm referring to has been largely neglected in the area of the industrial organisation as well. It consists of the possibility of smoothing the cost associated with R&D projects across multiple labs (or divisions, depending on circumstances).

This perspective is assessed here, taking as a departure point a monopoly model in which the regulator taxes GHG emissions in a time-consistent way, as illustrated by Petrakis and Xepapadeas (1999), Petrakis and Xepapadeas (2003), and the firm chooses the number of R&D labs and the optimal effort to be carried out in each of them (before tax policy is designed) and then produces the optimal output having observed the tax.

The main results of the analysis can be summarised in the following terms. To begin with, the very existence of R&D incentives is conditional upon the optimal policy to be a proper tax (as we are

[1] An exhaustive account of this evolution is in Requate (2005).

acquainted to think from the bulk of previous literature), while being altogether unaffected by the number of labs. Then, there emerges that profits are concave and single peaked in the number of labs, the privately optimal effort fragmentation being increasing in market size while falling short of the socially efficient one. In other words, all else equal, a benevolent planner would fragment R&D efforts more than a profit-seeking monopoly in order to boost the resulting cost-smoothing effect, due to the positive implications on consumer surplus via the price mechanism (which incorporates the tax), even if this implies some additional fixed costs.

The last step consists in checking whether the model delivers a validation of the Porter hypothesis, and – if so – in which form. According to Porter (1991), see also Porter and van der Linde (1995a), Porter and van der Linde (1995b), (i) environmental policies may spur firms to invest in either abatement or replacement technologies in order to soften the impact of regulation on their profits, so much so that (ii) they may end up delivering a higher welfare accompanied by a cleaner environment. The first implication is verified whenever firms find it profitable to invest in R&D activities rather than simply reduce emissions by diminishing production, while leaving technology unaltered. The second conjecture points to the possibility for firms' investments in green technologies to yield a socially efficient outcome. While the weak form of the Porter hypothesis envisages a validation of (i), the simultaneous validation of (i) and (ii) amounts to a win-win solution yielding a vindication of the hypothesis in its strong form. While the latter has been shown to emerge in a large number of theoretical models, we are still short of robust empirical evidence (which, however, is validating the weak form).[2]

Indeed, at the equilibrium of the ensuing model – under a proper taxation of GHG emissions – one finds a validation of the Porter hypothesis in its strong form, as the levels of profits and welfare are higher than those characterising the simpler scenario in which the firm's reaction to the tax is confined to an adjustment of its production plan. Moreover, the very fact that this result obtains in

[2]Detailed overviews of the debate on the Porter hypothesis can be found in Lanoie *et al.* (2011), Ambec *et al.* (2013), Lambertini (2013, 2017), Lambertini *et al.* (2017) and Ranocchia and Lambertini (2021).

correspondence of a time consistent tax policy endogenously designed by the regulator to maximise social welfare must be fully appreciated, as several theoretical investigations of the Porter hypothesis have been carried out under the assumption that the related environmental policy can be purposely shaped to achieve its validation in the strong form see, e.g., André *et al.* (2009), Lambertini and Tampieri (2012) and Lambertini (2013). This modelling choice is motivated by the intention – sometimes explicitly spelled out – of stressing that environmental regulation should not be permanent. In fact, the Porter hypothesis envisages a scenario in which a sufficiently strong policy stimulus should become immaterial as quickly as possible, and therefore consumers and firms could be willing to bear its transitory brunt. Having said that, the arising of a win-win solution in the presence of a welfare-maximising tax is surely more acceptable from social, political and economic standpoints alike.

The remainder of the chapter is structured as follows. Section 2 contains the layout of the model. The equilibrium analysis and its implications are illustrated in Section 3. Concluding remarks are in Section 4.

2. The Model

A pure monopolist operates in a market in which the representative consumer expresses the demand function $p = a - Q$, $a > 0$, for a homogeneous good, whose production takes place at decreasing returns to scale, summarised by the cost function $C(Q) = (b + cQ)Q$, $b, c > 0$. Production and/or consumption involve GHG emissions $\mathrm{E} = eQ$, with e measuring the amount of CO_2-equivalent particles per unit. The resulting environmental damage is $D = vE^2$.

Consequently, the government taxes emissions at rate t, and this may induce the firm to invest in green technologies to abate emissions. Defining the abatement effort as K, net emissions are $\mathrm{E}(K) = eQ - K$, whereby (provided t is indeed positive) the income generated by the tax is $TI = t\mathrm{E}(K) = t(eQ - K)$.

From the firm's standpoint, what matters is the cost function $\Gamma(K)$ associated with total R&D effort K. If, as one may sensibly suppose, also R&D activities are characterised by decreasing returns, the monopolist might indeed parcelise R&D activities into n identical labs in order to smooth R&D costs, thereby replacing a single cost function $\Gamma(K) = dK^2$, $d > 0$, with n symmetric cost functions equal to $\gamma(k) = dk^2$. All of this does not explicitly feature a generic degree of technological spillovers among labs, as one may postulate the existence of full information transmission across the organisational structure of the firm.

Hence, in the presence of a per-lab fixed setup cost F, the monopolist's profit function is

$$\pi = (A - Q - cQ)Q - t(eQ - nk) - n\left(dk^2 + F\right) \tag{1}$$

where $A \equiv a - b$. Note that the special case in which marginal production cost is constant obtains by posing $c = 0$ at any relevant point in the remainder of the analysis.

From the collective viewpoint, the relevant social welfare function is

$$\begin{aligned} SW = \pi + CS + TI - D = (A - Q - cQ)Q - n\left(dk^2 + F\right) \\ + \frac{Q^2}{2} - v(eQ - nk)^2 \end{aligned} \tag{2}$$

where the tax income cancels out because, once collected, it is redistributed to consumers through public expenditure.

As we know from Petrakis and Xepapadeas (1999), Petrakis and Xepapadeas (2003), the only time-consistent structure of the game is that where emission taxation is designed by the policy maker just before the market stage.[3] Accordingly, the game features four stages: at the first, the firm chooses the number of R&D labs that maximise its profits; at the second one, it identifies the single lab's effort k to the same aim, correctly anticipating the tax rate set by the public authority to maximise social welfare at the third stage; finally, at the fourth stage, the monopolist maximises its profits by setting quantity (or price). As usual, the solution concept is sub-game perfection attained by backward induction.

[3] All of this does not imply that the analysis of the time-inconsistent case is of no interest, as the policy maker may avail of a credible commitment device. In such a case, it is wise to perform a comparison between the two scenarios, as in Poyago-Theotoky and Teerasuwannajak (2002).

3. Solving the Game

The first order condition (FOC) at the fourth stage is

$$\frac{\partial \pi}{\partial Q} = A - 2(1+c) - t = 0 \tag{3}$$

which delivers the optimal monopoly output $Q^M = (A-t)/[2(1+c)]$ for a generic intensity of emission taxation. Plugging Q^M into (2) and proceeding backwards to the third stage, we may calculate the following FOC for the maximisation of social welfare:

$$\frac{\partial SW}{\partial t} = \frac{A(2v-1) - t[1+2(c+v)] - 4k(1+c)nv}{4(1+c)^2} = 0 \tag{4}$$

and the second-order condition (SOC)

$$\frac{\partial^2 SW}{\partial t^2} = -\frac{1+2(c+v)}{4(1+c)^2} \leq 0 \tag{5}$$

which is satisfied as a strict inequality across the whole relevant parameter range. Solving (4), one obtains the expression of the socially optimal policy instrument:

$$t^* = \frac{A(2v-1) - 4k(1+c)nv}{1+2(c+v)} \tag{6}$$

It is evident that the r.h.s. of (6) indeed defines a tax provided that (i) $v > 1/2$ and (ii) $k > A(2v-1)/[4(1+c)nv]$. It is worth noting that condition (i) amounts to requiring that the environmental damage be steeper than consumer surplus. More explicitly, (6) conveys the message that if the environmental impact of production/consumption is too soft, then the trade-off between consumer surplus and environmental damage may end up generating a subsidy instead of a tax, thereby causing the complete annihilation of abatement efforts.[4] We

[4]This is a problem repeatedly identified in a long-standing discussion encapsulated into the literature on these matters, and emerging in static and dynamic models alike. See, *inter alia*, Benchekroun and Long (1998), Montero (2002a), Poyago-Theotoky (2007) and Lambertini (2013, 2017).

will come back to this aspect in the remainder, after the identification of the equilibrium R&D effort. For the moment, it suffices to highlight that, if indeed $t^*, k > 0$, then

$$\frac{\partial t^*}{\partial k} = -\frac{4(1+c)nv}{1+2(c+v)} < 0 \tag{7}$$

Moreover,

$$\left|\frac{\partial^2 t^*}{\partial k \partial n}\right| = \frac{4(1+c)v}{1+2(c+v)} > 0 \tag{8}$$

Taken together, (7 & 8) entail the following

Lemma 1. *If the optimal policy instrument is a tax, and therefore R&D investments are positive, then the tax pressure becomes progressively softer as abatement efforts become more intense. This effect is fostered by any increase in the number of R&D labs.*

This result tells that R&D for green technologies softens the tax burden (which sounds very familiar), increasingly so as the parcelisation of total R&D increases through the creation of a larger number of labs, the latter being a much less familiar piece of information.

At the second stage, the profit function looks as follows:

$$\pi\left(Q^M, t^*\right) = \frac{A\left[A(1+c) + nk\left(4v(1+v) - 1 + 2c(4v-1)\right)\right] - \Theta}{\left[1+2(c+v)\right]^2} - nF \tag{9}$$

with

$$\Theta \equiv nk^2\left[4nv(1+c)(1+2c+v) + d\left(1+2(c+v)\right)^2\right] \tag{10}$$

The FOC w.r.t. k delivers

$$k^M = \frac{A\left[4v(v+1) - 1 + 2c(4v-1)\right]}{(1+2c+v)\left[8nv(1+c) + 2d(1+2c+v)\right]} \tag{11}$$

and the related SOC is always satisfied:

$$\frac{\partial^2 \pi\left(Q^M, t^*\right)}{\partial k^2} = -\frac{8n^2 v(1+c)(1+2c+v)}{(1+2c+v)^2} - 2d < 0 \tag{12}$$

Now, one must account for the fact that

$$k^M > 0 \Leftrightarrow 4v(v+1) - 1 + 2c(4v-1) > 0 \tag{13}$$

which holds for all $v > v_k \equiv -c - 1/2 + \sqrt{\left[1+c(3+2c)\right]/2} > 0$, strictly increasing and concave in c. Before proceeding any further, it must be noted that the above non-negativity condition is independent of n. That is,

Remark 1. The extent of R&D parcelisation has no impact on the positivity of the single lab's abatement effort.

This amounts to saying that the policy maker must not worry about the possibility for fragmentation to cause the annihilation of the firm's incentive to generate green technologies,[5] as this is a perspective connected with the *vexata quaestio*, concerning whether the socially optimal policy tool is a tax or not.

And indeed, whenever condition (13) is satisfied, the optimal tax can be rewritten as

$$t^*\left(k^M\right) = \frac{A\left[2v\left(2d\left(c+v\right)+n\left(1+c\right)\right)-b\left(1+2c\right)\right]}{\left[4nv\left(1+c\right)+d\left(1+2c+v\right)\right]\left(1+2c+v\right)} > 0 \qquad (14)$$

for all $v > v_k$ as the equation $t^*\left(k^M\right) = 0$ has two imaginary roots. Conversely, for all $v \in \left[0, v_k\right]$, the abatement effort is nil and the resulting tax is $t^*\left(0\right) = A(2v-1)/[1+2(c+v)]$. In fact, the latter is necessarily a subsidy since $v_k \in \left(1/2, \sqrt{2}/2\right)$ for all $c \in (0, \infty)$, and therefore $v_k < 1/2$ always. Moreover, it is easily ascertained that, if $v > v_k$, $\partial t^*(k^M)/\partial v > 0$ while $\partial k^M/\partial v > 0$.

The foregoing discussion can be summarised in

Proposition 1. *Provided* $v > v_k$, $k^M, t^*\left(k^M\right) > 0$ *for any finite number of research labs. In this parameter range, the single lab's abatement effort monotonically decreases in* v*, while the opposite holds for the tax. If instead* $v \in [0, v_k]$*, the optimal policy consists in subsidising production and the firm does not invest at all in abatement technologies.*

Having characterised the essential properties of the time-consistent equilibrium, it's time to focus upon the main subject matter of the analysis, namely, the efficient parcelisation of abatement efforts, to be determined at the initial stage under the assumption that $v > v_k$.

[5]Except for the case of infinitely many labs, which can be excluded *a priori* given the presence of the setup cost.

3.1. Jensen's inequality and the optimal number of R&D labs

The relevant magnitudes at the first stage of the game are the profit function, the aggregate abatement effort and social welfare:

$$K^M = nk^M = \frac{nA\left[4v\left(v+1\right)-1+2c\left(4v-1\right)\right]}{8nv\left(1+c\right)\left(1+2c+v\right)+d\left(1+2\left(c+v\right)\right)^2} \tag{15}$$

$$\pi\left(Q^M, t^*, k^M\right) = \frac{A^2\left[4d\left(1+c\right)+n\left(1+4v\left(1+2c+v\right)\right)\right]}{4[4nv\left(1+c\right)\left(1+2c+v\right)+d\left(1+2\left(c+v\right)\right)^2]} - nF \tag{16}$$

and $SW\left(Q^M, t^*, k^M\right) = \pi\left(Q^M, t^*, k^M\right) + CS\left(Q^M, t^*, k^M\right) + TI\left(Q^M, t^*, k^M\right) - D(Q^M, t^*, k^M)$, whose lengthy explicit expression is omitted for the sake of brevity.

The trivial observation of the fact that Jensen's inequality applies to quadratic cost curves calls for the proliferation of labs and would call for infinitely many labs, each one becoming arbitrarily small. What limits this incentive and delivers a finite privately efficient parcelisation of R&D activity is the presence of the exogenous fixed cost to be sunk with the creation of any single lab. This clearly emerges observing the relevant FOC:

$$\frac{\partial\pi\left(Q^M, t^*, k^M\right)}{\partial n} = \frac{A^2 d\left[4v\left(1+v\right)-1+2c\left(4v-1\right)\right]}{4[4nv\left(1+c\right)\left(1+2c+v\right)+d\left(1+2\left(c+v\right)\right)^2]^2} - F = 0 \tag{17}$$

where the first part of the expression on the r.h.s. is strictly positive in the relevant part of the parameter range. The associated SOC for concavity is

$$\frac{\partial^2\pi\left(\cdot\right)}{\partial n^2} = -\frac{2A^2\left(1+c\right)dv\left(1+2c+v\right)\left[4v\left(1+v\right)-1+2c\left(4v-1\right)\right]^2}{[4nv\left(1+c\right)\left(1+2c+v\right)+d\left(1+2\left(c+v\right)\right)^2]^3} \tag{18}$$

which is satisfied everywhere.

Solving (17) w.r.t. n, one finds these roots:

$$n_{\pm}^{M}=\frac{-2dF\left(1+2c+v\right)^{2}\pm A\left[4v\left(1+v\right)-1+2c\left(4v-1\right)\right]\sqrt{dF}}{8F\left(1+c\right)^{2}v^{2}\left(1+2c+v\right)^{2}} \tag{19}$$

with $n_{+}^{M}\geq 1>n_{-}^{M}$ for all[6]

$$A\geq\frac{2F[4v\left(1+c\right)\left(1+2c+v\right)+b\left(1+2\left(c+v\right)\right)^{2}]}{\sqrt{dF}\left[4v\left(1+v\right)-1+2c\left(4v-1\right)\right]} \tag{20}$$

Therefore, $n^{M}=n_{+}^{M}$, and it is easily verified that (i) n^{M} increases linearly in A; and the necessary and sufficient condition for $n^{M}\geq 2$ is

$$A\geq\frac{2F[8v\left(1+c\right)\left(1+2c+v\right)+b\left(1+2\left(c+v\right)\right)^{2}]}{\sqrt{dF}\left[4v\left(1+v\right)-1+2c\left(4v-1\right)\right]}\equiv\widehat{A} \tag{21}$$

Consequently, and recalling that $A\equiv a-b$, one may formulate

Proposition 2. *The privately efficient number of R&D labs increases monotonically in market size A, as measured under constant marginal production cost. The condition $A\geq\widehat{A}$ must be satisfied in order for investment smoothing across multiple labs to arise at equilibrium.*

The next step consists in assessing social preferences concerning the extent of R&D parcelisation chosen by the monopolist. Plugging n^{M} into $\partial SW(Q^{M},t^{*},k^{M})/\partial n$, it turns out that the partial derivative of social welfare is still positive, implying that, if it were in a position to control the fragmentation of R&D efforts (but not output and R&D efforts themselves), a social planner would create a larger number of labs as compared to the profit-seeking monopolist.

This fact can be visualised in Fig. 1, where $n^{M}\simeq 3$, while the peak of the welfare function takes place at $n\simeq 4$. The values of the model parameters have been fixed at $a=10$, $c=0.25$, $d=1.6$, $F=1.1$ and

[6]An intuitive property of n_{+}^{M} is that it is decreasing in c, all else equal. This ancillary implication is due to the fact that decreasing returns to scale in production clearly penalise gross profits and therefore limit the expansion of the number of labs.

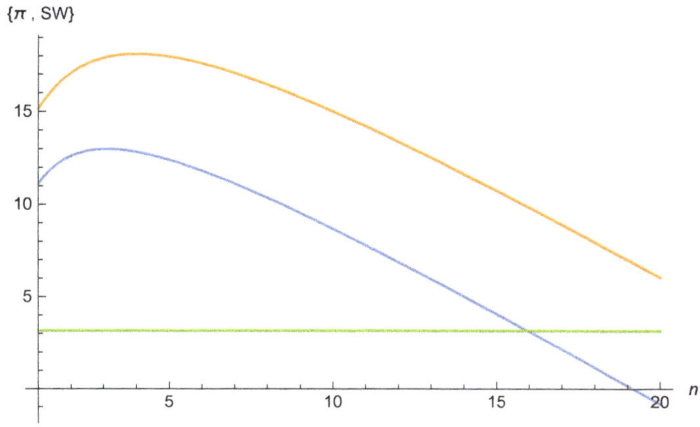

Fig. 1. Profits, social welfare and the privately optimal number of labs. **Colour codes** blue: π^M; orange: SW; green: n^M.

$v = 1.65$. the numerical simulation can be repeated at will, to show analogous outcomes. As an example, using $a = 10$, $c = 0$, $d = 1/2$, $F = 1/20$ and $v = \sqrt{(979 + 40\sqrt{10})/1902} - 1/2 \simeq 0.262$, the socially optimal number of labs is eight, while the profit-maximising number is still in the neighbourhood of $n^M \simeq 3$.

In a nutshell, the foregoing discussion boils down to the following

Proposition 3. *At the monopoly optimum, regulated by time-consistent emission taxation, investment smoothing falls short of the socially efficient level that a public authority would set, all else equal.*

In this respect, in order to grasp the intuition behind this result, it is appropriate to recall that we are accustomed to run across the opposite conclusion concerning the wasteful duplication of fixed costs, on the basis of a consolidated literature inherited from the theory of industrial organisation. To mention one, it holds for the case of excess entry with the associated wasteful duplication of sunk costs in Mankiw and Whinston (1986) and several follow-ups, as well as in the analysis of R&D incentives for process innovation, and the desirability of R&D cartels or joint ventures, as we know from d'Aspremont and Jacquemin (1988) and the ensuing discussion. In that literature, the pervasive result is that profit incentives bring about the inefficient replication of fixed costs curtailing social welfare. Here, instead, the replication of fixed costs is the key to the activation of investment smoothing as dictated by Jensen's inequality, and a public authority aware of the aforementioned trade-off affecting its policy instrument would favour fragmentation in excess of the monopoly optimum, insofar as the additional cost is more than offset by the reduction of R&D's marginal cost as well as the additional reduction of the environmental damage. The latter effect softens the impact of the tax passing through to consumers via the market price, and motivates the increase in R&D fragmentation in the public authority's mind.

An important corollary to the above findings is that the combination of time-consistent taxation by the policy maker and the optimal number of labs by the firm do validate the strong form of the Porter hypothesis, by delivering a win-win solution. This can be verified visually by looking at Figure 1, without any further calculation: both monopoly profits and social welfare monotonically increase in n, up to n^M. Indeed, this holds for all $n = 0, 1, 2, \ldots, n^M$. The inclusion of $n = 0$ may look weird at first glance, but is instead important as it refers to a situation in which the firm reacts to the tax adjusting output only.[7]

Having clarified this aspect, the fact that social welfare is still positively sloped in n at the private optimum may indeed sound disappointing for other reasons, but *de facto* is a self-explanatory validation of the win-win solution, which deserves to be formulated explicitly in

Corollary 1. *The choice of the profit-maximising number of R&D labs validates the strong form of the Porter hypothesis.*

To complement the exposition of the equilibrium outcome, there remains to formulate some considerations about the impact of the numerosity of R&D labs on total abatement effort K^M, and the resulting environmental damage, $D\left(Q^M, t^*, k^M\right)$.

The pattern of K^M is captured by the following derivatives:

$$\frac{\partial K^M}{\partial n} = \frac{Ad\left[1 + 2\left(c + v\right)\right]^2\left[4v\left(1 + v\right) - 1 + 2c\left(4v - 1\right)\right]}{2[4nv\left(1 + c\right)\left(1 + 2c + v\right) + d\left(1 + 2\left(c + v\right)\right)^2]^2} > 0 \quad (22)$$

[7]Observe that to validate the win-win solution it suffices to pose $n = 0$, and therefore also $F = 0$, in (17), to verify that it is strictly positive.

$$\frac{\partial^2 K^M}{\partial n^2} = -\frac{4A(1+c)\,dv\,(1+2c+v)\,[1+2(c+v)]^2\,\Omega}{[4nv(1+c)(1+2c+v)+d(1+2(c+v))^2]^3} < 0 \quad (23)$$

$$\Omega \equiv [4v(1+v) - 1 + 2c(4v-1)]^2$$

which show that K^M is increasing and concave in n. Obviously, this implies that, if building up a lab were cost-less, R&D fragmentation would be limitless.

The equilibrium level of environmental damage is

$$D\left(Q^M, t^*, k^M\right) = \frac{A^2 v\,(2d+n)^2\,[1+2(c+v)]^2}{4[4nv(1+c)(1+2c+v)+d(1+2(c+v))^2]^2} \quad (24)$$

which is everywhere decreasing and convex in n,[8] and it is evident that it cannot be driven to zero through any increase in R&D parcelisation. And the same obviously applies to GHG emissions. This amounts to saying that the abatement technology illustrated in this model (and in a large literature using the same ingredient) cannot deliver a fully green technology.

4. Concluding Remarks

The foregoing analysis offers a first glance at the relevance and consequences of investment smoothing in R&D projects for green innovations, going along with proper emission taxation, on relevant private and collective magnitudes. There neatly emerges that setting up several labs as a straightforward application of Jensen's inequality can be desirable in both respects, so much so to also bring about a confirmation of the win-win solution implied by the strong formulation of the Porter hypothesis.

However, the above is nothing more than a preliminary step, leaving aside many aspects that may play a relevant role, such as

[8] As stressed in Section 2, the definition of emission abatement implicitly assumes full spillovers. The presence of partial spillovers *à la* d'Aspremont and Jacquemin (1988) – which would make sense in oligopoly, with incomplete information transmission or leakage among labs – might engender non-monotone patterns. For instance, this happens in Lambertini (2017), in a Cournot oligopoly game delivering a concave and single-peaked abatement effort at the industry level.

the intensity of market competition, product differentiation, and of course alternative policy tools like emission trading systems and environmental standards. All of these extensions will hopefully drive future research.

Acknowledgements

I would like to thank Joanna Poyago-Theotoky for useful comments. I gratefully acknowledge the financial support received from the PRIN2017 grant no. 201782J9R9 "Experimental assessment of climate change economics" led by Marco Casari.

References

Ambec, S., Cohen, M., Elgie, S. and Lanoie, P. (2013). The Porter hypothesis at 20: Can environmental regulation enhance innovation and competitiveness? *Review of Environmental Economics and Policy* **7**, 2–22.

André, F., González, P. and Porteiro, N. (2009). Strategic quality competition and the Porter hypothesis, *Journal of Environmental Economics and Management* **57**, 182–94.

Benchekroun, H. and Long, N. (1998). Efficiency inducing taxation for polluting oligopolists, *Journal of Public Economics* **70**, 325–342.

Biglaiser, G. and Horowitz, J. K. (1995). Pollution regulation and incentives for pollution control research, *Journal of Economics and Management Strategy* **3**(4), 663–684.

d'Aspremont, C. and Jacquemin, A. (1988). Cooperative and noncooperative R&D in duopoly with spillovers, *The American Economic Review* **78**(5), 1133–1137.

Denicolo, V. (1999). Pollution-reducing innovations under taxes or permits, *Oxford Economic Papers* **51**, 184–199.

Downing, P. B. and White, L. J. (1986). Innovation in pollution control, *Journal of Environmental Economics and Management* **13**(1), 18–29.

Laffont, J. J. and Tirole, J. (1996a). Pollution permits and compliance strategies, *Journal of Public Economics* **62**, 85–125.

Laffont, J. J. and Tirole, J. (1996b). Pollution permits and environmental innovation, *Journal of Public Economics* **62**, 127–140.

Lambertini, L. (2013). *Oligopoly, the Environment and Natural Resources*, Routledge, Abingdon, Oxon, UK.

Lambertini, L. (2017). Green innovation and market power, *Annual Review of Resource Economics* **9**, 231–252.

Lambertini, L., Poyago-Theotoky, J. and Tampieri, A. (2017). Cournot competition and "green" innovation: An inverted-U relationship, *Energy Economics* **68**, 116–123.

Lambertini, L. and Tampieri, A. (2012). Vertical differentiation in a Cournot industry: The Porter hypothesis and beyond, *Resource and Energy Economics* **34**, 374–380.

Lanoie, P., Laurent-Lucchetti, J., Johnstone, N. and Ambec, S. (2011). Environmental policy, innovation and performance: New insights on the Porter hypothesis, *Journal of Economics and Management Strategy* **20**, 803–842.

Malueg, D. A. (1989). Emission credit trading and the incentive to adopt new pollution abatement technology, *Journal of Environmental Economics and Management* **18**, 52–57.

Mankiw, N. and Whinston, M. (1986). Free entry and social inefficiency, *RAND Journal of Economics* **17**, 48–58.

Martin, S. (1993). *Advanced Industrial Economics*, Blackwell, London, UK.

Milliman, S. R. and Prince, R. (1989). Firm incentives to promote technological change in pollution control, *Journal of Environmental Economics and Management* **17**, 247–265.

Montero, J.-P. (2002a). Market structure and environmental innovation, *Journal of Applied Economics* **5**, 293–325.

Montero, J.-P. (2002b). Permits, standards, and technology innovation, *Journal of Environmental Economics and Management* **44**(1), 23–44.

Parry, I. (1995). Optimal pollution taxes and endogenous technological progress, *Resource and Energy Economics* **17**, 69–85.

Petrakis, E. and Xepapadeas, A. (1999). Does government precommitment promote environmental innovation? in E. Petrakis, E. Sartzetakis and A. Xepapadeas (Eds.), *Environmental Regulation and Market Power*, pp. 145–161, Edward Elgar Publishing, Cheltenham, UK.

Petrakis, E. and Xepapadeas, A. (2003). Location decisions of a polluting firm and the time consistency of environmental policy, *Resource and Energy Economics* **25**(2), 197–214.

Porter, M. E. (1991). America's green strategy, *Scientific American* **264**(4), 168.

Porter, M. E. and van der Linde, C. (1995a). Green and competitive: Ending the stalemate, *Harvard Business Review* **September–October**, 120–134.

Porter, M. E. and van der Linde, C. (1995b). Toward a new conception of the environment-competitiveness relationship, *Journal of Economic Perspectives* **9**(4), 97–118.

Poyago-Theotoky, J. A. (2007). The organization of R&D and environmental policy, *Journal of Economic Behavior & Organization* **62**(1), 63–75.

Poyago-Theotoky, J. and Teerasuwannajak, K. (2002). The timing of environmental policy: A note on the role of product differentiation, *Journal of Regulatory Economics* **21**(3), 305–316.

Ranocchia, C. and Lambertini, L. (2021). Porter hypothesis vs. pollution haven hypothesis: Can there be environmental policies getting two eggs in one basket? *Environmental and Resource Economics* **78**, 177–199.

Requate, T. (2005). Timing and commitment of environmental policy, adoption of new technology, and repercussions on R&D, *Environmental and Resource Economics* **31**(2), 175–199.

Requate, T. and Unold, W. (2003). On the incentives of environmental policy to adopt advanced abatement technology: Will the true ranking please stand up? *European Economic Review* **47**(1), 125–146.

Sunnevåg, K. J. (2003). Auction design for the allocation of emission permits in the presence of market power, *Environmental and Resource Economics* **26**(3), 385–400.

Tirole, J. (1988). *The Theory of Industrial Organization*, MIT Press, Cambridge, Mass., US.

https://doi.org/10.1142/9789819816033_0003

Chapter 3

Imperfect Competition, Emissions Tax and the Porter Hypothesis

Flavio M. Menezes* and Jorge Pereira†

The University of Queensland, School of Economics, Brisbane, Australia

**f.menezes@uq.edu.au*

†*jorgepereira@bigpond.com*

This chapter investigates the conditions under which the design of an emissions tax can align social and private interests. Our contribution is to determine the general conditions for firms' profits and social welfare to be higher under the implementation of an emissions tax than under no tax. We consider n firms producing a homogeneous product and competing over supply schedules, which covers a continuum of imperfect competition equilibria from Bertrand to Cournot. We show that, as competition intensifies, the pass-through of the tax to consumers increases, to a point where the price rises more than offsets the net result of the investment outlay. Our analysis provides new insights into the trade-off between environmental policy, market competition and the so-called "win-win" outcome for firms and society.

Keywords: Technology, R&D, Environment, Policy, Emission tax, Subsidy, Porter hypothesis.

1. Introduction

An environmental policy such as an emissions tax is usually socially desirable as it corrects an externality. However, an environmental tax may have a negative impact on firms' profitability, which can create a perverse political economy, for example through lobbying of legislators. The private economic burden of an environmental tax may result in a social welfare enhancing tax not being adopted. This chapter investigates the conditions under which the design of an emissions tax aligns with social and business interests. That is, we characterise the market conditions under which an emissions tax leads to an increase in firms' profits and social welfare. Our results can be seen as determining conditions under which the strong version of the Porter hypothesis (Porter, 1991, Porter and van der Linde, 1995) holds.[1]

We consider the impact of an emissions tax in the context of an oligopolistic industry where n symmetric firms produce a homogeneous product. Production by this industry entails environmentally damaging emissions. Firms respond to the emissions tax by investing in emissions abatement R&D/technology and/or by decreasing their output. Each firm decides on its emissions reduction investment, which deterministically results in a level of emissions abatement. The firm then chooses a supply schedule, specifying how much it will produce at various prices. This approach allows us to parameterise the intensity of competition, which varies continuously from Cournot to Bertrand strategic behaviour (see Menezes and Quiggin (2012), Menezes and Quiggin (2020)).

Firms undertake the end-of-pipe type of emissions abatement, where gross emissions are subsequently decreased by implementing add-on measures, for example, by using a filter or scrubber technology (see Flagan and Seinfeld (2012), Hocking (2016), Bellas (1998)). The firms' investment in emissions abatement technology does not lead to gains in productivity (or attracts a "green" premium in price).

[1]See also Ambec *et al.* (2013).

Instead, in our model, the mechanism through which profits increase is the reduction in product market competition.[2]

In particular, we show that firms are more likely to benefit from an emissions tax when competition is more intense; firms have more to gain from a reduction in competition when it is more intense, and under some conditions these gains outweigh the costs imposed by the emissions tax. This necessary condition is described in terms of the emissions tax cost pass-through (the proportion of tax increase that is reflected in consumer prices). For an emissions tax to be profitable, the cost pass-through must be greater than the net emissions per unit of production, adjusted for the number of firms.

We then provide an example where we determine sufficient conditions for an emissions tax to be both welfare enhancing and to increase firms' profits. For firms to benefit from an optimal tax, the emissions abatement investment must be sufficiently efficient and under a given threshold, determined by the intensity of competition and the number of firms. In the case of a Cournot duopoly or a monopoly, we conclude that firms never benefit from an environmental tax. More intense market competition increases the gains from an emissions tax as it leads to a higher cost pass-through. This example complements the analysis of Delbono and Lambertini (2022) who show that, with linear demand and quadratic costs, and when two firms producing a homogeneous product compete in prices, win-win solutions arise for almost any level of environmental damage in any Bertrand–Nash equilibrium. Our example shows that win-win solutions can arise even when competition is less intense than in a Bertrand equilibrium.

This chapter is organised as follows. Section 2 describes the building blocks of the model, including product demand, emissions abatement technology and competition in supply schedules. In Section 3, we analyse how an emissions tax affects the profitability of firms. In Section 4, we establish the sufficient condition for an emissions tax to benefit firms. We also characterise the optimal (second best) emissions tax and the conditions under which private and social interests

[2]Heyes (2009) surveys theoretical and empirical research showing the potential for environmental regulation to reduce product market competition.

are aligned, i.e., the conditions under which a benevolent regulator would choose an optimal emissions tax that also benefits the firm. Section 5 presents our example and Section 6 concludes.

2. The Model

Consumers preferences for a homogeneous good are represented by the inverse demand function, $P(q_i, \mathbf{q}_-i)$ with $P(0, \mathbf{0}) = P_0 > 0$, $P'(\cdot) < 0, P''(\cdot) > 0$ for $q_i \geq 0$, where q_i denotes the amount produced by firm i, $i = 1, \ldots, n$. Firms face zero production costs, but the production of q_i units entail emitting $\mathrm{E}(q_i) = e_0 q_i$ units of pollution. Without loss of generality, we set $e_0 = 1$. If firm i invests $C(x_i)$ in emissions abatement, then i reduces its total emissions q_i by $x_i > 0$ with $C(0) = 0$, $C(\cdot) > 0$ and $C''(\cdot) \geq 0$. As we see below, the assumption that total emissions are reduced (instead of marginal emissions) implies that the profit function is additively separable in the two strategic variables q_i and x_i (see Poyago-Theotoky (2007)). For simplicity, the environmental damage caused by emissions is assumed to take a linear form:

$$D = \alpha \sum_{i=1}^{n} [q_i - x_i] \tag{1}$$

where $\alpha > 0$ is the marginal disutility of pollution. In the absence of a tax on emissions, firms do not invest in emissions abatement and, therefore, choose how much to produce without taking into account the externalities they cause. In contrast, firms can respond to a per-unit emissions tax t by either decreasing their output, or investing in emissions abatement R&D/technology, or both. In particular, a firm only invests in emissions abatement technology if there is a non-negative return from its investment:

$$tx_i - C(x_i) \geq 0 \tag{2}$$

In this setting, a tax on emissions leads to a reduction in the quantities produced by firms and increases investment in emissions abatement. The impact of the tax on profits, however, depends on the nature of competition and on the abatement technology, as shown in the next section.

We model imperfect competition by assuming that firms compete in supply schedules.[3] By considering families of more or less elastic supply schedules, it is possible to generate spaces of oligopoly games of which Bertrand and Cournot are polar cases. Specifically, firms compete in supply schedules given by:

$$q_i(\beta, \theta_i) = \beta P + \theta_i \tag{3}$$

The assumption of linearity in the supply schedule is not essential for the analysis, which relies on first-order conditions related to the slope of the supply curve (see Kao *et al.* (2014)). Following Menezes and Quiggin (2012, 2020), we assume a fixed value for β, the slope of the firm's supply function, and that firms choose θ_i. This assumption allows us to focus on the unique equilibrium, and avoid the multiplicity of supply function equilibria that exists in more general settings.[4] In our model, β can be interpreted as a measure of market competitiveness, where Cournot is obtained when $\beta = 0$ and Bertrand when $\beta \to \infty$. In addition to choosing θ_i, each firm i chooses the level of emissions abatement x_i.

3. The Impact of an Emissions Tax

In this section, we provide a necessary condition for an emissions tax to increase firms' profits in equilibrium. We write firm i's profit function in terms of its strategic variables θ_i, its choice of abatement x_i, and the strategic choice of other firms $\boldsymbol{\theta}_{-i}$ as:

$$\pi_i(\theta_i, \boldsymbol{\theta}_{-i}, x_i) = P(\theta_i, \boldsymbol{\theta}_{-i})q_i(\theta_i, \boldsymbol{\theta}_{-i}) - t[q_i(\theta_i, \boldsymbol{\theta}_{-i}) - x_i] - C(x_i) \tag{4}$$

Maximisation of profits yields the following first-order conditions:

$$\frac{\partial P(\theta_i, \boldsymbol{\theta}_{-i})}{\partial \theta_i} q_i(\theta_i, \boldsymbol{\theta}_{-i}) + (P(\theta_i, \boldsymbol{\theta}\_i) - t)\frac{\partial q_i(\theta_i, \boldsymbol{\theta}_{-i})}{\partial \theta_i} = 0 \tag{5}$$

[3]See, for example, (Grossman, 1981; Robson, 1981; Turnbull, 1983; Klemperer and Meyer, 1989; Grant and Quiggin, 1996; Delgado and Moreno, 2004; Vives, 2011; Menezes and Quiggin, 2012; Menezes and Quiggin, 2020) and Menezes and Pereira (2017).

[4]In Klemperer and Meyer (1989), for example, the Bertrand outcome is the unique equilibrium only under unbounded demand uncertainty and constant marginal costs.

and

$$t - \frac{\partial C(x_i)}{\partial x_i} = 0 \tag{6}$$

From (6), we can infer that any positive emissions tax always leads firms to invest in emissions abatement. Moreover, firm i's choice of x_i does not depend on the choices of other firms. Given that firms have identical abatement cost functions, in equilibrium we have $x_i = x_j = x^*, \forall i \neq j$. The decision on the choice of supply function (through the choice of θ_i), however, does depend on the choices of other firms. Our focus, therefore, is in the symmetric equilibrium, where $\theta_i = \theta_j = \theta^*, \forall i \neq j$ yielding the symmetric market equilibrium outcome $(P^*(n\theta^*), nq^*(\theta^*))$. The first order condition (5) can then be written as:

$$\frac{\partial P^*(n\theta^*)}{\partial \theta^*} q^*(\theta^*) + (P^*(n\theta^*) - t)(n + \beta \frac{\partial P^*(\theta^*)}{\partial \theta^*} = 0 \tag{7}$$

The equilibrium output for each firm can be expressed as:

$$P^*(\theta^*) = -\frac{(P^*(n\theta^*) - t)\left(n + \beta \frac{\partial P^*(n\theta^*)}{\partial \theta^*}\right)}{\frac{\partial P^*(n\theta^*)}{\partial \theta^*}} \tag{8}$$

Provided that $P^*(n\theta^*) - t > 0$, and (5) is satisfied, it can be readily checked that the second-order conditions for profit maximisation are also satisfied under our assumptions – a unique, symmetric Nash equilibrium exists. Next, we provide a condition which needs to be met for an emissions tax to have a positive impact on firms' profits in the symmetric equilibrium characterised by FOCs (5) and (6).

3.1. *The cost pass-through condition*

Omitting the arguments, denoting $P^{*\prime} = \frac{\partial P^*}{\partial \theta^*}$ and $P^{*\prime\prime} = \frac{\partial^2 P^*}{\partial \theta^{*2}}$, we define $F(P^*, t)$ using (7) as follows:

$$F(P^*, t) \equiv P^{*\prime}(\theta^* + \beta P^*) + (P^* - t)(n + \beta P^*) = 0 \tag{9}$$

The emissions tax cost pass-through can be determined by applying the implicit function theorem to the above expression:

$$\frac{dP^*}{dt} = \frac{\partial F/\partial t}{(\partial F/\partial \theta^*)/(\partial P^*/\partial \theta^*)}$$
$$= \frac{P^{*\prime}(n + \beta P^{*\prime})}{P^{*\prime}(n + 1 + 2\beta P^{*\prime}) + P^{*\prime\prime}[\theta^* + \beta(2P^* - t)]} \tag{10}$$

Following the notation presented in Weyl and Fabinger (2013), the cost pass-through can be written in terms of the elasticity of marginal surplus $\epsilon_{\text{ems}} = (1 + \frac{P^{*\prime\prime}Q}{P^{*\prime}})^{-1}$, as follows:

$$\frac{dP^*}{dt} = \frac{1}{1 + \left(\frac{1+\beta P^{*\prime}}{n+\beta P^{*\prime}}\right) 2 \left[\frac{1}{\epsilon_{\text{ems}} - \frac{(n-1)\beta P^{*\prime}}{n(1+\beta P^{*\prime})}}\right]} \tag{11}$$

The elasticity of marginal surplus (ϵ_{ems}) measures the curvature of the logarithm of demand. A log-convex demand always has $1/\epsilon_{\text{ems}} < 0$; if the demand is convex, then $1/\epsilon_{\text{ems}} < 1$. Important to note that in our model, the cost pass-through exceeds 1 if $\epsilon_{\text{ems}} < 0$. That is, the partial cost pass-through condition may not hold in the presence of strongly convex demand. For the remainder of this chapter, we will focus on the case where there is an emissions tax partial cost pass-through, i.e., $0 < \frac{dP^*}{dt} \leq 1$.[5]

We can now establish a necessary condition for firms to profit to increase with the emissions tax. The condition, specified in the next proposition, is not sufficient since firms' profits must still be greater than the profit without an emissions tax. In the next section, we present an example where we find a necessary and sufficient condition for profits to increase with an emissions tax.

Proposition 1. *Cost Pass-Through Condition for Profits to increase:*

For each firm's profit to increase with the emissions tax, the following condition needs to be met:

$$\frac{dP^*}{dt} > \frac{n}{n-1}\frac{p^*x^*}{q^* + \beta[P^* - t]} \tag{12}$$

[5]See Weyl and Fabinger (2013) for a comprehensive discussion of this issue.

Proof. A firm's profit in equilibrium can be expressed as:

$$\pi^*(t) = P^*q^* - t[q^* - x^*] - C(x^*)$$

For each firm's equilibrium profits to increase with the emissions tax, the following condition needs to be met:

$$\frac{d\pi^*}{dt} = \left[\frac{\partial P^*}{\partial \theta^*}q^* + (P^* - t)\frac{\partial q^*}{\partial \theta^*}\right]\frac{\partial \theta *}{\partial t} - q^* + x^* > 0 \tag{13}$$

Note that

$$\frac{\partial P^*}{\partial \theta^*} = \frac{\partial P}{\partial \theta_i} + (n-1)\frac{\partial P}{\partial \boldsymbol{\theta}_{-i}}; \frac{\partial q^*}{\partial \theta^*} = \frac{\partial q_i}{\partial \theta_i} + (n-1)\frac{\partial q_i}{\partial \boldsymbol{\theta}_{-i}} \tag{14}$$

Thus, (13) can be rewritten as:

$$\begin{aligned}\frac{d\pi^*}{dt} &= \left[\frac{\partial P}{\partial \theta_i} + (n-1)\frac{\partial P}{\partial \boldsymbol{\theta}_{-i}}\right]q^* + (P^* - t)\\ &\quad\times\left[\frac{\partial q_i}{\partial \theta_i} + (n-1)\frac{\partial q_i}{\partial \boldsymbol{\theta}_{-i}}\right]\frac{\partial \theta^*}{\partial t} - q^* + x^* > 0\end{aligned} \tag{15}$$

Given the linear supply schedule (3), we have:

$$\frac{\partial q_i}{\partial \theta_i} = 1 + \beta\frac{\partial P}{\partial \theta_i}; \frac{\partial q_i}{\partial \boldsymbol{\theta}_{-i}} = \beta\frac{\partial P}{\partial \boldsymbol{\theta}_{-i}} \tag{16}$$

Moreover, in the interior, symmetric equilibrium:

$$\frac{\partial P}{\partial \theta_i} = \frac{\partial P}{\partial \boldsymbol{\theta}_{-i}}; \frac{\partial P}{\partial \theta^*} = n\frac{\partial P}{\partial \theta_i} \tag{17}$$

Replacing (16) and (17) into (15), yields: (5)

$$\frac{d\pi^*}{dt} = \frac{(n-1)}{n}\frac{\partial P}{\partial \theta_i}[q^* + \beta(P^* - t)]\frac{\partial \theta^*}{\partial t} - q^* + x^* > 0$$

This implies that (12) is required for $\frac{d\pi^*}{dt} > 0$. □

Condition (12) requires that the emissions tax cost pass-through must be greater than the net emissions per unit of production, adjusted by the number of firms and the intensity of competition. Note that $\frac{n}{n-1}$ is equal to 2 under duopoly, tends to 1 as $n \to \infty$ and more generally decreases with n. That is, firms are more likely to find an environmental tax profitable as the number of firms increase. It is easy to see from (12) that β and n are substitutes[6] in the sense that the greater the β, the more likely the necessary condition for an increase in emissions tax to be profitable is met.

The key insight is that an emissions tax facilitates the exercise of market power, and the benefit for the firms is higher when the intensity of market competition is higher, or when the number of firms is larger. For example, while not formally defined in our setting, we can show that the cost pass-through condition is never met under a monopoly ($n = 1$). An emissions tax would lead the monopolist to reduce its quantity beyond the profit-maximising, monopoly quantity.

Note that for a firm to benefit from an emissions tax (sufficient condition), its profit must be greater than under no emissions tax, $\pi^*(t) > \pi^*(0)$. This general condition, which depends on specific functional forms, can be expressed as:

$$P^*(t)q^*(t) - P^*(0)q^*(0) > t[q^*(t) - x^*(t)] + C(x^*(t)) \tag{18}$$

The above condition simply states that, for a firm to benefit from an emissions tax, the increase in revenue due to the tax must compensate for the net cost of the tax.

4. Environmental Tax and Welfare

As the necessary condition for profitability of an emissions tax (12) requires the price to increase (and, therefore, the quantity to decrease) by a certain amount, consumer surplus will necessarily decrease with a tax. A decrease in quantity, however, decreases emissions, and thus increases welfare. It follows that an emissions tax

[6] Menezes and Quiggin (2012) provide a characterisation of the substitutability between n and β to determine the competitiveness of a market.

that increases firms' profits may not increase welfare, as the decline in consumer surplus may not be outweighed by the increase in profits and reduction in emissions. The focus of this section is to determine when an emissions tax can increase social welfare. In particular, we consider a social welfare function (as a function of the tax) that is additively separable in consumer surplus, producer surplus, the revenue from the emission tax, and the social environmental damage, as follows:

$$\begin{aligned} W(t) = CS(nq^*(t)) + n\pi^*(q^*(t), t) + nt[q^*(t) - x^*] \\ - \alpha n[q^*(t) - x^*(t)] \end{aligned} \tag{19}$$

Since both equilibrium quantities and prices are linear functions of the emissions tax, social welfare is a quadratic function of the emissions tax.

Proposition 2. *Cost Pass-Through Condition for Welfare to Increase*:

For social welfare to increase with the emissions tax, the following condition needs to be met:

$$\frac{dP^*(t)}{dt} < \frac{n(\alpha - t)\left[\frac{d\theta^*(t)}{dt} - \frac{dx^*(t)}{dt}\right]}{\beta[(n-1)P^*(t) + t - n\alpha] - q^*(t)} \tag{20}$$

Proof. Totally differentiating a firm's profit in equilibrium (omitting the arguments for simplicity) yields:

$$d\pi^* = \frac{n-1}{n}[q^* + \beta(P^* - t)]dP^* - (q^* - x^*)dt$$

Similarly, totally differentiating the welfare expression (19) yields:

$$\begin{aligned} dW &= -nq^*dP^* + (n-1)[q^* + \beta(P^* - t)]dP^* \\ &\quad - n(q^* - x^*)dt + n(q^* - x^*)dt + n(t - \alpha)(dq^* - dx^*) \\ &= [-q^* + \beta(n-1)(P^* - t)dP^* + n(t - \alpha)(dq^* - dx^*) \end{aligned}$$

Therefore,

$$\frac{dW}{dt} = [-q^* + \beta(n-1)(P^* - t)]\frac{dP^*}{dt} + n(t - \alpha)\left(\frac{dq^*}{dt} - \frac{dx^*}{dt}\right)$$

Replacing $\frac{dq^*}{dt} = \frac{d\theta^*(t)}{dt} + \beta\frac{dP^*}{dt}$. and rearranging the terms:

$$\frac{dW}{dt} = \beta[(n-1)(P^* - t) + n(t-\alpha)]$$

$$- q^*\frac{dP^*}{dt} + n(t-\alpha)\left(\frac{d\theta^*(t)}{dt} - \frac{dx^*}{dt}\right)$$

which results in the above condition. □

The numerator of (20) RHS is always non-positive because $\alpha \geq t$, $\frac{dx^*(t)}{dt} > 0$ and $\frac{d\theta^*(t)}{dt} < 0$. Given that the emission tax cost pass-through must be positive and is complete under a Bertrand setting $\left(0 < \frac{dP^*(t)}{dt} \leq 1\right)$ the denominator of (20) RHS must also be negative: $\beta[(n-1)P^*(t) + t - n\alpha] - q^*(t) < 0$. This is always satisfied in a Cournot setting ($\beta = 0$) and in a Bertrand setting ($P^* = t = \alpha$).

4.1. *Social and private gains from an increase in emissions tax*

The condition for the firm's profit to increase with an increase in the tax on emissions is given by (12). The condition for the social welfare to increase with an increase in the tax on emissions is given by (20). Combining these two conditions, and expressing it again in terms of the emissions tax cost pass-through, yields:

$$\frac{n}{n-1}\frac{q^*(t) - x^*(t)}{q^*(t) + \beta[P^*(t) - t]} < \frac{dP^*(t)}{dt}$$

$$< \frac{n(\alpha - t)\left[\frac{d\theta^*(t)}{dt} - \frac{dx^*(t)}{dt}\right]}{\beta[(n-1)P^*(t) + t - n\alpha] - q^*(t)} \tag{21}$$

This condition translates into a range of possible emissions taxes, assuming that the equilibrium profit function is convex ($\frac{d^2\pi_e}{dt''} > 0$) and the social welfare function is concave ($\frac{d^2W}{dt^2} < 0$). We can then now turn to examining when we expect this to occur. We first consider the profit function:

$$\begin{aligned}
\frac{d^2\pi^*}{dt^2} &= \frac{d}{dt}\frac{n-1}{n}\frac{dP^*}{dt}[q^* + \beta(P^* - t)] - (q^* - x^*) \\
&= \frac{n-1}{n}\frac{d^2P^*}{dt^2}[q^* + \beta(P^* - t)] + \frac{dP^*}{dt} \\
&\quad \times \left[\frac{dq^*}{dt} + \beta\left(\frac{dP^*}{dt} - 1\right)\right] - \left(\frac{dq^*}{dt} - \frac{dx^*}{dt}\right) \\
&= \frac{n-1}{n}\frac{dP^*}{dt}\left[\frac{dq^*}{dt} + \beta\left(\frac{dP^*}{dt} - 1\right)\right] - \left(\frac{dq^*}{dt} - \frac{dx^*}{dt}\right)
\end{aligned}$$

The above expression has to be positive to ensure convexity of the profit function. In this case, the emissions tax that minimises the profit function (t_{em}) can be obtained by solving the following equation ($\frac{d\pi^*}{dt} = 0$):

$$\frac{n-1}{n}\frac{dP^*}{dt}[q^* + \beta(P^* - t)] - (q^* - x^*) = 0$$

We now consider the social welfare function:

$$\begin{aligned}
\frac{d^2W}{dt^2} &= \frac{d}{dt}\left[-q^* + \beta(n-1)(P^* - t)\right]\frac{dP^*}{dt} + n(t-\alpha)\left(\frac{dq^*}{dt} - \frac{dx^*}{dt}\right) \\
&= -\frac{dq^*}{dt} - \beta(n-1)\left(1 - \frac{dP^*}{dt}\right)\Bigg]\frac{dP^*}{dt} + n\left(\frac{dq^*}{dt} - \frac{dx^*}{dt}\right)
\end{aligned}$$

The above expression must be negative to ensure concavity of the welfare function. In this case, the emissions tax that maximises the welfare function (t_{opt}) can be obtained by solving the following equation ($\frac{dW}{dt} = 0$):

$$[-q^* + \beta(n-1)(P^* - t)]\frac{dP^*}{dt} + n(t-\alpha)\left(\frac{dq^*}{dt} - \frac{dx^*}{dt}\right) = 0$$

The range of possible emissions taxes that ensures social and private gains (t_{w-w} to denote win-win outcomes), assuming that the equilibrium profit function is convex ($\frac{s^2\pi_e}{dt^2} > 0$) and the social welfare function is concave ($\frac{d^2W}{dt^2} > 0$), is given by:

$$t_{\text{em}} < t_{w-w} < t_{\text{opt}} \tag{22}$$

In the following sections we will use specific functional forms to illustrate the conditions under which private and social benefits can occur as a result of an emissions tax.

5. An Example

Following Singh and Vives (1984), the representative consumer has a quadratic (strictly concave) utility function, resulting in the following inverse demand function:

$$P = a - (q_i + \boldsymbol{q}_{-i}) \tag{23}$$

Without loss of generality, we will assume that $a = 1$. As in d'Aspremont and Jacquemin (1988), we assume that, if firm i invests $\frac{\nu}{2}x_i^2$ in emissions abatement R&D/technology, then firm i reduces its gross emissions q_i by x_i, where x_i represents the outcome of the firm's emissions reduction effort. Finally, ν relates to the efficiency or productivity of the abatement technology, where a higher value means lower efficiency. The investment in abatement technology is now expressed as:

$$C(x_i) = \frac{\nu}{2}x_i^2 \tag{24}$$

Firm i's profit function[7] is given by:

$$\pi_i(q_i, \boldsymbol{q}_{-i}, x_i) = (1 - q_i - \boldsymbol{q}_{-i})q_i - t(q_i - x_i) - \frac{\nu}{2}x_i^2 \tag{25}$$

The quantities can be expressed in supply schedules and the functional objective (profit function) above can also be expressed in terms of the strategic variables $\theta_i, \boldsymbol{\theta}_{-i}$ and x_i.

---

[7]Our model is equivalent to that of Lahiri and Symeonidis (2007) and Fikru and Gautier (2016). In their model, the abatement cost in the profit function is expressed in terms of emissions: $\pi_i(q_i, e_i) = (P - c)q_i - \frac{(\delta q_i - e_i)^2}{2} - e_i t_e$. Denoting $x_i = \delta q_i - e_i$ the profit function can now be written as $\pi_i(q_i, e_i) = (P - c)q_i - (\delta q_i - e_i)t_e - \frac{x_i^2}{2}$, which is similar to our model. Requate (2006) uses a generalised version of these cost functions: $C = C(q_i, e_i)$.

At the game's profit-maximising equilibrium conditions we obtain:

$$\theta^* = \frac{[1+(n-2)\beta] - t(1+n\beta)[1+(n-1+n)\beta]}{1+n[1+\beta(n-1)]} \tag{26}$$

$$x^* = \frac{t}{\nu} \tag{27}$$

The equilibrium quantities and prices can now be determined as follows:

$$q^* = \frac{(1-t)[1+\beta(n-1)]}{1+n[1+\beta(n-1)]} \tag{28}$$

$$P^* = \frac{nt[1+\beta(n-1)]}{1+n[1+\beta(n-1)]} \tag{29}$$

Substituting the equilibrium variables in the profit function we obtain:

$$\pi^*(t) = \frac{(1-t)^2[1+(n-1)\beta]^2}{1+n[1+\beta(n-1)]} + \frac{t^2}{2\nu} \tag{30}$$

Social welfare is defined by consumer surplus plus the profits of the n-firms (excluding taxes and subsidies) minus the environmental damage, as per the following expression:

$$\begin{aligned} W &= CS + n\bar{\pi}_i - D \\ &= \frac{nt(2\alpha - t) + (1-t)\nu(1+t-2\alpha)}{2\nu} \\ &\quad - \frac{(1-t)^2}{2[n+1+n\beta(n-1)]^2} + \frac{(1-t)(\alpha-t)}{n+1+n\beta(n-1)} \end{aligned} \tag{31}$$

We now proceed to illustrate when the general conditions established in the previous section for a win-win outcome from the introduction of an emissions tax will be met in our specific example.

5.1. *Tax on emissions and firm's profits*

The equilibrium profit function is quadratic and convex in relation to the emissions tax as depicted below (Figure 1):

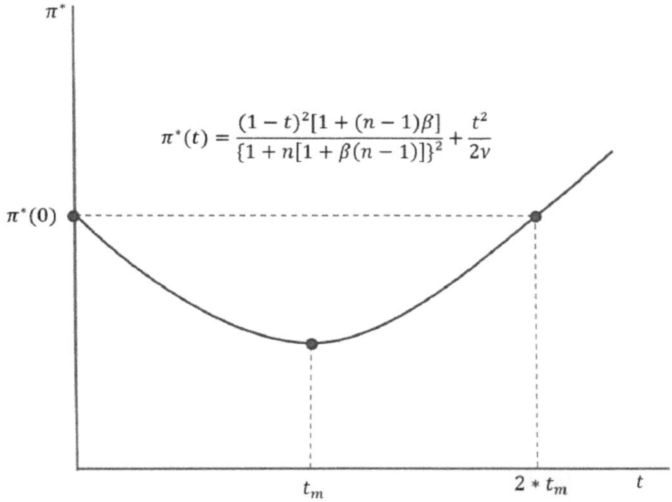

Fig. 1. Profit function.

The profit function reaches its minimum at $t = t_m$:

$$t_m = \frac{2\nu[1+(n-1)\beta]}{1+n(n+2)+2\nu+\beta(n-1)[(n(n+1)+\nu)]+(n-1)^2n^2\beta^2} \tag{32}$$

Given the quadratic and convex profit function (30), Proposition 1, which determines the cost pass-through condition for the firm's profit to increase with an increase in emissions tax, can simply be stated as:

$$t > t_m \tag{33}$$

For the firm to benefit from an emissions tax, its profit must be greater than under no emissions tax ($\pi^*(t) > \pi^*(0)$). This condition can be stated as:

$$t|_{\text{private\_benefit}} > 2 * t_m \tag{34}$$

The positive emissions condition ($q_i - x_i > 0$) must also be met, which translates into the following condition on the tax on emissions:

$$t < t|_{\text{pos\_em}} = \frac{\nu[1+(n-1)\beta]}{n+1+\nu+(n+\nu)(n-1)\beta} \tag{35}$$

Combining the two conditions we have:

$$2 * t_m < t|_{\text{private\_benefit}} < t|_{\text{pos\_em}} \tag{36}$$

That is, there is a range of emissions tax rates, complying with the above inequality, if $2 * t_m < t|_{\text{pos\_em}}$, or

$$\frac{4\nu[1+(n-1)\beta]}{1+n(n+2)+2\nu+\beta(n-1)[(n(n+1)+\nu)]+(n-1)^2n^2\beta^2} < \frac{\nu[1+(n-1)\beta]}{n+1+\nu+(n+\nu)(n-1)\beta} \tag{37}$$

which simplifies into the following inequality:

$$3+2\nu-n(n-2)+2\beta(n-1)[\nu-n(n-1)]-(n-1)^2n^2\beta^2 < 0 \tag{38}$$

The above condition (38) can also be expressed as a condition on ν technology efficiency):

$$\nu < \frac{[n-3+n\beta(n-1)][n+1+n\beta(n-1)]}{2+2(n-1)\beta} \tag{39}$$

or as a condition on β (intensity of competition):

$$\beta > \frac{\nu-n(n-1)+\sqrt{(n+\nu)^2+3n^2}}{n^2(n-1)} \tag{40}$$

Expression (39) simply states that, for a firm to benefit from a range of emissions tax rates, its technology efficiency in abating emissions must be high enough, implying a lower value of that satisfies equation (39). Note that for $n > 3$ and assuming Cournot competition ($\beta = 0$), if the emissions abatement technology is efficient enough ($\nu < \frac{1}{2}(n-3)(n+1)$), firms will always benefit from an emissions tax.

Furthermore, a firm will only benefit from an emissions tax if the intensity of competition is above a threshold set by the condition expressed in (40). If the emissions abatement technology is not efficient enough, the intensity of competition must be high and comply with (40) for a firm to benefit from an emissions tax.

Expression (39) can be rewritten a condition on n for the case of a n-firm Cournot setting ($\beta = 0$):

$$n > \sqrt{2(\nu + 2)} + 1 \tag{41}$$

For a duopoly ($n = 2$) condition (40) can be simplified as:

$$\beta > \frac{\nu - 2 + \sqrt{(2 + \nu)^2 + 12}}{4} \tag{42}$$

To study the interaction between β and n in relation to the threshold above which firms benefit from an emissions tax, let us define (from (38)) the following constraint function:

$$F(n, \beta) = 3 + 2\nu - n(n-2) + 2\beta(n-1)[\nu - n(n-1)] - (n-1)^2 n^2 \beta^2 \tag{43}$$

Applying the implicit function theorem:

$$\begin{aligned}\frac{\partial \beta}{\partial n} &= -\frac{\partial F(n, \beta)\partial n}{\partial F(n, > beta)\partial \beta} \\ &= \frac{1 - n + \beta[\nu - 1 + n(4 - 3n)] + \beta^2[(3 - 2n)n - 1]}{(n-1)[n(n-1)(1 + n\beta) - \nu]}\end{aligned} \tag{44}$$

Under the last two equations it is easy to prove that $\frac{\partial \beta}{\partial n} > 0$. In other words, the intensity of competition and the number of firms are substitutes for the condition under which a firm's profits increase with an increase in emissions tax, as illustrated in the following figure.

The shaded area in Fig. 2 represents the combination of intensity of competition and number of firms under which firms benefit from an emissions tax, i.e., that satisfy the condition set out in equation (38). The lower boundary of this area shifts down (lower boundary values for β and n) when the efficiency of emissions abatement technology increases (the value of ν decreases). Along the vertical axis we can find the threshold value of the intensity of competition for a duopoly, as per equation (42). Along the horizontal axis, we can find the threshold value of the number of firms in a Cournot setting, as per equation (41). As the number of firms (n) and/or the intensity of competition (β) increase, the firms don't need to be as efficient in their emissions abatement activities, in order to benefit from an emissions tax.

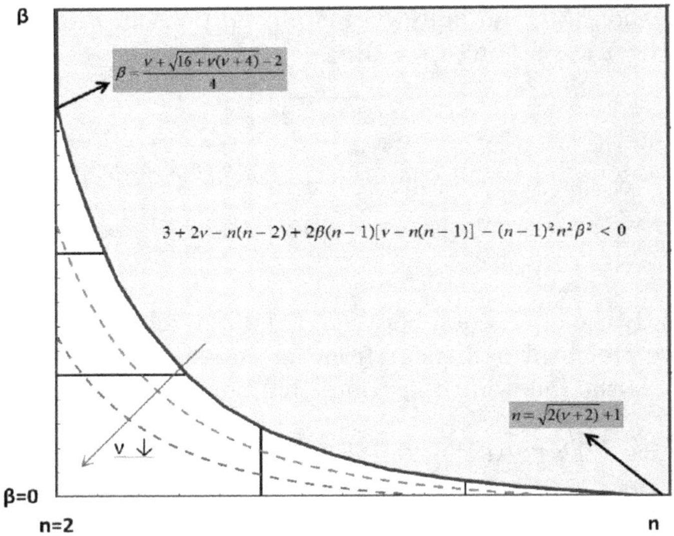

Fig. 2. Intensity of competition (β) and number of firms (n).

As per our analytical framework, we can observe that a monopoly and a Cournot duopoly never benefit from an emissions tax.

Having shown that firms can actually benefit from an environmental tax policy under certain conditions, we now ask whether a benevolent government would ever choose an emissions tax rate that satisfies these conditions. To this end, in the next section, we determine the optimal (second best) emissions tax to find the conditions under which private and social interests align.

5.2. *Tax on emissions and social welfare*

The regulator sets its emissions tax to maximise the social welfare, taking into account the equilibrium quantities/prices and investment in emissions abatement that firms choose in order to maximise their profits.

A tax on emissions will reduce consumer surplus and environmental damage but will have an ambiguous impact on producer surplus.

Given the specific functional forms used, the equilibrium social welfare, equation (31), is quadratic and concave in relation to the emissions tax (t), as depicted in the following graph (Figure 3).

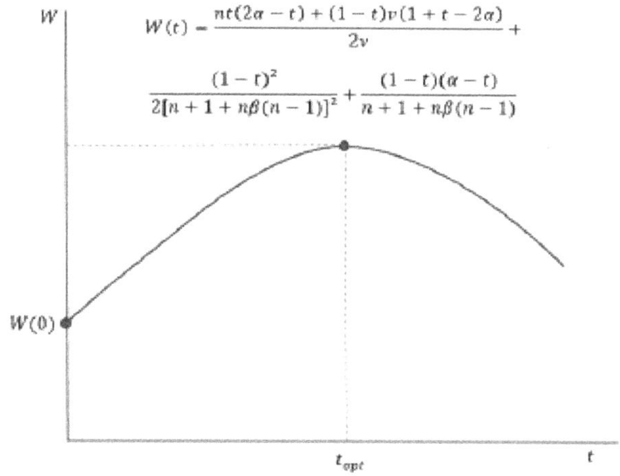

Fig. 3. Welfare.

The welfare function is maximised at the optimal emissions tax (second best)[8]

$$t_{\text{opt}} = \frac{\alpha[n+1+n(n-1)\beta][n+1+\nu+(n+\nu)(n-1)\beta] - (a-c)\nu[1+(n-1)\beta]}{1+n[1+(n-1)\beta][n+2+\nu+(n+\nu)(n-1)\beta]} \tag{45}$$

Remark 1. From the linear supply schedules the Cournot duopoly game or corresponding market structure can be analysed by setting the competitiveness parameter $\beta = 0$. The Bertrand duopoly game or corresponding market structure can be analysed by setting the competitiveness parameter $\beta \to \infty$. The optimal pollution or emissions tax in a Cournot setting is given by:

$$t^C = \frac{\alpha(1+n)(1+n+\nu)\nu(a-c)}{1+n(2+n+\nu)} \tag{46}$$

The optimal pollution or emissions tax in a Bertrand setting is given by:

$$t^B = \alpha \tag{47}$$

[8]Analysing the second-order conditions, it is clear that this expression is indeed a maximum as $\frac{\partial^2 W(t_e)}{\partial t_e^2} = \frac{n1+n[1+(n-1)\beta][n+2+\nu+(n+\nu)(n-1)\beta]}{\nu[n+1+n(n-1)\beta]^2} < 0$.

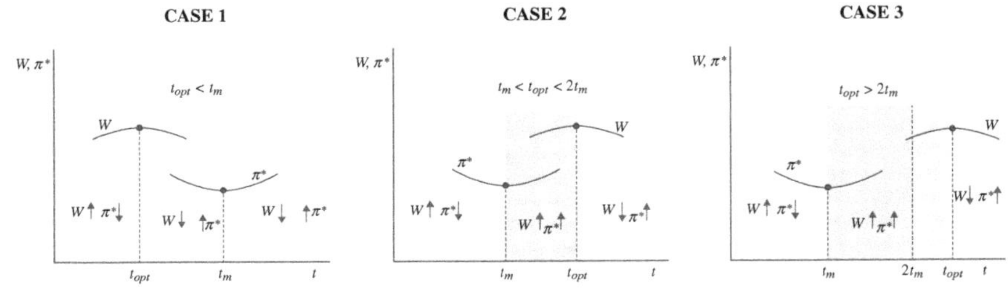

Fig. 4. Private and social outcomes from an emissions tax.

Proposition 2, which determines the cost pass-through condition for the welfare to increase with an increase in emissions tax, can simply be stated as:

$$t < t_{\text{opt}} \tag{48}$$

In the next Section we will analyse the conditions under which an emissions tax can be socially and privately beneficial.

5.3. *Private and social gains from an emissions tax*

For firms to benefit from an optimal emissions tax, the optimal tax rate must be greater than the tax rate above which firms benefit from an emissions tax but under the positive emissions tax (CASE 3). The general condition can be set as

$$t|_{\text{pos\_em}} > t_{\text{opt}} > 2 * t_m \tag{49}$$

where the three emissions tax thresholds are given by (45), (35) and (32).

Note that, under the established model conditions $t|_{\text{pos\_em}} > t_m$, always. However, $t|_{\text{pos\_em}} > t_{\text{opt}}$, results in the following condition:

$$\alpha < \frac{\nu}{n+\nu}1 - \frac{1}{[1+n+\nu+(n-1)(n+\nu)\beta]^2} \tag{50}$$

Case 1. $(t_{\text{opt}} < t_m)$

$$\alpha < \frac{\nu[1+(n-1)\beta][3(n+1)+2\nu+(n-1)(3n+2\nu)\beta]}{k_1 k_2} \tag{51}$$

where

$$k_1 = 1 + n + \nu + (n-1)(n+\nu)\beta$$

and

$$k_2 = 1 + n(2+n) + 2\nu + 2(n-1)[n(n+1) + \nu]\beta + (n-1)^2 n^2 \beta^2$$

The limiting condition on α is smaller in the above expressions than in (50).

Case 2. ($t_m < t_{\text{opt}} < 2t_m$)

$$\nu < \frac{[n-3+(n-1)n\beta][1+n+(n-1)n\beta]}{2[1+(n-1)\beta]} \tag{52}$$

and

$$\alpha > \frac{\nu[1+(n-1)\beta][3(n+1)+2\nu+(n-1)(3n+2\nu)\beta]}{k_1 k_2} \tag{53}$$

If $n \leq 3$, this additional condition applies: $n + n\beta(n-1) > 3$. In other words, CASE 2 will never occur under a Cournot duopoly.

Case 3. ($t_{\text{opt}} > 2t_m$)

$$\nu < \frac{[n-3+(n-1)n\beta][1+n+(n-1)n\beta]}{2[1+(n-1)\beta]} \tag{54}$$

and

$$\alpha > \frac{\nu[5+5n(n+2)+2\nu(2n+1)+k_3]}{k1k2[1+n+(n-1)n\beta]} \tag{55}$$

where

$$\begin{aligned} k_3 = {} & (n-1)(3n+1)[5(n+1)+4\nu]\beta + (n-1)^2 \\ & \times [5n(2+3n) + 2(1+6n)\nu]\beta^2 + (n-1)^3 n(5n+4\nu)\beta^3 \end{aligned}$$

If $n \leq 3$, this additional condition applies: $n + n\beta(n-1) > 3$. In other words, CASE 3 will never occur under a Cournot duopoly.

At the level of emissions tax where the firm's profit is equal to the profit with no emissions tax, for society to also benefit from an emissions tax, social welfare must also be increasing with an increase in emissions tax. Under the positive emissions condition (38), the level of emissions tax at the firm's profit break-even point, where the firm's profit with an emissions tax is equal to its profit without the tax ($t = 2 * t_m$). The proposition below provides sufficient conditions for win-win outcomes.

Proposition 3. *Assuming that the positive emissions condition (38) is met and under an emissions tax, firms' profits are higher than under no tax and social welfare increases when emissions tax increases, if the following conditions are met:*

$$\alpha > \frac{\nu[1+(n-1)\beta]K_1}{K_2K_3K_4} \quad \text{and} \quad \nu < \frac{K_2^2}{2+2(n-1)\beta} \tag{56}$$

where

$$\begin{aligned} K_1 &= 5 + 2\nu + n(10 + 5n + 4\nu) + 2\beta(n-1) \\ &\quad \times [\nu + n(5 + 5n + 4\nu)] + n\beta^2(n-1)^2(5n + 4\nu) \\ K_2 &= [1 + n + n\beta(n-1)] \\ K_3 &= [n + 1 + \nu + (n + \nu)(n-1)\beta] \end{aligned}$$

and

$$K_4 = (n+1)^2 + 2\nu + 2(n-1)(n + n^2 + \nu)\beta + (n-1)^2n^2\beta^2$$

Proof. The above condition on α results from substituting the emissions tax given by (34) into the inequality $\frac{dW}{dt} > 0$ and solving it for α. In order to ensure positive quantities, as per (39), under optimal emissions tax $\alpha < 1$, therefore:

$$\frac{\nu[1+(n-1)\beta]K_1}{K_2K_3K_4} < 1 \tag{57}$$

$$\nu < \frac{K_2^2}{2+2(n-1)\beta} \tag{58}$$

□

The above proposition simply states that, for firms to benefit from an emissions tax, whilst welfare increases with an increase in emissions tax, the marginal disutility of emissions (the cost that society allocates to environmental damage) must be high enough and above the threshold set by Proposition 3. The firm must also be efficient in undertaking emissions abatement (lower value of ν). When the above conditions are met, the social benefits from an increase in emissions tax are aligned with the private benefits.

Under a Bertrand setting (prices are strategic substitutes), these conditions are always met as the above conditions reduce to: $\alpha > 0$. In other words, in a price competition setting (Bertrand) with an emissions tax, firms' interests (profits) are always aligned with social interests as shown by Delbono and Lambertini (2022). Under a Cournot setting (quantities are strategic substitutes), the above conditions are simplified as follows:

$$\alpha > \frac{\nu[5(n+1)^2 + 2\nu(1+2n)]}{(n+1)(n+1+\nu)[(n+1)^2 + 2\nu]} \text{ and } \nu < \frac{(1+n)^2}{2} \tag{59}$$

In the case of a Cournot duopoly, the positive emissions condition states that firms will never benefit from a tax on emissions.

6. Concluding Remarks

This chapter investigates the conditions under which an emissions tax can lead to both social and private benefits. Considering a homogeneous product, symmetric n-firm oligopoly setting, we find that a welfare enhancing emissions tax can also benefit profit-maximising firms. Importantly, we do not assume that investment in emissions abatement leads to gains in productivity (or attracts a green premium in price).

Our key insight is that for an emissions tax to lead to an increase in profits, the emissions tax cost pass-through (the proportion of the emissions tax increase that is reflected in consumer prices) must be greater than the net emissions per unit of production, adjusted for the number of firms. As the intensity of competition increases, firms are more likely to benefit from an emissions tax, as it facilitates the exercise of market power. In the special cases of a monopoly or a Cournot duopoly, this condition is never met. This result may assist in understanding the political economy of emissions tax; more competitive industries are more likely to support the introduction of an emissions tax.

For the special case of linear demand function and linear emissions, we are also able to determine the sufficient conditions for social welfare and the private interests (firms' profits) to be aligned. For firms to benefit from an emissions tax, whilst welfare increases with an increase in emissions tax, the marginal disutility of emissions (the cost that society allocates to environmental damage) must be above a critical level determined by the extent of the market, the intensity of competition, the number of firms and the abatement technology efficiency. Under a Bertrand setting (prices are strategic substitutes), these conditions are always met, i.e., with an emissions tax, firms' interests (profits) are always aligned with social interests.

In our model, the investment in emissions reduction technology, which is undertaken as a response to the introduction of an emissions tax, is set independently of market competition. For example, in a Cournot duopoly, it turns out that the increase in price that follows as the emissions tax is passed through to consumers, is not enough to recover the net result of the investment outlay. As competition intensifies, the pass-through of the tax to consumers increases, to a point where the price rises more than offsets the net result of the investment outlay. The separation of the investment and quantity/price decisions implies that firms may earn positive profits under a Bertrand setting. The profits can be viewed as a tax credit.

Our analysis allows a better understanding of the trade-off between environmental policy, market competition and the so-called "win-win" outcome for firms and society.

References

Ambec, S., Cohen, M., Elgie, S. and Lanoie, P. (2013). The Porter hypothesis at 20: Can environmental regulation enhance innovation and competitiveness? *Review of Environmental Economics and Policy* **7**, 2–22.

Bellas, A. S. (1998). Empirical evidence of advances in scrubber technology, *Resource and Energy Economics* **20**(4), 327–343.

d'Aspremont, C. and Jacquemin, A. (1988). Cooperative and noncooperative R&D in duopoly with spillovers, *The American Economic Review* **78**(5), 1133–1137.

Delbono, F. and Lambertini, L. (2022). Optimal emission taxation and the Porter hypothesis under bertrand competition, *Annals of Public and Cooperative Economics* **93**(3), 755–765.

Delgado, J. and Moreno, D. (2004). Coalition-proof supply function equilibria in oligopoly, *Journal of Economic Theory* **114**(2), 231–254.

Fikru, M. G. and Gautier, L. (2016). Mergers in Cournot markets with environmental externality and product differentiation, *Resource and Energy Economics* **45**, 65–79.

Flagan, R. C. and Seinfeld, J. H. (2012). *Fundamentals of Air Pollution Engineering*, Courier Corporation, Mineola, New York, US.

Grant, S. and Quiggin, J. (1996). Capital precommitment and competition in supply schedules, *The Journal of Industrial Economics* **44**(4), 427–441.

Grossman, S. J. (1981). Nash equilibrium and the industrial organization of markets with large fixed costs, *Econometrica* **49**(5), 1149–1172.

Heyes, A. (2009). Is environmental regulation bad for competition? a survey, *Journal of Regulatory Economics* **36**(1), 1–28.

Hocking, M. B. B. (2016). *Handbook of Chemical Technology and Pollution Control*, Elsevier, Amsterdam.

Kao, T., Menezes, F. M. and Quiggin, J. (2014). Optimal access regulation with downstream competition, *Journal of Regulatory Economics* **45**, 75–93.

Klemperer, P. D. and Meyer, M. A. (1989). Supply function equilibria in oligopoly under uncertainty, *Econometrica* **57**(6), 1243–1277.

Lahiri, S. and Symeonidis, G. (2007). Piecemeal multilateral environmental policy reforms under asymmetric oligopoly, *Journal of Public Economic Theory* **9**(5), 885–899.

Menezes, F. M. and Pereira, J. (2017). Emissions abatement R&D: Dynamic competition in supply schedules, *Journal of Public Economic Theory* **19**(4), 841–859.

Menezes, F. M. and Quiggin, J. (2012). More competitors or more competition? market concentration and the intensity of competition, *Economics Letters* **117**(3), 712–714.

Menezes, F. M. and Quiggin, J. (2020). The strategic industry supply curve, *The Journal of Industrial Economics* **68**(3), 523–555.

Porter, M. E. (1991). America's green strategy, *Scientific American* **264**(4), 168.

Porter, M. E. and van der Linde, C. (1995). Toward a new conception of the environment-competitiveness relationship, *Journal of Economic Perspectives* **9**(4), 97–118.

Poyago-Theotoky, J. A. (2007). The organization of R&D and environmental policy, *Journal of Economic Behavior & Organization* **62**(1), 63–75.

Requate, T. (2006). Environmental policy under imperfect competition, in T. Tietenber and H. Forlmer (Eds.), *The International Yearbook of*

Environmental and Resource Economics, pp. 120–207, Edward Elgar Publishing, Cheltenham, UK.

Robson, A. J. (1981). Implicit oligopolistic collusion is destroyed by uncertainty, *Economics Letters* **7**(1), 75–80.

Singh, N. and Vives, X. (1984). Price and quantity competition in a differentiated duopoly, *The RAND Journal of Economics* **15**(4), 546–554.

Turnbull, S. J. (1983). Choosing duopoly solutions by consistent conjectures and by uncertainty, *Economics Letters* **13**(2–3), 253–258.

Vives, X. (2011). Strategic supply function competition with private information, *Econometrica* **79**(6), 1919–1966.

Weyl, E. G. and Fabinger, M. (2013). Pass-through as an economic tool: Principles of incidence under imperfect competition, *Journal of Political Economy* **121**(3), 528–583.

https://doi.org/10.1142/9789819816033_0004

Chapter 4

Profitable Environmental Corporate Social Responsibility with a Public Eco-Firm

Sang-Ho Lee[*,‡] **and Chul-Hi Park**[†,§]

[*] *Chonnam National University, Department of Economics, Gwangju, Korea*

[†] *Gwangju National University of Education, Department of Social Studies Education, Gwangju, Korea*

[‡] *sangho@chonnam.ac.kr*

[§] *newhuman@gnue.ac.kr*

We consider a vertical structure scenario with a public eco-firm producing abatement goods under mixed ownership and a polluting firm that adopts environmental corporate social responsibility (ECSR). In examining the strategic interaction between the degree of private ownership and ECSR incentives, we find that the efficiency of abatement technology crucially affects profitable ECSR and its welfare effects. Where there is a high degree of private ownership in a public eco-firm, as the degree of private ownership increases, ECSR can be used to reduce an emission tax, which increases ECSR's possible strategic role. Furthermore, an increase in ECSR can improve (decrease) social welfare with an inefficient (efficient) abatement technology. However, where there is a low degree of private ownership, the increased input price under privatisation can crowd out the ECSR incentive and reduce its possible space, while an increase of ECSR always improves social welfare regardless of the efficiency of abatement technology. Our findings suggest that green technology development in an eco-industry determines the feasible design of green policy through privatising a public eco-firm under the strategic ECSR incentive.

Keywords: Public echo-firm, Abatement, Environmental CSR (corporate social responsibility), Private vs. public ownership.

1. Introduction

This study analyses polluting firms' ECSR in the emergence of public eco-firm producing abatement goods under mixed ownership.

1.1. *Environmental corporate social responsibility*

The issue of climate change has been elevated to the board level on the corporate agenda. Due to increasing public concerns about environmental damage and financial pressure from institutional investors, many leading companies engage in ECSR activities. For example, many listed firms in the G250 Fortune Index (a list of the largest 250 multinational companies) reveal their concerns about ECSR. According to KPMG (2017), 67% of the world's top companies set internal carbon reduction targets in 2017. Furthermore, an Open Compliance and Ethics Group (OCEG) global survey of 530 corporate executives reveals that 32% are planning to base compensation for executives on environmental, social, and governance (ESG) factors (DiNapoli, 2021).[1]

As ECSR has become a global business practice, significant attention from policymakers and academic researchers has increased. In accordance with the environment-competitiveness relationship and the creation of shared value (e.g., Porter and van der Linde, 1995) under ECSR, there has been growing interest in its strategic use in

[1]An interesting aspect of the emerging corporate response is that executive compensation is being linked to climate performance, that is, companies are reformulating their strategies for emission-reduction activities (Financial Times, The Guardian, 2021). According to an OCEG global survey of 530 corporate executives, 32% planned to base executive compensation on ESG factors, while 20% already did (DiNapoli, 2021). Furthermore, 45% of the companies listed on the FTSE 100 had an ESG factor in either the annual bonus, the long-term incentive plan (LTIP), or both, linked to environmental issues, such as decarbonisation and energy transition (Price Waterhouse Cooper, 2022; Ritz, 2022).

recent business and economics literature. For example, many recent studies have investigated the strategic use of ECSR in a managerial delegation framework, referred to as green managerial delegation. Liu *et al.* (2015) examined firms' voluntary initiatives towards abatement activities and emission reduction and showed that adopting ECSR can improve a firm's reputation among green consumers, thus representing a competitive strategy. Hirose *et al.* (2017, 2020) employed a strategic managerial incentive design in which owners could encourage managers to run the firm based on green managerial incentives, demonstrating that ECSR can enhance the profitability of polluting firms. Some studies have also incorporated the role of the government in determining emission taxes and examined the relationship between these taxes and strategic ECSR under green managerial delegation. Poyago-Theotoky and Yong (2019) introduced an explicit environmental incentive to a managerial compensation contract with an emission tax. They showed that, compared with a standard sales compensation contract, the environmental delegation contract results in more abatement, lower emission tax, higher profits, and social welfare. Fukuda and Ouchida (2020) and Wang (2021) also explored the relationship between the government's emission tax and ECSR for a firm in a monopoly setting and showed that ECSR enhances the consumer surplus, profits, and social welfare, though it is not always beneficial for the environment. In a Cournot–Bertrand comparison, Buccella *et al.* (2022, 2023) and Xu *et al.* (2022) analysed the strategic choice of adopting abatement technology under an emission tax to incentivise firms to pursue emission-reducing actions. While Buccella *et al.* (2022, 2023) emphasised the relative size of society's ecological awareness, Xu *et al.* (2022) highlighted the timing of the relationship between an emission tax and ECSR. Additionally, Park and Lee (2023) and Xu *et al.* (2023) extended these models by combining the two compensation schemes, identifying an optimal combination of double delegation contracts. However, they focused on a simple Cournot case without considering consumers' willingness to pay (WTP) for green products or product differentiation.

1.2. *Emergence of a public eco-firm*

Global concerns about climate change require strong environmental protection and significant government intervention. Stricter environmental regulations have contributed to the emergence of eco-industries, such as wastewater treatment and air pollution control. Environmentally specialised eco-firms provide abatement goods and services to mitigate pollution and manage environmental resources efficiently. The importance of the eco-industry has been recognised by numerous national and international institutions and researchers, such as the Organisation for Economic Co-operation and Development (OECD, 1999; Berg *et al.*, 1998; Ecotech Research and Consulting Ltd., 2002; Kennett and Steenblik, 2005).[2] In particular, Lee and Park (2019, 2021) examined a green managerial incentive design in the presence of an eco-industry and revealed that the sequential adoption of ECSR by polluting firms under price competition enhances their profitability.

Pollution management using the abatement of goods has become more important in the policy-making process, given that these environmental products and clean technologies are largely supplied by the eco-industry. Many governments have recognised the importance of the eco-industry and enacted various policies to encourage them. In particular, they have significantly increased policy attention towards public institutions and organisations for public firms to be key players in this eco-industry. For example, the Korean eco-industry market increasingly imports environmental technology: 22% by the public sector and 78% by the private sector in 2012. Recently, many governments in advanced countries have also invested in the research and development (R&D) of eco-technology, such as CleanTECH San Diego in the USA, Lahti Regional Development Company in Finland, Solar Valley Mitteldeutschland in Germany, and Water Cluster in Israel.

Recent studies have investigated the policy consequences of privatising public eco-firms or nationalising private ones in mixed oligopolies where public eco-firms compete with private ones, reflecting the increased attention of policymakers in this

[2]For a recent analysis of the eco-industry, we can also refer to the works of David and Sinclair-Desgagné (2005), Canton *et al.* (2008, 2012), David *et al.* (2011), Lee and Park (2011, 2019, 2021), Kim and Lee (2014, 2016), and Kim *et al.* (2018), among others.

regard.[3] Particularly in the presence of an eco-industry, the literature on mixed oligopolies and externalities also focuses on the vertical market structure. Park *et al.* (2022) followed earlier research (Pal and Saha, 2015; Xu *et al.*, 2016; Poyago-Theotoky and Yong, 2019), identifying the optimal degree of privatisation when a mixed oligopoly produces both goods and pollution. They imagine an upstream mixed oligopoly that provides an abatement good as an input to downstream firms. The government sets both the extent of privatisation upstream and a subsidy to induce downstream firms to purchase abatement goods. These tools influence output and pollution and, thus, their optimal use of privatisation policy. They show that depending on the environmental damage from pollution, any level of privatisation (including none or complete) can be optimal. This finding is inconsistent with research on mixed oligopolies, where the optimal degree of privatising a public firm is important. They show that the presence of a not overly inefficient public eco-firm improves welfare by reducing the extent of double marginalisation and saving real resources. Moreover, whenever this is the case, partial privatisation of the firm can often further enhance welfare by reducing the cost disadvantage of an entirely public firm.

In this chapter, we consider a vertically related market structure where the emission tax is levied on the net emissions of a polluting monopoly producing final goods that emit emissions, whereas a public eco-firm produces the abatement goods reducing emissions. We examine the effects of voluntary ECSR by the polluting monopoly and partial privatisation policy to the public eco-firm. We highlight that the efficiency of abatement technology crucially affects the profitable ECSR and its welfare effects. Our findings suggest that green technology development in an eco-industry determines the feasible design of green policy through privatising a public eco-firm under the strategic ECSR incentive.

[3] In an OECD report, Kowalski *et al.* (2013) noted that, among the 2,000 largest public companies in the world, over 10% are either public firms or have significant government ownership, and their sales are equivalent to approximately 6% of the global GDP.

2. The Model

We consider a vertically related market where a (downstream) polluting firm sells consumption goods to consumers and an (upstream) eco-firm sells abatement goods to the polluting firm. We accordingly assume a linear inverse demand function of consumption goods, $f(Q) = 1 - Q$. The polluting firm's production of Q generates pollution emissions, e, taxed at the rate of $t \geq 0$ on emissions.[4] Then, it can reduce its emissions (and, thus, its tax burden) by purchasing abatement goods of A from the eco-firm at the price of r, reducing emissions to $e = Q - A$. The total cost function of the polluting firm is given as $C_p(Q) = cQ + rA$, where c is the unit cost of production, which is set at $c = 0$ without loss of generality.[5] Then, the profit of polluting firm P under an emissions tax regime is as follows:

$$\pi_p = f(Q)Q - rA - te \tag{1}$$

We also assume that the cost function of an eco-firm E is given as $C_E(A) = \gamma A^2$, where $\gamma > 0$ denotes the coefficient of the production cost of abatement goods. Then, the profit of the eco-firm is as follows:

$$\pi_E = rA - \gamma A^2 \tag{2}$$

Environmental damage is assumed as a quadratic function of net emissions, defined as $de^2 = d(Q - A)^2$, where d is the marginal cost of emissions, normalised as $d = 1$, for analytic simplicity. The social welfare is, then, defined as the sum of consumer surplus and firms'

---

[4]We can use $t \geq (t_0 > 0)$, where t_0 is defined as a socially acceptable rate of emission tax, which is assumed that $t_0 > 0$. In that case, we have a positive minimum level of emission tax rate, which might reduce the feasible region of ECSR in our analysis, while our findings are robust. Furthermore, this assumption can exclude the possibility of the optimal non-negative value of emission tax in the analysis. Note that this happens when the monopoly power of the polluting firm is sufficiently high and thus, its dead-weight loss outweighs the social cost of externalities by the polluting firm. See the works of Buchanan (1969) and Lee (1998) for more discussion on this debate.

[5]It is also assumed that in-house abatement (environmental R&D investment) is costly to undertake by the polluting firm itself and thus, outsourcing abatement is economically feasible when the price of abatement goods r is sufficiently low.

profits minus environmental damage:

$$W = \int_0^Q (1 - u)\mathrm{d}u - \gamma A^2 - de^2 \tag{3}$$

We consider different organisational structures between the polluting and an eco-firm. On the one hand, for the polluting firm, we consider a green managerial delegation scenario where owners and managers are separated while the owners can commit to ECSR. We assume that, given the concern of the owners of the polluting firm for its emission level (and thus, tax burden), their managers are mandated to undertake ECSR activities as far as ECSR initiatives do not reduce their profits, compared with their initial profit level without ECSR. Thus, we concentrate on the profitable approach to ECSR by the owners of the firm, namely, profitable ECSR. Then, the managers seek to maximise the weighted sum of profits while fractionally reducing the emissions levels caused by the firm's production processes. Specifically, we define the managers' objective function as[6]

$$T_p = \pi_p - \theta e^2 \tag{4}$$

where $\theta \geq 0$ denotes the degree of ECSR that is chosen by the owners. On the other hand, regarding the eco-firm, we consider a governmental managerial delegation model, where owners and managers are separated while the firm is partially owned by the government and private investors. Following the work of Park *et al.* (2022), which applies the model of partial privatisation in the work of Matsumura (1998) to the eco-industry, we consider a partially privatised eco-firm in which the objective function is the weighted sum of own profit and

[6]While recent studies have adopted different incentive weights on ECSR in green managerial delegation contracts, we adopt a typical setup from the works of Buccella *et al.* (2022) and Xu *et al.* (2023) who employed ECSR incentives as compensation for firm's reductions in its own emission levels. For other incentives, for example, Hirose *et al.* (2017), Lee and Park (2019, 2021), Xu *et al.* (2022), Xing and Lee (2023), and Park and Lee (2023) employ environmental damage, while Poyago-Theotoky and Yong (2019), Buccella *et al.* (2023), and Xu *et al.* (2023) employ emission tax reductions.

social welfare:

$$T_E = \alpha \pi_E + (1 - \alpha) W \tag{5}$$

where α denotes the ownership share of the private sector that corresponds to the degree of privatisation determined by the welfare-maximising government, assumed to manage social welfare under the contract of non-negative profit of a public eco-firm. That is, we impose the following assumption for interior solutions on the whole analysis.[7]

Assumption 1. Non-negative profit of the Eco-firm, $\pi_E > 0$.

In the analysis, we focus on the profitable role of ECSR in the strategic interaction with the government's optimal emission tax rate. The equilibrium solutions can be analysed by considering the outcome of the sequential game. We first consider the management level, where the degree of privatisation (α) and the level of ECSR (θ) are given, and then examine the effects of ECSR decisions by the owners. The timing of this game is as follows: In the first stage, firm E sets the price of abatement goods for maximising its objectives in equation (5), whereas the government sets the emission tax for maximising social welfare in equation (3). In the second stage, firm P chooses the production level of final goods and purchasing level of abatement goods for maximising its objectives in equation (4). Then, equilibrium outcomes are sub-game perfect Nash equilibrium and solved by backward induction.

3. The Analysis

To analyse the feasibility of ECSR, we first assume that $\theta > 0$. Then, in the second stage, the first-order conditions for firm P are as follows:

$$\begin{aligned} \frac{\partial T_p}{\partial q} &= 1 - 2Q - t + 2(A - Q)\theta = 0 \\ \frac{\partial T_p}{\partial A} &= t - r + 2(Q - A)\theta = 0 \end{aligned} \tag{6}$$

[7] We can show that full nationalisation is impossible without governmental deficit since $\pi_E(\alpha = 0) = \frac{-1}{(1+3\gamma)^2} < 0$ in the following analysis.

By solving the above simultaneously, the equilibrium outcomes are as follows:

$$Q = \frac{1-r}{2} \quad \text{and} \quad A = \frac{1-r}{2} - \frac{r-t}{2\theta} \tag{7}$$

Note that, for the non-negative emission level, that is, $\mathrm{E} = Q - A \geq 0$, the price of abatement goods should not be lower than the emission tax, that is, $r \geq t$ as far as $\theta > 0$ in the equilibrium.

Again, assuming $\theta > 0$ in the first stage, the first-order conditions for firm E and the government are as follows:

$$\frac{\partial T_E}{\partial r} = \frac{\begin{array}{c}2(\gamma - (\alpha+\gamma)(2r-t))\theta + ((1-r)(3\alpha+2\gamma)\\ -(1+r))\theta^2 - 2(r-t)(1-\alpha+\gamma)\end{array}}{4\theta^2} \tag{8}$$

and

$$\frac{\partial W}{\partial t} = \frac{(r-t)(1+\gamma) - (1-r)\gamma\theta}{2\theta^2}$$

By solving the above simultaneously, the equilibrium outcomes are as follows:

$$\begin{aligned}
r^* &= \frac{\alpha(\gamma + (3+\gamma)\theta) - (1-\gamma)\theta}{2\alpha(1+2\gamma) + (1+3\gamma+\alpha(3+\gamma))\theta}\\
t^* &= \frac{2\alpha\gamma - \theta(1-\alpha(3-\gamma) - \gamma + 2\gamma\theta}{2\alpha(1+2\gamma) + (1+3\gamma+\alpha(3+\gamma))\theta}\\
Q^* &= \frac{(1+\gamma)(\alpha+\theta)}{2\alpha(1+2\gamma) + (1+3\gamma+\alpha(3+\gamma))\theta}\\
A^* &= \frac{\alpha+\theta}{1\alpha(1+2\gamma) + (1+3\gamma+\alpha(3+\gamma))\theta}\\
e^* &= \frac{\gamma(\alpha+\theta)}{1\alpha(1+2\gamma) + (1+3\gamma+\alpha(3+\gamma))\theta}\\
\pi_p^* &= \frac{(\alpha+\theta_D)^2((1+\gamma)^2 + 2\gamma^2\theta)}{(1\alpha(1+2\gamma) + (1+3\gamma+\alpha(3+\gamma))\theta)^2}\\
\pi_E^* &= \frac{(\alpha+\theta_D)(\alpha\gamma - (1-\alpha(3+\gamma))\theta)}{(1\alpha(1+2\gamma) + (1+3\gamma+\alpha(3+\gamma))\theta)^2}
\end{aligned} \tag{9}$$

and

$$W^* = \frac{(1+\gamma)(\alpha+\theta)(\alpha(3+5\gamma) + (1+3\gamma+2\alpha(3+\gamma))\theta)}{2(1\alpha(1+2\gamma) + (1+3\gamma+\alpha(3+\gamma))\theta)^2}$$

3.1. *Profit effects of ECSR*

We now examine the effects of ECSR. First, we can show that with a low (high) degree of privatisation, both consumption and abatement goods increase (decrease) as ECSR increases and thus, total emissions increase (decreases), i.e., $\frac{\partial Q^*}{\partial \theta}, \frac{\partial A^*}{\partial \theta} \gtrless 0 \Leftrightarrow a \lesseqgtr \frac{1+\gamma}{3+\gamma} (= \alpha^W)$, or equivalently, $\gamma \gtrless \frac{3\alpha - 1}{1-\alpha} (= \gamma^W)$. This is because the input price of abatement goods is low (high) with a low (high) degree of privatisation, and thus, the polluting firm employing ECSR can produce more (less) consumption goods by purchasing more (less) abatement goods. However, it also depends on the efficiency of the production of abatement goods by the public eco-firm; that is, with a high (low) degree of abatement inefficiency, as ECSR increases, both consumption and abatement goods increase (decrease). This finding is also derived because, given the degree of privatisation, the input cost of abatement goods is relatively costly (cheap) under the high (low) inefficiency of abatement technology, and the input price is high (low); thus, the polluting firm employing ECSR can produce less (more) consumption goods by purchasing less (more) abatement goods. Note that $\frac{\partial Q^*}{\partial \theta}, \frac{\partial A^*}{\partial \theta} > 0$ if $a < \frac{1}{3}$. Thus, under the given the higher government ownership, ECSR can increase both consumption and abatement goods and thus, welfare.[8] However, the changes in both consumption and abatement goods regarding the level of ECSR are independent of the degree of ECSR. Finally, we have $r^* > t^*$ and $\frac{\partial t^*}{\partial \theta} \gtrless 0 \Leftrightarrow \gamma \lesseqgtr \frac{\sqrt{8\alpha(5\alpha-1)(\alpha+\theta)2+16\alpha^2\theta^2+(1+3\alpha)\theta^2(8\alpha+(1+3\alpha)\theta)}-2\alpha(1-\alpha+2\theta)-(1+3\alpha)\theta^2}{2(\alpha(1+3\alpha)+8\alpha\theta+(3+\alpha)\theta^2)}$ representing the strategic relationship between the emission tax and the ECSR level. If the production of abatement goods is inefficient, that is, γ is large, a higher level of ECSR decreases the emission tax since it would be better for the social welfare if the level of ECSR was increased by the polluting firm rather than increasing the production of abatement goods by the eco-firm. Similarly, if the production of abatement goods is efficient, that is, γ is small, higher level of ECSR

[8]Note that $\frac{\partial Q^*}{\partial \theta} \gtrless \frac{\partial A^*}{\partial \theta} \Leftrightarrow \alpha \lesseqgtr \alpha^W$ or $\Leftrightarrow \gamma \gtrless \gamma^W$ and thus $\frac{\partial e^*}{\partial \theta} \lesseqgtr 0 \Leftrightarrow \alpha \gtrless \alpha^W$ or $\Leftrightarrow \gamma \gtrless \gamma^W$.

Note also that $\frac{\partial r^*}{\partial \gamma} \gtrless 0 \Leftrightarrow \alpha \gtrless \alpha^W$ or $\Leftrightarrow \gamma \lesseqgtr \gamma^W$ while $\frac{\partial r^*}{\partial \gamma} > 0$.

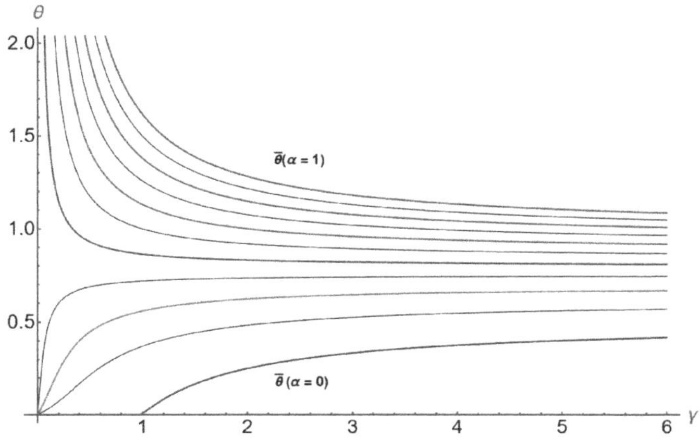

Fig. 1. Feasibility of ECSR.

increases the emission tax since it would be better for the social welfare if the level of ECSR as well as the production of abatement goods were increased.

Lemma 1. *Feasibility of ECSR: There exists an upper bound of ECSR;* $0 < \theta < \bar{\theta} = \text{Min}[\theta_t, \theta_{\pi_E}]$, *where* θ_t *satisfies* $t \gtreqless 0 \Leftrightarrow \theta \lesseqgtr \theta_t$ *and* θ_{π_E} *satisfies* $\pi_E \gtreqless 0 \Leftrightarrow \theta \lesseqgtr \theta_{\pi_E}$.

For vivid understanding, numerical simulations in Fig. 1 show the upper bound of ECSR in the feasibility of ECSR in which θ is critically dependent upon the level of privatisation (α). Note that the upper bound of ECSR is always positive for $\forall \gamma > 0$ unless the degree of privatisation is low; that is, $\alpha > \frac{1}{3+3\gamma}$ (if γ is sufficiently low, $\alpha > \frac{1}{3}$).

Lemma 1 states that the degree of privatisation α is critical in determining the feasible range of ECSR when the government and the owners of the polluting firm interact. If the degree of privatisation is low, that is, $0 < \alpha < \frac{1}{3(1+\gamma)}$, the government should consider the non-negative profit of the eco-firm to ensure the adoption of ECSR by the owners of the polluting firm.[9] Otherwise, the government should consider the relative levels between the emission tax and the price

[9]Under full nationalisation policy, the profit of a public eco-firm is always negative and, thus, neither full nationalisation nor ECSR is feasible.

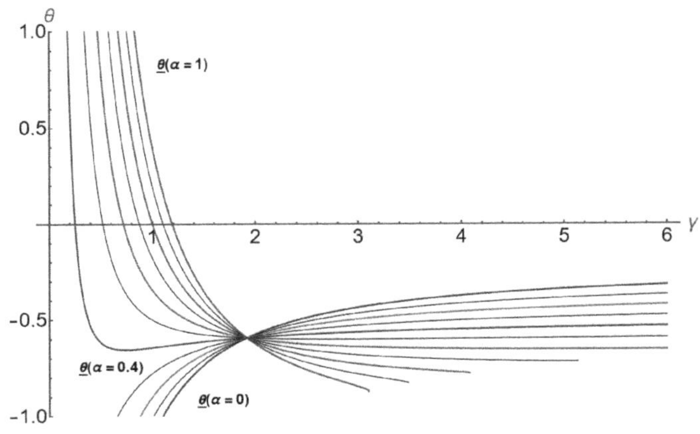

Fig. 2. Profitability of ECSR.

of abatement goods in regulating the public eco-firm; hence, as the government privatises firm E, its profit increases. Therefore, it does not need to be concerned about the non-negative profit, i.e., $\frac{\partial \pi_E}{\partial \alpha} = \frac{\theta(1+\gamma+(3+\gamma)\theta)(2\alpha(1+\gamma)+((1+\gamma)(3-\alpha)-2\alpha)\theta)}{(2\alpha(1+2\gamma)+(1+3\gamma+\alpha(3+\gamma))\theta)^3} > 0$.

Lemma 2. *Profitability of ECSR: There exists a threshold of ECSR that guarantees higher profit of the polluting firm, compared with the profit level without ECSR;* $\theta > \text{Max}[\theta, \underline{\theta}]$, *where* θ *satisfies* $\Delta_{\pi_P} \gtreqless 0 \Leftrightarrow \theta \gtreqless \theta$.

Numerical simulations in Fig. 2 show that the profitable ECSR always arises with the higher degree of abatement technology, that is, $\gamma > 1.19$, while the profitable ECSR never arises with the lower degree of privatisation, that is, $\alpha < \frac{1}{3}$.

Lemma 2 also states that the degree of privatisation α is critical in determining the profitable range of ECSR when the government and the owners of the polluting firm interact.

Lemmas 1 and 2 represent the feasibility and profitability conditions of ECSR, respectively, which imply that the level of privatisation (α) critically shapes both conditions. In particular, we find that only when $\alpha > \frac{1}{3}$ the feasibility and the profitability of ECSR can be assured for any $\gamma > 0$. In other words, under the full nationalisation policy, the feasibility of ECSR does not arise if γ is sufficiently low. For example, when we set $\alpha = 2/5$, Fig. 3 shows that the feasibility

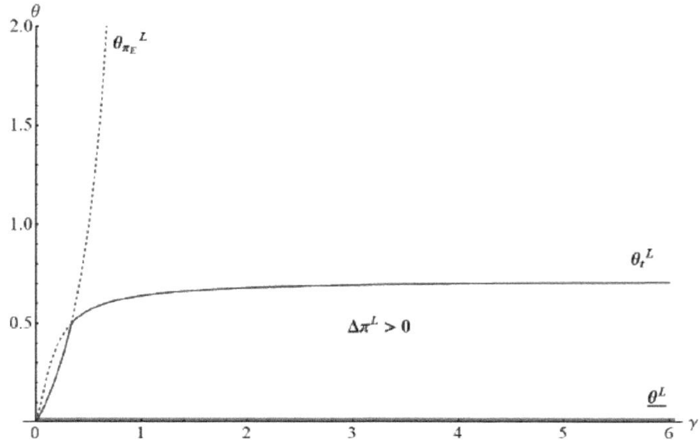

Fig. 3. $\underline{\theta}$ and $\bar{\theta}$ with a low degree of privatisation, $\alpha = \frac{1}{4}$.

condition of ECSR (θ) is higher than the profitability condition of ECSR (θ) unless γ is sufficiently low.

In the following, we show two examples regarding the degree of privatisation. The first example pertains to a low degree of privatisation, i.e., $0 < \alpha < \frac{1}{3}$, where all feasible ranges of ECSR are profitable for the polluting firm. The second reflects a high degree of privatisation, i.e., $\frac{1}{3} < \alpha \leq 1$, where a threshold for profitable ECSR exists.

First, for a low degree of privatisation, suppose $\alpha = \frac{1}{4}$. Then, we derive Fig. 3.

For a high degree of privatisation, suppose $\alpha = \frac{3}{4}$. In this case, we derive Fig. 4.

Proposition 1. *Under the given degree of privatisation, a polluting firm has the incentive to adopt ECSR to increase its profits in the regions of* $\text{Max}[0, \underline{\theta}] < \theta < \bar{\theta}$.

Proposition 1 emphasises profitable ECSR in the strategic interaction with the optimal emission tax adjusted by the government in the decision process of the price of abatement goods. However, as far as γ is not sufficiently low, the aggressive production of abatement goods is not always beneficial to society since it is costly. Thus, the government has the option to induce the polluting firm to adopt ECSR, which might be less costly than the case of direct expansion of the production of abatement goods, while higher ECSR causes

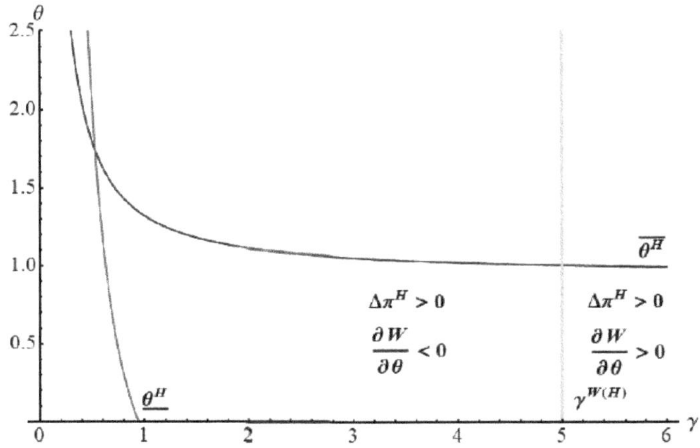

Fig. 4. $\underline{\theta}$ and $\bar{\theta}$ with a high degree of privatisation, $\alpha = \frac{3}{4}$.

the extraction of the production of final goods. Therefore, the government can consider the polluting firm's profitability by comparing the welfare cost/benefit between the production cost of abatement goods (which fixes the externality problem) and the welfare loss in the consumption of final goods (which causes allocative inefficiency).

3.2. *Welfare effects of ECSR*

Finally, we investigate the effects of profitable ECSR on social welfare, critically dependent upon the level of privatisation (α) and the efficiency of abatement technology (γ). Differentiating welfare with respect to the degree of ECSR yields $\frac{\partial W^*}{\partial \theta} \gtrless 0 \Leftrightarrow \alpha \lesseqgtr \alpha^W \Leftrightarrow \gamma \gtreqless \gamma^W$, that is, the welfare effect is not dependent on the degree of ECSR but on the degree of privatisation and the efficiency of abatement technology.

Furthermore, α^W has the minimum value at $1/3$ for $\forall \gamma > 0$. Thus, with a low degree of privatisation, the profitable choice of ECSR can always increase social welfare. However, with a higher degree of privatisation, the welfare effect of the profitable ECSR choice depends on the efficiency of the abatement technology. In other words, under the given efficiency of abatement technology, the profitable choice of ECSR can increase (decrease) social welfare when the degree of privatisation is low (high). Equivalently, under the given degree of privatisation, the profitable choice of ECSR can increase (decrease) social welfare when the abatement technology is inefficient (efficient). For example, when we set $\alpha = \frac{1}{4}$, as shown in Fig. 3, feasible ECSR is the profitable ECSR choice and is desirable for society. However, when we set $\alpha = \frac{3}{4}$, as shown in Fig. 4, we can find the regions for welfare-improving profitable ECSR. In particular, given the feasibility condition of ECSR ($\bar{\theta}$) and the profitability condition of ECSR ($\underline{\theta}$), if $\gamma > \gamma^{W(H)}(= 5)$, the profitable choice of ECSR always improves social welfare.

Proposition 2. *Unless the degree of privatisation is low, profitable ECSR can increase social welfare with an inefficient abatement technology. However, when the degree of privatisation is low, profitable ECSR can increase social welfare regardless of the efficiency of abatement technology.*

We further examine the effects of privatisation on the profitable ECSR and social welfare. In the previous analysis in Figs. 1 and 2, we showed that, as the degree of privatisation increases, both the feasibility condition of ECSR ($\bar{\theta}$) and the profitability condition of ECSR ($\underline{\theta}$) move up. This finding implies that the profitability of ECSR depends on the efficiency of the abatement technology. For example, we can set the two different degrees of privatisation between $\frac{1}{3} < \alpha^L(= \frac{1}{4}) < \alpha^H(= \frac{3}{4}) < 1$ and draw the ranges between θ and θ, respectively, in Fig. 5.

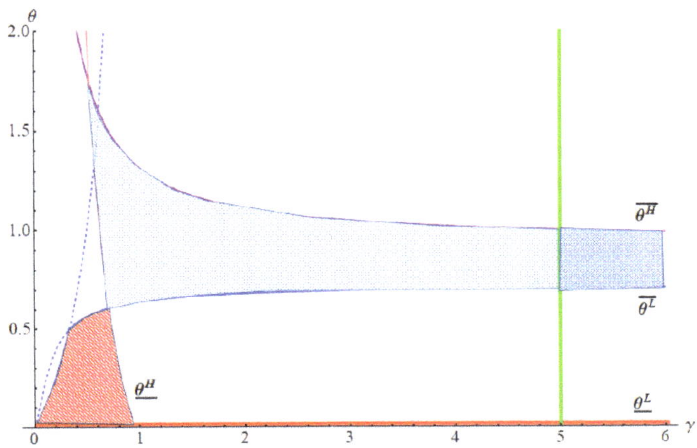

Fig. 5. The effects of privatisation on ECSR.

We now compare the changes in the feasibility and profitability ranges in Fig. 5 between $\alpha^L(=\frac{1}{4})$ and $\alpha^H(=\frac{3}{4})$. First, the blue area reflects the increased area of the profitability conditions of ECSR, which can decrease social welfare if $\gamma < \gamma^{W(H)}(=5)$. It represents that given the efficiency of abatement technology, the increased degree of privatisation policy can encourage the profitable ECSR, while the welfare effect of privatisation policy depends on the efficiency of abatement technology. Second, the red area indicates the decreased area between the feasibility conditions of ECSR, implying that the increased degree of the privatisation policy can crowd out profitable ECSR choices, especially when the production of abatement goods is efficient.

Proposition 3. *Privatisation policy can encourage the profitable ECSR with an inefficient abatement technology, while it might crowd out the profitable ECSR with an efficient abatement technology.*

4. Concluding Remarks

We consider a vertical structure model with emission externalities where a public eco-firm under mixed ownership produces abatement goods that can be utilised by a polluting firm in the final goods market. The public eco-firm cares about environmental damage and welfare when it provides abatement goods, while the government can indirectly regulate an input price with a lower level. We impose the non-negative profit condition for a public eco-firm where the mixed ownership firm does not run losses, thereby restricting the full nationalisation policy in the eco-industry. Within the context of an emission tax where the polluting firm might adopt profitable ECSR to lessen the tax burden, we examine the strategic relationship between ECSR incentives and the degree of mixed ownership of a public eco-firm.

We find that the efficiency of abatement technology crucially affects profitable ECSR and social welfare. When there is a high degree of private ownership in a public eco-firm, as the degree of private ownership in a public eco-firm increases, ECSR can be strategically used to reduce an emissions tax, while abatement goods price increases, due to double marginalisation effect in the vertical structure, which increases the possible strategic spaces of ECSR. Furthermore, privatising a public eco-firm with an inefficient abatement technology can improve social welfare because the polluting firm purchases less abatement goods, which is socially expensive to produce. Thus, privatising a public eco-firm can increase the level of ECSR, which can improve social welfare only when inefficient green technology is applied by a public eco-firm. However, when there is a low degree of private ownership, as the degree of private ownership in a public eco-firm increases, the increased input price reduces profitable ECSR incentives, shrinking the possible strategic space for ECSR. Thus, there exists a crowding-out effect in the abatement goods price regulation on the polluting firm's incentive to engage in ECSR while an increase of ECSR always improves social welfare regardless of the efficiency of abatement technology.

In the analysis, we impose the non-negative profit condition whereby the mixed ownership of the public eco-firm does not run losses. This constraint could be relaxed when government subsidisation is allowed. However, such subsidisation could come with its own cost of public financing that reduces social welfare, thus introducing another trade-off in the welfare. For example, while the emission tax revenue can provide a double-dividend effect, which can also be used for public finance, an emission tax has its own distorting effects on labour supply, which can have the same excess burden as a tax on labour income. Furthermore, the primary benefit of public ownership under the governmental deficit is that a public enterprise can achieve social goals by increasing allocative efficiency and decreasing environmental externalities. Nevertheless, the public eco-firm may mismanage its assets in such a way that they cause managerial production inefficiencies, which causes welfare loss. In some cases, higher public ownership might be less efficient than their private sector counterparts, especially when the public eco-firm is operated under political pressure rather than economic interests. Therefore, when the government activates both privatisation and competition policies in the eco-industry, the strategic effects not only in the relations between ECSR and emission tax but also in the relations between the degree of private ownership and the efficiency of abatement technology should be scrutinised by the cooperation between environment and competition authorities.

Appendix: Proofs of Lemmas

Proof of Lemma 1. First, for $\pi_{E^*} \geq 0$, it should be satisfied that $0 < \theta < \theta_{\pi_E} = \frac{\alpha\gamma}{1-\alpha(3+\gamma)}$ when $\alpha < \frac{1}{3+\gamma}$. If $0 < \alpha < \frac{1}{3+\gamma}$, then $\pi_{E^*} > 0 \Leftrightarrow 0 < \theta < \theta_{\pi_E} = \frac{\alpha\gamma}{1-\alpha(3+\gamma)}$. If $\alpha > \frac{1}{3+\gamma}$, then $\pi_{E^*} > 0$ for $\forall \alpha, \gamma$ and $\theta > 0$.

Second, for $t^* > 0$, it should be satisfied that $0 < \theta < \theta_t = \frac{(\gamma-1)(1-\alpha)+2\alpha+\sqrt{(\gamma-1-\alpha(\gamma-3))^2+16\alpha\gamma^2}}{4\gamma}$. Then, $\theta_t = \theta_{\pi_E} \gtreqless 0 \Leftrightarrow \alpha \gtreqless \frac{1}{3(1+\gamma)}$ and $\frac{1}{3(1+\gamma)} < \frac{1}{3+\gamma}$.

Therefore, the upper bound of ECSR with $\pi_{E^*} \geq 0$ and $t^* > 0$ is as follows:

If $0 < \alpha < \frac{1}{3(1+\gamma)}$, then $\bar{\theta} = \text{Min}[\theta_t, \theta_{\pi_E}] = \theta_{\pi_E}$.

If $\frac{1}{3(1+\gamma)} < \alpha < 1$, then $\bar{\theta} = \text{Min}[\theta_t, \theta_{\pi_E}] = \theta_t$.

□

Proof of Lemma 2. Let $\Delta\pi_D$ be the profit difference of the polluting firm between the profits with and without ECSR activities, that is, $\Delta\pi_D \equiv \pi_{D^*}|_{\theta=0}$. Then, we have the following:

$$\Delta\pi_P \overset{\geq}{\underset{<}{}} 0 \Leftrightarrow \theta \overset{\geq}{\underset{<}{}} \underline{\theta}$$

$$= \frac{\left[\dfrac{\alpha^2(1+\gamma)^2(3+\gamma)^2-(1+\gamma)^3(3+7\gamma)+\alpha\Big(6+2\gamma\big(16+\gamma(18-\gamma(16+29\gamma))\big)\Big)}{+(1+\gamma)\big(\alpha(3+\gamma)-(1+\gamma)\big)\sqrt{\begin{array}{l}\alpha^2(1+\gamma)^2(3+\gamma)^2+(1+\gamma)^2(3+7\gamma)^2\\ +2\alpha\Big(9+\gamma\big(42+\gamma(48-\gamma(26+57\gamma))\big)\Big)\end{array}}}\right]}{16\gamma^2(1+2\gamma)^2}$$

Note that $\underline{\theta}$ can be negative and thus, $\Delta\pi_P > 0$ only if $\theta > \text{Max}[0, \underline{\theta}]$.

□

References

Berg, H., Öhman, M. C., Troëng, S. and Lindén, O. (1998). Environmental economics of coral reef destruction in Sri Lanka, *Ambio* **27**(8), 627–634.

Buccella, D., Fanti, L. and Gori, L. (2022). "Green" managerial delegation theory, *Environment and Development Economics* **27**(3), 223–249.

Buccella, D., Fanti, L. and Gori, L. (2023). Environmental delegation versus sales delegation: A game-theoretic analysis, *Environment and Development Economics* **28**(5), 469–485.

Buchanan, J. M. (1969). External diseconomies, corrective taxes, and market structure, *The American Economic Review* **59**(1), 174–177.

Canton, J., David, M. and Sinclair-Desgagné, B. (2012). Environmental regulation and horizontal mergers in the eco-industry, *Strategic Behavior and the Environment* **2**(2), 107–132.

Canton, J., Soubeyran, A. and Stahn, H. (2008). Environmental taxation and vertical cournot oligopolies: How eco-industries matter, *Environmental and Resource Economics* **40**, 369–382.

Costello, M. (2002). Qualitative research with clients: Longer-term experiences of a work-focused service (No. 171), Ecotech Research and Consulting Ltd., Corporate Document Services.

David, M., Nimubona, A.-D. and Sinclair-Desgagné, B. (2011). Emission taxes and the market for abatement goods and services, *Resource and Energy Economics* **33**(1), 179–191.

David, M. and Sinclair-Desgagné, B. (2005). Environmental regulation and the eco-industry, *Journal of Regulatory Economics* **28**, 141–155.

DiNapoli, J. (2021). Most executives think their ESG programs fall short, survey finds, survey, *Reuters*, https://www.reuters.com/business/sustainable-business/most-executives-think-their-esg-programs-fall-short-survey-finds-2021-09-15.

Fukuda, K. and Ouchida, Y. (2020). Corporate social responsibility (CSR) and the environment: Does CSR increase emissions? *Energy Economics* **92**, 104933.

Hirose, K., Lee, S.-H. and Matsumura, T. (2017). Environmental corporate social responsibility: A note on the first-mover advantage under price competition, *Economics Bulletin* **37**(1), 214–221.

Hirose, K., Lee, S.-H., Matsumura, T., *et al.* (2020). Noncooperative and cooperative environmental corporate social responsibility, *Journal of Institutional and Theoretical Economics* **176**(3), 549–571.

Kennett, M. and Steenblik, R. (2005). *Environmental Goods and Services: A Synthesis of Country Studies*, Vol. 3, OECD Publishing, Paris, France.

Kim, S.-L. and Lee, S.-H. (2014). Eco-technology licensing under emission tax: Royalty vs. fixed-fee, *Korean Economic Review* **30**(2), 273–300.

Kim, S.-L. and Lee, S.-H. (2016). The licensing of eco-technology under emission taxation: Fixed fee vs. auction, *International Review of Economics & Finance* **45**, 343–357.

Kim, S.-L., Lee, S.-H. and Matsumura, T. (2018). Eco-technology licensing by a foreign innovator and privatization policy in a polluting mixed duopoly, *Asia-Pacific Journal of Accounting & Economics* **25**(3–4), 433–448.

Kowalski, P., Büge, M., Sztajerowska, M. and Egeland, M. (2013). State-owned enterprises: Trade effects and policy implications, Technical Report, OECD.

Lee, S.-H. (1998). R&D spillovers, technology cartel, and monopoly regulation, *International Economic Journal* **12**(3), 77–88.

Lee, S.-H. and Park, C.-H. (2011). Environmental regulations on vertical oligopolies with eco-industry, *Korean Economic Review* **27**(2), 311–327.

Lee, S.-H. and Park, C.-H. (2019). Eco-firms and the sequential adoption of environmental corporate social responsibility in the managerial delegation, *The B.E. Journal of Theoretical Economics* **19**(1), 20170043.

Lee, S.-H. and Park, C.-H. (2021). Corporate environmentalism in a managerial delegation and abatement subsidy policy, *Asia-Pacific Journal of Accounting & Economics* **28**(5), 546–561.

Liu, C.-C., Wang, L. F. and Lee, S.-H. (2015). Strategic environmental corporate social responsibility in a differentiated duopoly market, *Economics Letters* **129**, 108–111.

Matsumura, T. (1998). Partial privatization in mixed duopoly, *Journal of Public Economics* **70**(3), 473–483.

OECD (1999). The environmental goods and services industry: Manual for data collection and analysis, Technical Report, OECD/Eurostat, Paris, https://doi.org/10.1787/9789264173651-en.

Pal, R. and Saha, B. (2015). Pollution tax, partial privatization and environment, *Resource and Energy Economics* **40**, 19–35.

Park, C.-H. and Lee, S.-H. (2023). Emission taxation, green R&D and managerial delegation contracts with environmental and sales incentives, *Managerial and Decision Economics* **44**(4), 2366–2377.

Park, C.-H., Lee, S.-H. and Nakamura, T. (2022). Voluntary green commitment and optimal privatization policy in a mixed eco-industry, *Asian Journal of Law and Economics* **13**(2), 149–171.

Porter, M. E. and van der Linde, C. (1995). Toward a new conception of the environment-competitiveness relationship, *Journal of Economic Perspectives* **9**(4), 97–118.

Poyago-Theotoky, J. and Yong, S. K. (2019). Managerial delegation contracts, "green" R&D and emissions taxation, *The B.E. Journal of Theoretical Economics* **19**(2), 20170128.

Price Waterhouse Cooper (2022). Global investor survey 2022, Technical Report, Price Waterhouse Cooper, https://www.pwc.com/gx/en/global-investor-survey/PwC-Global-Investor-Survey-2022.pdf.

Ritz, R. A. (2022). Linking executive compensation to climate performance, *California Management Review* **64**(3), 124–140.

Wang, C. (2021). Monopoly with corporate social responsibility, product differentiation, and environmental R&D: Implications for economic, environmental, and social sustainability, *Journal of Cleaner Production* **287**, 125433.

Xing, M. and Lee, S.-H. (2023). Non-cooperative and cooperative environmental R&D under environmental corporate social responsibility with green managerial coordination, *Managerial and Decision Economics* **44**(5), 2684–2696.

Xu, L., Chen, Y. and Lee, S.-H. (2022). Emission tax and strategic environmental corporate social responsibility in a Cournot – Bertrand comparison, *Energy Economics* **107**, 105846.

Xu, L., Cho, S. and Lee, S.-H. (2016). Emission tax and optimal privatization in Cournot – Bertrand comparison, *Economic Modelling* **55**, 73–82.

Xu, L., Su, F. and Lee, S.-H. (2023). Strategic corporate social responsibility and partial privatization policy with foreign penetration, *The Japanese Economic Review* **74**(2), 251–278.

https://doi.org/10.1142/9789819816033_0005

Chapter 5

The Effects of Environmental Taxes on the Private and Social Incentives to FDI

Mario Martínez Fernández[*,‡], **Rafael Moner-Colonques**[*,§], **and Jose J. Sempere-Monerris**[*,†,‖]

[*] *University of Valencia, Department of Economic Analysis and ERI-CES, Valencia, Spain*

[†] *CORE/LIDAM, UCLouvain, Louvain-la-Neuve, Belgium*

[‡] *marferm5@alumni.uv.es*

[§] *rafael.moner@uv.es*

[‖] *jose.j.sempere@uv.es*

We develop an imperfect competition model of trade with environmental damages where firms decide between foreign direct investment (FDI) and exports prior to competition in quantities. We shall also characterise countries' choices according to welfare. The comparison of equilibria allows us to identify a potential market failure and whether the highest possible welfare is attained. Our analysis shows that an environmental tax equal to marginal damage brings private and social interests together and the highest possible welfare is reached in more cases relative to no intervention. Also, there is a tax, greater than the marginal damage, that eliminates the welfare dilemma, but a market failure remains. Finally, environmental taxes may influence firms' internationalisation choices and eventually lead to lower environmental damages.

Keywords: Environmental tax, International duopoly, Private and social choices, Emission tax, Capital FDI vs. Export strategy, Location choice.

1. Introduction

> Finally, as the world becomes increasingly crowded, the interaction between trade policies and environmental policies will become more important. I would predict that much of the actual trade policy debate over the next decade or two will deal with environmental and resource use issues. Accordingly, since many of the relevant industries are of the oligopoly type, it will be important to integrate resource and environmental concerns into models of strategic trade policy. Brander (1995)

A key characteristic of the globalisation of the world economy has been the liberalisation and expansion of global foreign direct investment (FDI) flows (Cole *et al.*, 2017). World FDI reached \$1,294 billion in 2022 and was hardly \$164 billion in 1992. It is well known that the growth of multinational enterprise (MNE) activity in the form of foreign direct investment (FDI) has grown at a faster rate than most other international transactions, particularly trade flows between countries (Blonigen, 2005). Global patterns of trade and FDI show a remarkable growth over the last decades (late 80s onwards). A closer look at aggregate data unveils that developed countries account for a great proportion of outward FDI and are also recipients of FDI – one of the stylised macro facts documented in Markusen (1995). At the firm level, multinationals are important in industries with firm-specific assets and high levels of R&D relative to sales (micro fact). Although FDI is important for growth and development it is also seen as a source of negative environmental consequences for host countries/regions. While renewable energy investments have grown considerably, developing countries have attracted a very low share (UNCTAD, 2023).

With these elements at hand, researchers have intensified their efforts to study the environmental consequences of FDI flows. One important aspect which has merited particular attention is to what extent environmental regulation influences firms' location decisions, that is, whether firms relocate their plants to less environmentally-friendly countries to compete in the international markets – this is referred to as the pollution haven hypothesis. OECD Statistics on environmental policy stringency indexes reveal that, although their levels in many developing countries show an increasing trend, they remain noticeably below those in developed countries. Firms' expansion strategies to other markets are shaped not only by rivals' decisions, which ultimately determine the intensity of competition, but also by environmental policy considerations. In this context, one wonders whether the private incentives of firms towards FDI are aligned with social incentives. This chapter is thus a theoretical contribution to the FDI-environment debate by developing a model where firms with market power, located in different countries, decide on how to serve the foreign market, whether by setting up a plant (FDI strategy) or by exports (E strategy). It will be argued that a conflict exists in such strategic settings and that the conflict is more important in the presence of environmental damage. Our analysis will conclude by showing how an environmental tax may contribute to bring private and social interests closer together with regard to firms' internationalisation strategies. In other words, how location choices respond to environmental policies.

Pollution is a by-product inevitably linked to production, and while the latter is a source of social welfare, the former is socially undesirable. The consideration of international oligopoly competition makes the problem a complex one. Governments may use instruments, such as environmental taxes, to contend with pollution at the local level. Although there is a variety of reasons that explain a firm's decision to invest abroad, environmental regulations are an additional determinant of such decisions. Governments may be tempted to adopt lax regulations, aimed at not harming much the competitiveness of domestic firms which, on the other hand, may certainly attract foreign firm investment willing to avoid more severe regulations in their countries of origin; this could lead to larger output and more local pollutions. In contrast, stricter regulation would reduce the intensity of foreign competition, although consumer surplus may be lower and so is environmental damage. The following questions arise: in the absence of environmental taxes, do firms' choices between FDI and exports result in the highest attainable welfare levels? What is the effect of an environmental tax on firms' internationalisation decisions? Can the right choice of the tax align private and social interests more often? The purpose of this chapter is to develop an imperfect competition model of trade where firms decide between FDI and exports prior to competition in quantities. Alternatively, we shall characterise countries' choices according to welfare objectives before firms compete. The comparison of equilibria when either firms or countries play allows us to identify a potential market failure. Market structure is endogenised and the analysis will proceed in steps. Firstly, the baseline model will be presented in which environmental damages are assumed away; this will illustrate the possible conflict area between private and social interests regarding the FDI versus E choice by focusing solely on strategic reasons for FDI in international competition and whether the highest possible welfare is attained. Secondly, the model with environmental damages is introduced conducting the same analysis. Thirdly, we study the role of environmental taxes in bringing private and social interests together and in getting the highest possible welfare and lowest environmental damages. For the sake of the analysis, the model is fairly symmetric to show the following. A setting without environmental damages does not exhibit a private-social conflict, yet, for low enough values of setting up a foreign plant, welfare under an export strategy is higher than under FDI, which is the equilibrium firm choice. The consideration of environmental damages (i) makes a market failure to appear and, (ii) enlarges the range of setup costs for which the highest attainable welfare is not achieved. Our analysis shows that an environmental tax equal to marginal damage brings private and social interests together and the highest possible welfare is reached in more cases. Besides, there is a tax, greater than marginal damage, that eliminates the welfare dilemma, but a market failure remains. Some numerical examples show that (i) for large setup costs, intervention shifts firms' choices from exports to FDI and implies lower environmental damages compared to no intervention, (ii) for lower values of setup costs, intervention shifts firms' play to export and damages are reduced, and, (iii) differences in environmental taxes lead to opposite equilibrium strategies for firms with FDI occurring in the country with a less stringent policy; such outcomes need not correspond with higher welfare levels or lower damages. Therefore, firms' internationalisation strategies do react to environmental policies.

Before moving to the model, we survey the most relevant and related literature in the next section. Section 3 presents the model, where different subsections develop the case without environmental damages, with damages and no intervention, and with damages and intervention; results are shown throughout the analysis. Then a few numerical examples are given in Section 3.4, and some concluding remarks close the chapter.

2. Literature Review

Traditional theories on foreign direct investment (FDI) emphasise that a firm must possess some advantages over local firms that compensate for inherent costs and risks of doing business abroad, as structured by Dunning (1981) in the well-known ownership, location, and internalisation (OLI) framework. Those theories typically disregard strategic interactions in explaining FDI decisions. There exist a number of contributions which formally address the export versus FDI decision in a game-theoretic setting and include Horstmann and Markusen (1987), Horstmann and Markusen (1992), Smith (1987), Motta (1992), Motta and Thisse (1994), Rowthorn (1992), Campa *et al.* (1998), Markusen (2002), Dixon (2006), and (Barac and Moner-Colonques, 2016, 2022), among many others. The paper by Horstmann and Markusen (1992) develops a model with two countries and two firms, each headquartered in a different country, where firms play a two-stage game. In the first stage, firms simultaneously decide over three options regarding plant location: (a) not to serve any country, which means a zero plant strategy; (b) to have a plant in their domestic country and serve the other country via exports – and incur some trade/transportation costs, which is a one plant strategy; or (c) to have a plant in each country becoming multinational – this corresponds to FDI and additional fixed costs – which means a two plant strategy. In the second stage, firms compete in quantities à la Cournot. They show how firms' decisions endogenously determine the equilibrium market structure. The intuition rests on the proximity-concentration trade-off. The two-firm, two-plant structure arises when plant setup costs are low relative to transportation costs, that is, both firms would engage in FDI. Similarly, the two-firm, one plant exporting duopoly occurs for relatively large plant setup costs. Although a welfare comparison is not conducted, the authors note that small tax-policy variations may drive changes in the equilibrium market structure with important welfare effects.

Intuitively, one would then expect to observe FDI as a substitute for exporting when tariff rates are high. This insight, known as the tariff-jumping argument, can be contradicted in strategic settings where foreign entrants face competition from domestic firms. A non-monotonic relationship between FDI and tariffs is provided by Motta (1992) and Campa *et al.* (1998). It is also possible to rationalise unconventional FDI decisions by proposing a sequential setting where the potential multinational makes her choice in advance, as done in Markusen (2002) and Dixon (2006). Which firm enters early through FDI and is imitated later by another is modelled in Barac and Moner-Colonques (2022); leadership in FDI by the more efficient firm arises when setup costs are low enough, which is best for consumers, however, total welfare might be higher were firms opting for opposite internationalisation strategies. Also, other game-theoretical work has studied the rationale for FDI founded on consumer-based arguments such as: (Moner-Colonques *et al.*, 2007, 2008; Rob and Vettas, 2003; Saggi, 1998) and technology-based arguments (Ethier and Markusen, 1996; Fosfuri and Motta, 1999).

Another strand of the literature has looked into the environmental implications of FDI flows – see Rauscher (2005) for a survey on the literature on foreign trade and the environment. The reader may consult Cole *et al.* (2017) for a recent review on the relationship between FDI and the environment. Initial theoretical contributions anticipate that trade and capital will flow from countries with tough regulations to countries with lax regulations. This is consistent with the so-called pollution haven hypothesis according to which FDI is attracted to low regulation havens. In an early contribution, Baumol and Oates (1988) made that point by noting that developed countries have higher regulations and therefore a comparative disadvantage in the production of dirty goods. Markusen *et al.* (1993) and Motta and Thisse (1994) provide theoretical support on the relevance of environmental policy and firm location. More specifically, Markusen *et al.* (1993) is a variation of Horstmann and Markusen (1992) described above. The model features a two-stage game where firms first decide on the number of plants before competing. Production generates regional pollution, which diminishes consumer utility. There is an exogenous per unit pollution tax in one of the regions. Now, the location decisions are a function of the pollution tax. The authors show that changes in the tax will bring variations in firm profits and hence modify location decisions. Different market structures entail different levels of pollution, consumer surplus and welfare. Their numerical analyses unveil that the private decision of firms regarding location may lead to outcomes in which welfare is not maximal.

Both the above findings regarding the welfare effects of FDI in strategic settings and the fact that empirical evidence is not conclusive on the pollution haven hypothesis have shifted attention to further investigating the role of environmental regulation in firms' location decisions. The seminal paper by Markusen *et al.* (1995) features the governments of two regions that compete in terms of their environmental policies and how they affect plan location. Thus, if the disutility of pollution is not too large, then the regions compete by setting low environmental taxes ending up in an equilibrium with more plants (FDI) and more pollution. Celik and Orbay (2011) analysis throws a similar result. In the presence of uncertainty about the pollution damage caused by the foreign firm's production, a developing country will fix a pollution tax that stimulates FDI when the marginal damage of pollution is low enough; although this enhances welfare, it results in too much local pollution. The idea that stringent environmental regulations may not deter FDI or induce firm relocation can be found in (Dijkstra *et al.*, 2011; Sanna-Randaccio and Sestini, 2012) and (Elliott and Zhou, 2013), to name a few. The former shows that FDI is chosen since it implies a higher environmental tax which raises the domestic firm's cost; this ultimately leads to lower welfare levels. The latter reveals the incentive to FDI when entry by domestic firms is deterred. Sanna-Randaccio and Sestini (2012) emphasises the relevance of market size for discouraging relocation in an international duopoly model. Firm heterogeneity is assumed in Sanna-Randaccio *et al.* (2017) to conclude that, with unilateral climate policy, no relocation does not ensure a fall in global emissions. Finally, environmental taxes also affect firms' incentives to adopt and develop less polluting technologies Requate (2005). The interplay between taxes, abatement effort and location for a monopolist in undertaken by Petrakis and Xepapadeas (2003); an emission tax set in advance affects the location decision of the firm, which eventually engages in environmental innovation. Differences in firms' environmental innovation will produce differences in emissions rates technologies. Sanna-Randaccio *et al.* (2017) offer an intuition of what to expect regarding plant location with unilateral climate policy, as noted above. At any rate, Lambertini *et al.* (2017) unveil that, when the tax is endogenously determined, there is an inverted-U relationship between competition and green R&D. There is empirical evidence on the globalisation of green R&D. Noailly and Ryfisch (2015) find that about 17% of green patents result from R&D investments carried out by multinationals outside their home countries. Further formal analyses are required to investigate on how environmental policy influences FDI location choices and green R&D investments undertaken both by foreign and host firms.

This chapter contributes to the understanding of the conflicts that arise between the private and social equilibrium choices of internationalisation strategies as well as the welfare desirability of the resulting market structure in the presence of environmental damages. The analysis is carried out in an international trade duopoly model. Interestingly enough, our research unveils how the proper choice of an environmental tax can align private and social interests in more cases as compared to no intervention; we will also note how taxes indeed influence firms' choices regarding their internationalisation strategies and the resulting environmental damages.

3. The Model

The setting is in the spirit of Horstmann and Markusen (1992) and Markusen *et al.* (1993). Consider an oligopoly model of trade comprising two countries, 1 and 2. Firm 1 is initially located in country 1, and firm 2 is initially located in country 2. The cost of the domestic plant is already sunk. Markets are segmented and firms serve both markets. Each firm serves domestic consumers from production in the domestic country. Foreign consumers can be served either by setting up a plant in the foreign country (FDI), or by exporting to the foreign country (E). Firms compete in quantities (Cournot) in each market and the marginal cost of production is constant and equal to $c \geq 0$. For simplicity, we assume that each unit of output produced generates one unit of pollution and that pollution is local. If a firm chooses to export, then it incurs an additional per-unit export cost $\tau \geq 0$. This cost can be interpreted as due to natural (e.g., transportation costs) or artificial (e.g., tariffs) barriers to trade. We will refer to τ as trade costs. If, instead, a firm establishes a plant in the foreign country then it incurs a setup cost $F \geq 0$. These costs reflect the well-known proximity-concentration trade-off in the model. The inverse demand function in each country is given by:

$$p_i = A - (q_{1i} + q_{2i}) \quad \text{for } i = 1, 2 \tag{1}$$

where p_i is the price in country i, $A > c \geq 0$ represent the market size and q_{1i} and q_{2i} represent the output by firm 1 and firm 2 respectively, sold in country i. The interaction between firms forms a two-stage game. In the first stage firms simultaneously decide how to serve the foreign market, either through FDI or through E, which endogenously determines market structures. The four resulting combinations lead to four simultaneous- move quantity sub-games at the second stage. In order to illustrate the potential conflict between the private and the social incentives to FDI, we shall also solve the game in which the first stage is modelled as the interaction between countries' choices according to welfare objectives, i.e., the social game. In this way, if the equilibrium obtained when firms choose does not coincide with that obtained when countries do, a conflict or a market failure is identified. The equilibria of these two-stage games are characterised when

(1) there are no environmental damages,
(2) there are environmental damages and no-intervention and,
(3) there are environmental damages with intervention.

3.1. *No environmental damages*

We begin by solving the second stage. The profit maximisation problem in each sub-game can be specified as follows:

$$\begin{aligned} \max_{q_{11},q_{12}} \pi_1 &= (A - q_{11} - q_{21} - c)q_{11} + (A - q_{12} - q_{22} - c)q_{12} \\ &\quad - \lambda_1 \tau q_{12} - (1 - \lambda_1)F \end{aligned} \tag{2}$$

$$\begin{aligned} \max_{q_{21},q_{22}} \pi_2 &= (A - q_{11} - q_{21} - c)q_{21} + (A - q_{12} - q_{22} - c)q_{12} \\ &\quad - \lambda_2 \tau q_{21} - (1 - \lambda_2)F \end{aligned} \tag{3}$$

where λ_i takes the value 1 if firm i chooses to export; λ_i takes the value zero if instead firm i opts for FDI. With this short-hand notation, the solution to the system of first-order conditions

$\frac{\partial \pi_1}{\partial q_{11}} = 0$, $\frac{\partial \pi_1}{\partial q_{12}} = 0$, $\frac{\partial \pi_2}{\partial q_{21}} = \frac{\partial \pi_2}{\partial q_{22}} = 0$ is given by:

$$\begin{aligned} q_{11}^* &= \frac{(A - c + \lambda_2 \tau)}{3} & q_{12}^* &= \frac{(A - c - 2\lambda_1 \tau)}{3} \\ q_{21}^* &= \frac{(A - c - 2\lambda_2 \tau)}{3} & q_{22}^* &= \frac{(A - c + \lambda_1 \tau)}{3} \end{aligned} \tag{4}$$

So, the equilibrium outputs when both firms choose to export – sub-game (E, E) – amounts to taking $\lambda_1 = \lambda_2 = 1$ in the above expressions; the first element in (E, E) refers to the choice made by firm/country 1 and the second element to that made by firm/country 2. The equilibrium outputs in the other three sub-game structures follow naturally. It is assumed that $(A-c)/2 > \tau$ to ensure positive equilibrium outputs in all sub-games. It is easy to check that total output (in a given country) is largest when both firms engage in FDI, followed by outcome (FDI, E), then (E, FDI) and the smallest total output arises under exports by both firms. Trade costs naturally diminish output exported and favour the output domestically produced by the home firm. Any firm always prefers to face an exporter. We next report the equilibrium profits in each sub-game:

$$\pi_1(\mathrm{E},\mathrm{E}) = \pi_2(\mathrm{E},\mathrm{E}) = \frac{(A - c + \tau)^2}{9} + \frac{(A - c - 2\tau)^2}{9} \tag{5}$$

$$\pi_1(\mathrm{FDI},\mathrm{FDI}) = \pi_2(\mathrm{FDI},\mathrm{FDI}) = \frac{(A - c)^2}{9} + \frac{(A - c)^2}{9} - F \tag{6}$$

$$\pi_1(\mathrm{E},\mathrm{FDI}) = \pi_2(\mathrm{FDI},\mathrm{E}) = \frac{(A - c)^2}{9} + \frac{(A - c - 2\tau)^2}{9} \tag{7}$$

$$\pi_1(\mathrm{FDI},\mathrm{E}) = \pi_2(\mathrm{E},\mathrm{FDI}) = \frac{(A - c + \tau)^2}{9} + \frac{(A - c)^2}{9} - F \tag{8}$$

where the first term corresponds to equilibrium profits in the domestic country and the second term is that in the foreign country. With the equilibrium profits expressions at hand the first stage equilibrium can be characterised. Firm 1 will prefer FDI rather than E, provided that firm 2 exports, when the next inequality holds: $\pi_1(\mathrm{FDI},\mathrm{E}) > \pi_1(\mathrm{E},\mathrm{E})$, that is,

$$F < \frac{4\tau(A - c - \tau)}{9} \equiv \hat{F} \tag{9}$$

Similarly, firm 1 will prefer FDI rather than E, provided that firm 2 chooses FDI when $\pi_1(\text{FDI}, \text{FDI}) > \pi_1(\text{E}, \text{FDI})$ which leads to the same above condition on the size of the setup cost F. Therefore, and given the symmetry assumed, *the Nash equilibrium in stage one is a) both firms choose FDI when $F < \hat{F}$ or b) both firms export when $F > \hat{F}$*

Since consumer surplus (the first term in the below expressions) in this case is equal to half the square of total output sold in a particular country, the welfare expressions for each sub-game are the following:

$$W_1(\text{E}, \text{E}) = W_2(\text{E}, \text{E}) = \frac{(2A - 2c - \tau)^2}{18} + \frac{(A - c + \tau)^2}{9} + \frac{(A - c - 2\tau)^2}{9} \tag{10}$$

$$W_1(\text{FDI}, \text{FDI}) = W_2(\text{FDI}, \text{FDI}) = \frac{2(A - c)^2}{9} + \frac{(A - c)^2}{9} + \frac{(A - c)^2}{9} - F \tag{11}$$

$$W_1(\text{E}, \text{FDI}) = W_2(\text{FDI}, \text{E}) = \frac{2(A - c)^2}{9} + \frac{(A - c)^2}{9} + \frac{(A - c - 2\tau)^2}{9} \tag{12}$$

$$W_1(\text{FDI}, \text{E}) = W_2(\text{E}, \text{FDI}) = \frac{(2A - 2c - \tau)^2}{18} + \frac{(A - c + \tau)^2}{9} + \frac{(A - c)^2}{9} - F \tag{13}$$

What would then be the equilibrium market structure if countries decide between E and FDI? Country 1 will opt for FDI rather than E, provided country 2 chooses exports, when $W_1(\text{FDI}, \text{E}) > W_1(\text{E}, \text{E})$ that results in the same above condition. Similarly, provided that country 2 opts for FDI. We may conclude that *there is no conflict between private and social incentives regarding the internationalisation choices of either exports or FDI.* This result follows from the fact that total output – and hence consumer surplus – is the same for a given choice by the foreign firm. The consumer surplus terms

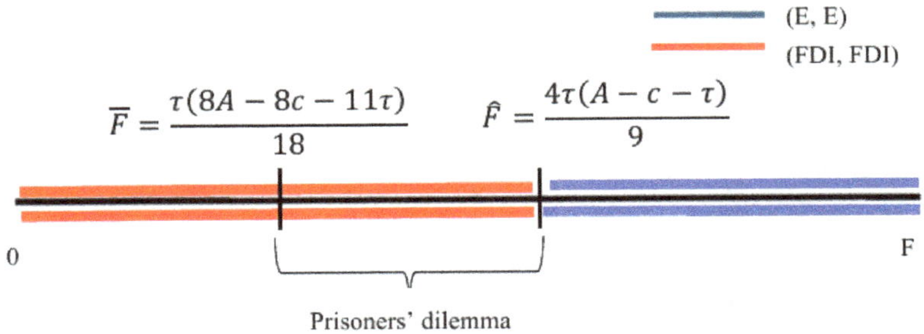

Fig. 1. No environmental damages. Equilibria as a function of setup costs and prisoners' dilemma cases.

cancel out and the same threshold $\hat{F}$ shows up – this is also due to the segmented markets assumption.

Since there are two possible equilibria in dominant strategies, it is interesting to rank the equilibrium welfare levels under such equilibria. The difference $W_i(\text{FDI}, \text{FDI}) > W_i(\text{E}, \text{E})$ is positive as long as:

$$F < \frac{\tau(8A - 8c - 11\tau)}{18} \equiv \bar{F} \tag{14}$$

It is readily checked that $\bar{F} < \hat{F}$ which uncovers an interval of setup cost values reflecting a disagreement between the welfare attained at equilibrium and the largest possible one, defining a prisoners' dilemma. For $\bar{F} < F < \hat{F}$, *firms choose FDI in equilibrium and yet welfare is higher under exports.* This idea is represented in Fig. 1. The coloured line above the black line shows the equilibrium when firms make the internationalisation decisions (blue identifies the (E, E) equilibrium, whereas the (FDI, FDI) equilibrium appears in red). The same code applies for the coloured line below for countries' choices. Thus, when F is in the defined interval there is both a private and a social incentive to FDI, although the equilibrium is not Pareto optimal due to strategic play.

3.2. *Environmental damages and no intervention*

We now consider environmental damages and assume that every unit of output produced generates one unit of pollution and that pollution is local. The environmental damage function is linear in output (emissions) produced in each country, weighted by the marginal damage of pollution, denoted by $d, d > 0$. Rather obviously the equilibrium choices for firms between exports and FDI are determined by the same above threshold $\hat{F}$, now denoted $\hat{F}^d$, superscript d refers to damages. However, if countries were playing the first stage where they simultaneously decide between exports and FDI, then the threshold on F will be a function of the marginal damage. Note that damages are associated with all output produced in that country. It is easily checked that damages, say for country one, are largest under (E, FDI), followed by (FDI, FDI), then by (E, E) and damages are the smallest under (FDI, E). In the case of (E, E) environmental damages would follow from all output produced by firm i in country i, whether it is sold at home or abroad, that is, $d\frac{(2A-2c-\tau)}{3}$. This term is to be subtracted from $W_i(\mathrm{E}, \mathrm{E})$ above yielding $W_i^d(\mathrm{E}, \mathrm{E})$. The same logic is applied to obtain the corresponding welfare levels in the presence of environmental damages. Taking this into account, country 1 will choose FDI rather than E, provided country 2 chooses exports, when $W_1^d(\mathrm{FDI}, \mathrm{E}) > W_1^d(\mathrm{E}, \mathrm{E})$, that is, when,

$$F < \frac{4\tau(A - c - \tau) + 3d(A - c - 2 > \tau)}{9} \equiv \tilde{F}^d \tag{15}$$

The same inequality follows from $W_1^d(\mathrm{FDI}, \mathrm{FDI}) > W_1^d$ $(\mathrm{E}, \mathrm{FDI})$, The construction of country 2's best response leads to the same above threshold.

It is easy to see that $\hat{F}^d < \tilde{F}^d$ since $\tilde{F}^d = \hat{F}^d + \frac{d(A-c-2\tau)}{3}$.

Consequently, the next result can be stated: *There is a range of values of the setup costs, i.e., for $\hat{F}^d < F < \tilde{F}^d$, where the private equilibrium is (E, E) whereas the social equilibrium is (FDI, FDI).* The introduction of environmental damages creates a disparity in the thresholds on F that determine the equilibrium market structure, which unveils a market failure. In fact, the disparity widens as marginal damage increases. The strategic play by a country must now consider that damages lower the corresponding welfare level. Noting the ranking of damages given above, the damage for (FDI, FDI) implies a lower number subtracting when compared with (E, FDI), something similar occurs when comparing (FDI, E) with (E, E). Thus, relative to the no damages scenario, welfare differences are higher and, consequently, there are more parameter values of F for which countries would choose an FDI strategy.

To close the argument, we need to rank the welfare levels under the two possible equilibrium outcomes. The difference $W_i^d(\text{FDI}, \text{FDI}) - W_i^d(\text{E}, \text{E})$, in the presence of environmental damages is positive as long as:

$$F < \bar{F} - \frac{\tau d}{3} \equiv \bar{F}^d \tag{16}$$

It is straightforward to see that $\bar{F}^d < \bar{F}$. Therefore, the parameter region for which a prisoners' dilemma arises is different: *For,* $\bar{F}^d < F < \hat{F}^d$ *firms choose FDI in equilibrium and yet welfare is higher under exports.* We observe that the interval becomes larger in the presence of environmental damages. This calls for some policy intervention to reduce the private-social conflict and possibly identify a parameter region for values of F such that the private play by oligopolistic firms indeed results in the highest welfare.

3.3. *Environmental damages with intervention*

In this section, we wish to study the role of an exogenous and the same environmental tax that is imposed by both countries. The introduction of a tax will ultimately produce changes in firms' choices, i.e., in equilibrium market structure, and different market structures have implications for pollution levels, output (consumer surplus), firm profit and government tax revenue. Whether the private and the social interests can more often be aligned is the objective of this section.

More specifically, an environmental tax decreases all output that is produced in the taxing country. Thus, in sub-game (E, FDI), the environmental tax by country one will apply to all output produced by firm one and to firm two's output produced in the plant at country one; the tax set by country two will affect firm two's production that is sold domestically. Then, output by firm one sold at home and output by firm two produced and sold in country one is decreased by the tax in country one. Output exported to country two is pushed down by the tax in country one while it is pushed up by the tax in country two; the effect of these taxes on output produced and sold by firm two at home is reversed. However, in case both countries set the same environmental tax equilibrium outputs would be reduced by the size of the tax divided by the number of firms plus one. Assume, for the sake of the presentation, that it is indeed the case and that the tax is proportional to environmental damage, therefore the tax $t_1 = t_2 = t = \alpha d$. Equilibrium quantities are given by,

$$\begin{aligned} q_{11}^{**} &= \frac{(A - c + \lambda_2 \tau - \alpha d)}{3} \quad & q_{12}^{**} &= \frac{(A - c + \lambda_1 \tau - \alpha d)}{3} \\ q_{21}^{**} &= \frac{(A - c + 2\lambda_2 \tau - \alpha d)}{3} \quad & q_{22}^{**} &= \frac{(A - c + \lambda_1 \tau - \alpha d)}{3} \end{aligned} \tag{17}$$

With the same interpretation of λ_i as above and now assuming $(A - c - \alpha d)/2 > \tau$ and $(A - c)/d > \alpha$ to ensure positive equilibrium outputs.

Because output determines equilibrium profits, we expect a change in the threshold on F that distinguishes the private equilibrium. Similarly, the welfare expressions now include an additional term associated with tax revenue so that we anticipate different thresholds both when countries choose their internationalisation strategies and when establishing which welfare level is highest.

Thus, conducting the analysis as in the previous sections, we find that the threshold on the setup cost that makes FDI a dominant strategy for firms is the following,

$$F < \hat{F}^d - \frac{4\tau}{9}\alpha d \equiv \hat{F}_\alpha^d \tag{18}$$

Which is smaller than the threshold without a tax $\hat{F}^d$ because of the negative effect that the tax has on output and profits, where subscript α identifies the thresholds with intervention. The game in which countries select the internationalisation strategies has (FDI, FDI) as an equilibrium whenever,

$$F < \hat{F}_\alpha^d - \frac{(\alpha - 1)d(A - c - 2\tau - \alpha d)}{3} \equiv \tilde{F}_\alpha^d \tag{19}$$

Likewise, welfare under (FDI, FDI) with intervention exceeds that under (E, E) as long as,

$$F < \bar{F}^d - \frac{\tau}{9}\alpha d \equiv \bar{F}_\alpha^d \tag{20}$$

The interval for the setup costs in which there is a market failure is given by $\tilde{F}_\alpha^d - \hat{F}_\alpha^d$, which is reduced to zero for $\alpha = 1$, and therefore there is no private-social conflict as in the initial setting with no environmental damages, although this threshold is smaller than $\hat{F}$. In fact, $\alpha = 1$ implies that countries would play exports just as firms would do. For a small tax (i.e., lower than marginal damage), $0 < \alpha < 1$, there is a conflict area where firms choose exports, whereas countries play FDI, noting that this area would certainly be smaller than without intervention. Finally, for taxes larger than damages, the conflict flips to firms choosing FDI and countries playing exports.

Similarly, the interval for the setup costs in which there is a prisoners' dilemma is given $\hat{F}^d_\alpha - \bar{F}^d_\alpha$ which can be written as $\hat{F}^d_\alpha - \bar{F}^d_\alpha = \hat{F}^d_\alpha - \bar{F}^d - \frac{\tau}{3}\alpha d$ so that the range of values of the setup costs corresponding to a prisoners' dilemma situation shrinks with intervention. As before, there is a value of α, such that the dilemma vanishes, which equates $\alpha = 1 + \frac{\tau}{2d}$ Altogether, a tax that is equal to marginal damage aligns private and public incentives to FDI and a prisoners' dilemma arises less often. Figure 2 summarises the aforementioned results under no intervention and a small tax.

As suggested above, the introduction of an environmental tax affects agents' payoffs and modify the thresholds that determine the

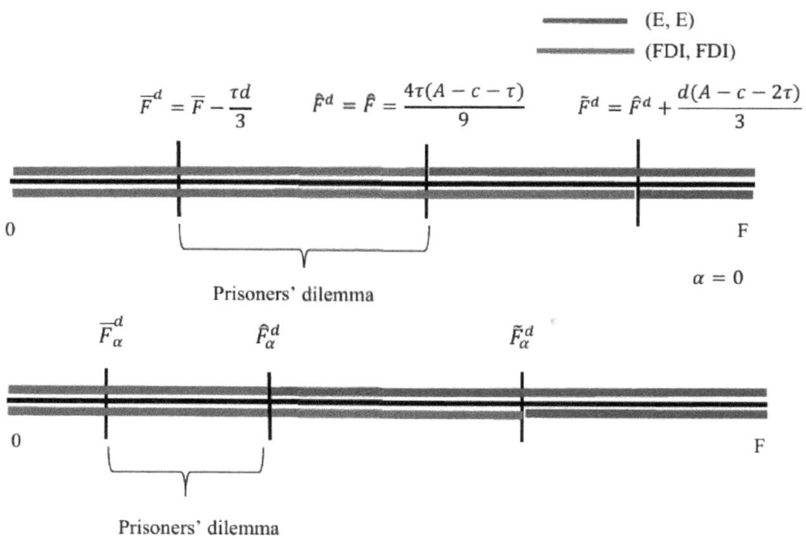

Fig. 2. Environmental damages. Equilibria and prisoners' dilemma cases under no intervention (top) and a small tax (bottom).

private and social choices as well as the social desirability of either internationalisation mode. Consider a small value of α, that is, a small environmental tax. The magnitudes of output reductions are not too important. Of course, profits are smaller and rather naturally the values of setup costs for firms to engage in FDI must be lower than in the absence of a tax, i.e., $\hat{F}_{\alpha}^{d} < \hat{F}^{d}$. Because of the previous effect, it is easy to conclude that damages are slightly lower when there is a tax. It also happens that $\tilde{F}_{\alpha}^{d} < \tilde{F}^{d}$. The welfare comparisons with a tax now include profits plus consumer surplus, which are lower, minus the damages, which are also lower; the former reductions are more important than the gains of smaller damages so that again lower values of setup costs are needed for FDI to result in the highest possible welfare, i.e., $\bar{F}_{\alpha}^{d} < \bar{F}^{d}$ In fact, the effect of the tax in shifting down the threshold $\hat{F}_{\alpha}^{d}$ is more significant than its effect on $\bar{F}_{\alpha}^{d}$. Therefore, the use of an environmental tax makes the prisoners' dilemma interval to shrink.

3.4. *Some numerical examples*

The tables below report some numerical examples that allow us to gain some further insights into the effects of different internationalisation strategies on welfare and environmental damages.

Table 1 shows, in the top game (part a), profits of firms for the case in which environmental damages exist yet there is no tax (Section 3.1): the first number of each pair is the profit for firm 1 while the second is the profit for firm 2. Profits in each pair are the equilibrium profits that correspond with given firms' choices between exports (E) and foreign direct investment (FDI), that is, for a given market structure. Similarly, in the bottom game (part b), equilibrium welfare pairs are reported.

The value of the setup cost, $F = 5$, has been chosen to illustrate that, without intervention, there is a market failure because $\hat{F}^{d} = 4$ and $\tilde{F}^{d} = 6$. The Nash equilibrium in the private game is (E, E) whereas that when countries play is (FDI, FDI). Environmental damages are lower under exports (4.75) as compared to those under FDI which are equal to five. This example discloses a prisoners' dilemma from a social perspective since welfare under exports exceeds that under FDI, but since $\hat{F}^{d} = 4 < F$, firms choose (E, E) and the highest social welfare is attained. The conflict interval in

Table 1. Equilibrium private and social choices with no tax and large setup cost.

(a) private game

Firm 1/Firm 2	FDI	E
FDI	17.22; 17.22	19.56; 18.22
E	18.22; 19.56	20.56; 20.56

(b) social game

Country 1/Country 2	FDI	E
FDI	34.44; 34.44	36.86; 33.44
E	33.44; 36.86	35.86; 35.86

Note: Parameter values: $A = 10$, $c = 0$, $d = 0.75$, $\tau = 1$, $\alpha = 0$ and $F = 5$.

Table 2. Equilibrium private and social choices with a tax equal to marginal damage and large setup cost.

(a) private game

Firm 1/Firm 2	FDI	E
FDI	14.01; 14.01	16.18; 58.35
E	15.35; 16.18	17.51; 17.51

(b) social game

Country 1/Country 2	FDI	E
FDI	33.03; 33.03	33.19; 34.36
E	34.36; 33.19	34.53; 34.53

Note: Parameter values: $A = 10$, $c = 0$, $d = 0.75$, $\tau = 1$, $\alpha = 0$ and $F = 5$.

this example arises for $\bar{F}^d = 3.58 < F < \hat{F}^d = 4$. This means that its size is $\hat{F}^d = 4 - \bar{F}^d = 0.42$.

The presentation of Table 2, like Table 1, shows firms' profits and welfare levels when both countries set the same environmental tax on damages; it corresponds with the case of a tax that is equal to marginal damage, that is, for $\alpha = 1$.

It can be seen that the Nash equilibrium in the private and the social game is (E, E) so that the environmental tax has eliminated the market failure and also the prisoners' dilemma situation. The thresholds on the size of the setup cost that determine the private and the social equilibrium are equal for $\alpha = 1$. In this numerical example, the conflict interval arises for $\bar{F}^d_\alpha = 3.5 < F < \hat{F}^d_\alpha = 3.67$, the tax makes this interval smaller. We see that when the setup cost is large enough, a tax equal to marginal damage aligns all agents' incentives. Note that environmental damages under exports (4.375) are smaller than under FDI (4.625), which in turn are lower than damages under exports and no intervention. The same aforementioned qualitative results arise for all values of F in the interval $\hat{F}^d = 4 < F < \tilde{F}^d = 5$. The next table looks at the case of a lower setup cost.

We now see that initially, without intervention, no market failure arises since firms have FDI as its dominant strategy and the same happens for countries. As with the case of a large setup cost, there is a prisoners' dilemma in the game played by countries and, also, in the game played by firms. Table 5 shows the effects of intervention.

As already noted, a tax equal to marginal damage corrects for the disagreement between private and social choices; export is "played" in equilibrium. It also eliminates the prisoners' dilemma situation. However, the nature of the no market failure without and with intervention is different; intervention has shifted the equilibrium to exports, where environmental damages are lower.

Setting a larger tax, the one that eliminates the prisoners' dilemma interval, confirms the conclusions reached from Tables 3 and 4. In line with the received literature on the proximity-concentration trade-off, one expects FDI for low enough setup costs. This is what we observe in Table 3. Intervention influences the resulting market structure since now private and social choices shift to exports. An environmental tax has produced positive effects since environmental damages under exports (4.125) are lower than under FDI (4.375). The above conclusions remain qualitatively similar for $\tilde{F}^d_{\alpha=1} = \bar{F}^d_{\alpha=1} = 3.67 < F < \hat{F}^d = 4$.

The conclusion is that environmental taxes are useful tool in models of trade with imperfect competition. They reduce the conflict interval regarding firms' internationalisation strategies. However, the

Table 3. Equilibrium private and social choices with no tax and small setup cost.

(a) private game

Firm 1/Firm 2	FDI	E
FDI	18.42; 18.42	20.76; 18.22
E	18.22; 20.76	20.56; 20.56

(b) social game

Country 1/Country 2	FDI	E
FDI	35.64; 35.64	38.06; 33.44
E	33.44; 38.06	35.86; 35.86

Note: Parameter values: $A = 10$, $c = 0$, $d = 0.75$, $\tau = 1$, $\alpha = 0$ and $F = 3.8$.

Table 4. Equilibrium private and social choices with a tax equal to marginal damage and small setup cost.

(a) private game

Firm 1/Firm 2	FDI	E
FDI	15.21; 15.21	17.38; 15.35
E	15.35; 17.38	17.51; 17.51

(b) social game

Country 1/Country 2	FDI	E
FDI	34.23; 34.23	34.39; 34.36
E	34.36; 34.39	34.53; 34.53

Note: Parameter values: $A = 10$, $c = 0$, $d = 0.75$, $\tau = 1$, $\alpha = 1$ and $F = 3.8$.

private equilibrium may result in lower environmental damages and so a more careful policy decision might eventually be influenced by the weight that policymakers would attach to damages.

The strategic setting that we model has not looked at optimal taxes. In any case, a taxing government must weigh the incentives to impose a rather weak environmental tax and avoid harming the competitiveness of the home firm too much, against adopting a more

Table 5. Equilibrium private and social choices with a tax larger than marginal damage and small setup cost.

(a) private game

Firm 1/Firm 2	FDI	E
FDI	13.21; 13.21	15.27; 13.57
E	13.57; 15.27	15.63; 15.63

(b) social game

Country 1/Country 2	FDI	E
FDI	33.14; 33.14	32.02; 34.63
E	34.63; 32.02	33.50; 33.50

Note: Parameter values: $A = 10$, $c = 0$, $d = 0.75$, $\tau = 1$, $\alpha = 1.67$ and $F = 3.8$.

stringent tax, which would cut down damages and consumer surplus too. Environmental taxes imply an additional variable cost and faced with different tax levels per country, may invite firms to relocate their production in countries with laxer regulations and continue polluting elsewhere. This is known in the literature as the Pollution Haven Hypothesis, according to which firms relocate to less environmentally friendly countries to compete in international markets. The numerical example in Table 6 considers that country 1 implements a tax $\alpha_1 d$ that is smaller than the tax implemented by country 2, $\alpha_2 d$. For the sake of the presentation the chosen values in the previous Tables are employed.

The Nash equilibrium in the private game is (E, FDI), an equilibrium in line with the predictions of the Pollution Haven Hypothesis. It can be seen that the equilibrium profits of the firm initially located in the country with a more stringent tax, firm 2, are lower than those of her rival: moving production to country 1 allows her to improve profits, regardless of the choice by firm 1. From a welfare perspective, we observe that the country with a laxer policy achieves notable welfare levels when her firm is an exporter. Although environmental damages are higher, they are offset by the gains in firm profits and consumer surplus and exports is a dominant strategy for country 1. The Nash equilibrium in the social game is (E, E), which does not coincide with the private equilibrium. Thus, asymmetric taxes

Table 6. Equilibrium private and social choices with different taxes and large setup cost.

(a) private game

Firm 1/Firm 2	FDI	E
FDI	13.01; 13.01	16.35; 12.85
E	16.18; 14.01	19.51; 13.85

(b) social game

Country 1/Country 2	FDI	E
FDI	32.03; 32.94	32.40; 33.82
E	35.19; 31.61	35.57; 32.49

Note: Parameter values: $A = 10$, $c = 0$, $d = 0.75$, $\tau = 1$, $\alpha_1 = 1$, $\alpha_2 = 1.67$ and $F = 5$.

also unveil the conflict between the private and social incentives towards FDI leading to market failures. In fact, the welfare levels of both countries are higher under (E, E) compared to (E, FDI). In this example, aggregate welfare under (FDI, FDI) and (E, E) is larger than under (E, FDI) whereas total environmental damages are the second highest in the private equilibrium (E, FDI). Therefore, asymmetries in the stringency of environmental taxation are likely to lead to opposite equilibrium strategies for firms and such outcomes may neither be those with higher welfare levels nor lower damages. Note that the choice of optimal taxes is not straightforward since, as noted through this chapter, their levels affect the threshold values that determine firms' internationalisation decisions and hence different market structures imply a piece-wise welfare function to be maximised – small differences in the tax may lead to great differences in terms of welfare.

4. Concluding Remarks

A simple model of international oligopoly competition with environmental pollution has been developed to illustrate the conflicts that arise between the private incentives of firms towards FDI and its welfare desirability. Compared to a setting without damages, it has been shown that strategic firm interaction regarding internationalisation choices accentuate the private-social tensions when production generates pollution. This opens the chance for policy intervention: environmental taxes may bring together the private and social interests in more cases. Apart from looking at the comparison between equilibrium profits and welfare levels, our analysis draws attention to the fact that private choices may produce lower environmental damages. Hence, no intervention could be advisable in countries with goals tilted to climate change remedies.

Although the model considered provides an intuition of the effects brought about by the internationalisation process of firms, it is important to acknowledge that the analysis has been carried out under fairly symmetric assumptions. As confirmed by previous research, asymmetries in country size, oligopoly size and costs are worth of analysis and would help our understanding about foreign firms' expansion strategies; they would offer conclusions that could empirically be checked. A fruitful area of future research is to study the environmental consequences of FDI regarding investments in cleaner technologies. There is mixed evidence on whether foreign firms are greener than domestic firms. Most interestingly, there remains the question of examining to what extent the presence of FDI may encourage environmental improvements by domestic firms and host country welfare. How environmental regulations impact investments in cleaner technologies and how they interact with FDI decisions are absolutely fundamental issues for the current FDI-climate debate. Similarly, carbon-border-adjustments by countries with stringent regulations merit to be included in the research agenda.

References

Barac, M. and Moner-Colonques, R. (2016). Internationalization strategies in oligopoly with heterogeneous firms, *Bulletin of Economic Research* **68**(S1), 66–77.

Barac, M. and Moner-Colonques, R. (2022). Leadership in internationalization strategies, *The Manchester School* **90**(3), 293–318.

Baumol, W. J. and Oates, W. E. (1988). *The Theory of Environmental Policy*, Cambridge University Press, Cambridge, UK.

Blonigen, B. A. (2005). A review of the empirical literature on FDI determinants, *Atlantic Economic Journal* **33**, 383–403.

Brander, J. (1995). Strategic trade policy, in G. M. Grossman and K. Rogoff (Eds.), *Handbook of International Economics* **3**, 1395–1455, Elsevier.

Campa, J., Donnenfeld, S. and Weber, S. (1998). Market structure and foreign direct investment, *Review of International Economics* **6**(3), 361–380.

Celik, S. and Orbay, B. Z. (2011). Location choice under trade and environmental policies, *Economic Modelling* **28**(4), 1710 –1715.

Cole, M. A., Elliott, R. J. and Zhang, L. (2017). Foreign direct investment and the environment, *Annual Review of Environment and Resources* **42**(1), 465–487.

Dijkstra, B. R., Mathew, A. J. and Mukherjee, A. (2011). Environmental regulation: An incentive for foreign direct investment, *Review of International Economics* **19**(3), 568–578.

Dixon, S. (2006). Multinational corporations, stackelberg leadership, and tariff-jumping, *Review of International Economics* **14**(3), 414–426.

Dunning, J. H. (1981). *International Production and the Multinational Enterprise*, London: George Allen and Unwin Ltd.

Elliott, R. J. R. and Zhou, Y. (2013). Environmental regulation induced foreign direct investment, *Environmental and Resource Economics* **55**, 141–158.

Ethier, W. J. and Markusen, J. R. (1996). Multinational firms, technology diffusion and trade, *Journal of International Economics* **41**(1–2), 1–28.

Fosfuri, A. and Motta, M. (1999). Multinationals without advantages, *Scandinavian Journal of Economics* **101**(4), 617–630.

Horstmann, I. J. and Markusen, J. R. (1987). Strategic investments and the development of multinationals, *International Economic Review* **28**(1), 109–121.

Horstmann, I. J. and Markusen, J. R. (1992). Endogenous market structures in international trade (natura facit saltum), *Journal of International Economics* **32**(1–2), 109–129.

Lambertini, L., Poyago-Theotoky, J. A. and Tampieri, A. (2017). Cournot competition and "green" innovation: An inverted-U relationship, *Energy Economics* **68**, 116–123.

Markusen, J. R. (1995). The boundaries of multinational enterprises and the theory of international trade, *Journal of Economic Perspectives* **9**(2), 169–189.

Markusen, J. R. (2002). Incumbency, preemption, and persistence, in J. R. Markusen (Ed.), *Multinational Firms and the Theory of International Trade*, pp. 61–75, MIT Press, Cambridge, Mass., US.

Markusen, J. R., Morey, E. R. and Olewiler, N. D. (1995). Competition in regional environmental policies when plant locations are endogenous, *Journal of Public Economics* **56**(1), 55–77.

Markusen, J. R., Morey, E. R. and Olewiler, N. D. (1993). Environmental policy when market structure and plant locations are endogenous, *Journal of Environmental Economics and Management* **24**(1), 69–86.

Moner-Colonques, R., Orts, V. and Sempere-Monerris, J. J. (2007). Asymmetric demand information and foreign direct investment, *Scandinavian Journal of Economics* **109**(1), 93–106.

Moner-Colonques, R., Orts, V. and Sempere-Monerris, J. J. (2008). Entry in foreign markets under asymmetric information and demand uncertainty, *The Southern Economic Journal* **74**(4), 1105–1122.

Motta, M. (1992). Multinational firms and the tariff-jumping argument: A game theoretic analysis with some unconventional conclusions, *European Economic Review* **36**(8), 1557–1571.

Motta, M. and Thisse, J.-F. (1994). Does environmental dumping lead to delocation? *European Economic Review* **38**(3–4), 563–576.

Noailly, J. and Ryfisch, D. (2015). Multinational firms and the internationalization of green R&D: A review of the evidence and policy implications, *Energy Policy* **83**, 218–228.

Petrakis, E. and Xepapadeas, A. (2003). Location decisions of a polluting firm and the time consistency of environmental policy, *Resource and Energy Economics* **25**(2), 197–214.

Rauscher, M. (2005). International trade, foreign investment, and the environment, *Handbook of Environmental Economics* **3**, 1403–1456.

Requate, T. (2005). Timing and commitment of environmental policy, adoption of new technology, and repercussions on R&D, *Environmental and Resource Economics* **31**(2), 175–199.

Rob, R. and Vettas, N. (2003). Foreign direct investment and exports with growing demand, *The Review of Economic Studies* **70**(3), 629–648.

Rowthorn, R. E. (1992). Intra-industry trade and investment under oligopoly: The role of market size, *The Economic Journal* **102**(411), 402–414.

Saggi, K. (1998). Optimal timing of FDI under demand uncertainty, in J. L. Mucchielli, P. J. Buckley and V. V. Cordell. (Eds.), *Globalization and Regionalization: Strategies, Policies and Economic Environments*, Haworth Press, New York.

Sanna-Randaccio, F. and Sestini, R. (2012). The impact of unilateral climate policy with endogenous plant location and market size asymmetry, *Review of International Economics* **20**(3), 580–599.

Sanna-Randaccio, F., Sestini, R. and Tarola, O. (2017). Unilateral climate policy and foreign direct investment with firm and country heterogeneity, *Environmental and Resource Economics* **67**, 379–401.

Smith, A. (1987). Strategic investment, multinational corporations and trade policy, *European Economic Review* **31**(1–2), 89–96.

UNCTAD (2023). World investment report. Technical Report, United Nations.

https://doi.org/10.1142/9789819816033_0006

Chapter 6

On the Relative Effectiveness of Voluntary Agreements and Mandatory Regulation, When Consumers are Environmentally Conscious*

Christos Constantatos† **and Apostolos Ioannis Martis**‡

University of Macedonia, Department of Economics, Thessaloniki, Greece

†*cconst@uom.edu.gr*

‡*amartis@uom.edu.gr*

We examine the impact of environmental policies in imperfectly competitive markets, when consumers care about the environmental damage of their consumption, and firms respond to consumers' worries using end-of-pipe abatement. We focus on the choice of tax base between emissions and output, considering a flexible regulator who offers a Voluntary Agreement (VA) in the form of stick & carrot approach: the regulator offers a credible menu of tax rates based on firms' abatement, and the firm chooses its abatement and the tax rate that will apply on its output or emissions. We find that the emissions tax base provides higher welfare for most levels of consumers' environmental consciousness because the

***Funding Information**: This work is part of a project that has received funding from University of Macedonia Research Fund under the Basic Research 2023 funding programme.

output tax may lead to over-abatement. Moreover, for low (high) levels of consumers, environmental consciousness, an emission (output) tax provides better environmental conditions. Comparing with the previous results where the regulator resorts to mandatory regulation, we find that the emissions tax when the regulator offers a VA menu leads to higher welfare. In contrast, in the case of the output tax, the decision between committing to a tax rate (mandatory regulation) or not (VA) depends on the level of environmental consciousness. Considering the environmental impact of a VA relative to mandatory taxation, the output (emissions) tax is generally superior when the regulator is not (is) able to commit.

Keywords: Green consumers, Environmental taxes, Monopoly.

1. Introduction

Consumer sensitivity over environmental issues ties consumption decisions to producers' environmental performance. This creates incentives for firms to ameliorate their environmental performance in order to increase demand. However, due to the externality nature of the problem, consumer awareness may not suffice in order to attain sufficiently clean environment, thus calling for regulatory intervention. We examine two such types of intervention, emissions and output taxes and compare their efficiency when the environmental damage caused by a good's production can be reduced at the expense of a fixed cost, like end-of-pipe abatement (use of filters). Since fixed investments go in pair with imperfect competition, we focus on cases where firms have market power, and to avoid complications due to strategic interactions among firms we restrict our analysis to the case of monopoly.

Our main focus is on situations where the regulator does not commit to a given tax rate before firms make their long-run abatement decisions. First, we assume that commitment is not possible and examine the relative efficiency of two frequently used tax bases, emissions and output, in terms of welfare. Second, assuming that commitment is possible, we analyse whether it is optimal for the regulator to commit to a tax rate, or wait to observe the firm's abatement decision before announcing the tax rate. Full commitment to the tax characteristics (base and rate) corresponds to traditional mandatory regulation. Announcing a tax base and offering a tax menu relating tax rates to abatement decisions is closer to the idea of a *Voluntary Agreement* (VA, more on that later). Crucial parameter in all our analysis is the level of consumers' social responsibility (SR) towards environmental issues.

When the tax can affect the abatement decision, the choice of tax base is crucial in determining equilibrium output, emissions, and welfare, as shown in Constantatos *et al.* (2021) (CPS, hereafter) where the tax rate is announced before the firm's abatement decision. However, if the tax rate is imposed after abatement investment has already taken place, the regulator is indifferent about the tax base, since any feasible outcome can be obtained using either base, by adjusting the tax rate accordingly.[1] Thus, a tax base announcement from a regulator lacking commitment power can be considered credible, since the regulator has no incentive to renege and change the tax base after the firm realises its abatement investment.[2] The firm, however, when making its abatement decision *anticipates* the upcoming taxation and adjusts accordingly. Our results confirm that when the firm knows that the regulator will choose the tax rate optimally, the firm's abatement decision is crucially affected by the tax base it expects the regulator to use.

Let us for the moment assume that the regulator announces a tax base but not a tax rate, and ask *why the firm may be faster in adopting abatement than the regulator choosing the tax rate?* First, because designing and voting a new tax may be a slow process, sufficiently long from its initial inception to the final vote as to provide the firm with the necessary time to adjust their abatement level before the tax is finally adopted. In this case, the firm knows that by increasing abatement it can hope for a lower tax rate.[3] Second, because the regulator *may choose* to avoid committing into a tax rate before firms do commit to their abatement decision, in order to

[1]This holds since emissions bear a stable relation to output. For instance, if each unit of output generates h units of emissions, a tax rate on emissions h times the tax rate on output leads to the same real outcome (consumption, abatement, emissions, welfare).

[2]This is obviously not true concerning a tax rate announcement.

[3]Situations where the regulator is slow to react and/or lacks commitment power can also be found in Poyago-Theotoky and Teerasuwannajak (2002), Petrakis *et al.* (2005), Requate (2005), and Poyago-Theotoky (2007). The first paper deals

create higher abatement incentives. Instead of imposing a single tax rate, the regulator offers a menu of tax rates, allowing the firm to select from it by installing the required abatement mechanism. This menu must be credible and in the absence of commitment power it can only correspond to the regulator's best reply to the firm's choice of abatement.

The idea of a credible tax menu corresponds to a VA, where – contrary to traditional mandatory taxation under which the regulatory authority unilaterally designs an imposes the tax – the regulated subjects are allowed to have a say on the tax terms.[4] In Lyon and Maxwell (2003), several examples are presented where eminent companies in the US reduced their emissions in order to positively affect both, the media and the Climate Challenge Action Plan, which was used to reduce greenhouse gas emissions. These examples stress two main points. First, that a firm's participation in a VA is not necessarily driven by a direct legislative threat, and second that governments public awareness offer benefits to firms in exchange to participation in a VA. Arora and Cason (1995) find that firms with large amount of emissions are more likely to participate in a VA,[5] and usually over-comply with the standards required in the VA. Also, public awareness enhances firms' environmental performance and encourages them to participate in VA.[6] Usually, a VA allows firms to obtain lower tax rates (or even subsidies) in exchange for higher investment in abatement. Such agreements are always exposed to opportunistic behaviour by the second mover. By reserving this position to himself, the regulator avoids being deceived, but becomes potential deceiver himself, since he is able to first make a promise in order to induce a given behaviour and then adopt a tax rate different than the promised one. Thus, unless one assumes commitment power to

with the impact of taxation on product differentiation, the second with the importance of the number of firms, while the other two with the impact of tax on environmental R&D in the presence of R&D spillovers. None of these papers considers environmental consciousness and/or output taxation.

[4] "VAs are designed to link private benefits with the voluntary provision of public goods" (Delmas and Montes-Sancho, 2010).

[5] Their work examines empirically firm characteristics related to a firms' participation in the US Environmental Protection Agency's 33/50 Program.

[6] Arora and Cason (1995) build a full-information two-stage model with consumers who value environmental quality, yet have different willingness-to-pay for it, and show that under publicly available information, firms tend to over-comply.

one or both parties, only VAs containing time-consistent promises can be credible.

The above discussion reflects upon modelling choices. Mandatory taxation is modelled as a multi-stage game where at the first stage the regulator announces the regulation terms and at later stages firms make their decisions (see for instance Constantatos *et al.* (2021)). VAs on the other hand, are often modelled as a bargaining process between the regulator and the firm (see Segerson and Miceli (1998)). However, given the sunk-cost nature of end-of-pipe abatement investments and the fact that the regulator has the power to unilaterally modify the tax rules at any moment, both approaches ignore that a regulator's initial decision is most likely time-inconsistent: the regulator may wish to renege on his initial decision after the firm has undertaken the expected action. Only when the regulator possesses substantial commitment power initial decisions and/or agreements can be credible.

In this work we assume that the regulator first announces a tax base, and a monopolist firm reacts by choosing abatement (its long-run decision). After observing abatement the regulator determines a tax rate that applies upon the already announced tax base and then the monopolist chooses output. Note that while the regulator has no commitment power over the tax rate, the fact that at the third stage he is indifferent with respect to the tax base choice allows his initial announcement to be credible.

Our work shows that in an imperfectly competitive environment, as consumer consciousness increases, the abatement incentive provided by an output tax increases, while that provided by an emissions tax decreases. Increases in consumer consciousness generally call for lowering the tax rates, whether on emissions or output, since consumers internalise part of the environmental externality by reducing demand. A reduction of the output-tax rate works like an output subsidy, boosting production. Since abatement is a fixed cost, higher output lowers the cost of abatement per unit of output, naturally providing a greater abatement incentive.[7] On the other

[7]The optimal output tax may become negative (output subsidy), while we do not allow for emissions subsidies. This, however, it is not what is crucial, since increases in output are caused by reductions in the output tax rate, whether that rate is positive.

hand, a reduction of the emissions tax rate due to an increase in consumer consciousness corresponds to making emissions less costly, thus curtailing the firm's incentive for abatement. Therefore, the efficiency of an environmental tax based on emissions decreases as consumers become more environmentally conscious.

The aforementioned interaction between environmental consciousness and the efficiency of each tax base is also present in cases where the regulator does commit to a tax rate, as shown in CPS. However, when the regulator is unable or unwilling to commit to a tax rate, an additional incentive to increase abatement is added, namely the firm's incentive to factor pointing towards higher abatement is added, the factors determining this interaction are coupled with an additional abatement incentive, due to the firm's effort to affect the tax rate via its choice of abatement. We show that as consumer consciousness increases and the tax rates are reduced in consequence, the credible tax menu that the regulator may offer exacerbates the propensity of the output tax towards higher abatement, while it moderates the emission-tax's tendency towards lower abatement. As a consequence, no matter the level of consumer environmental consciousness, the emissions base yields higher welfare when the regulator offers a tax menu instead of committing to a single tax rate. For the output base the conclusion is mixed: for low levels of consciousness the tax menu yields higher welfare, but as consciousness increases the over-abatement effect kicks-in causing welfare to decrease rapidly (this result is true when output subsidies are allowed).

Categorising environmental taxes according to (a) their base, and (b) whether there is or not a commitment to a given rate, our analysis shows that a menu of emissions tax rates based on observed abatement (i.e., an emissions tax without commitment to a tax rate) represents for most levels of consumer consciousness the second-best alternative to full regulation (i.e., regulation of both, output and abatement). Even for the small interval of consciousness levels for which an emissions tax without commitment does not represent the second best, it constitutes the third-best alternative producing welfare levels slightly lower than that of the second-best. Thus, if the level of environmental consciousness cannot be accurately measured, offering a tax rate menu based on observed abatement represents perhaps the safest regulation.

The rest of the chapter is organised as follows: Section 2 provides some literature review, Section 3 presents the model, Section 4 derives the equilibrium with each type of tax under the no commitment assumption, Section 5 compares the results of Section 4 to those obtained in CPS under tax rate commitment, and Section 6 concludes.

2. Literature

This work stands in the junction of three strands of the literature. The first deals with the comparison between emissions and output taxes, the second with the importance of environmental consciousness in affecting behaviour and tax efficiency, and the third concerns the commitment power of the regulator to a given tax rate when facing new abatement conditions.

The discussion of negative externalities in most textbooks leads to the Pigouvian tax levied either on emission or output, assuming, explicitly or implicitly, that output and emission taxes are equivalent. This equivalence is based on the assumption that the amount of emission produced per unit of output is immutable, ignoring the realistic possibilities of engaging in abatement. Recognising that a given level of output may yield different levels of emissions, breaks up the equivalence of output and emission taxes. A significant literature has been developed examining the optimal choice of environmental tax instrument in different settings. Schmutzler and Goulder (1997) compare emissions and output taxes in a partial equilibrium framework and in the presence of imperfect monitoring of emissions, while Fullerton *et al.* (2001) and Cremer and Gahvari (2001) in a general equilibrium framework. Aoyama and Silva (2022) compare the effectiveness of output and emission taxation in promoting the adoption of advanced abatement technology without addressing the effect of consumers' environmental awareness. Closest to our work, Constantatos *et al.* (2021) compare the two tax bases in terms of welfare taking into account environmental awareness, but only considering the case where the regulator can commit to a single tax rate.

The increasing importance of green consumerism has raised the question of the appropriate adjustments to the traditional environmental tax and subsidy policies and furthermore initiated a discussion regarding the effectiveness of information campaigns and advertising, aiming at increase environmental awareness, as an additional policy instrument (see for example, Petrakis *et al.* (2005), Nyborg *et al.* (2006), Brouhle and Khanna (2007) and Sartzetakis *et al.* (2012)). The literature has approached the emergence of green consumers using different frameworks. Most of the models assume that green consumers differentiate products based on their environmental attributes inducing some firms to produce a "greener" variety of the product. This differentiation has been examined mainly within a framework of vertical differentiation (Bansal and Gangopadhyay, 2003; García-Gallego and Georgantzís, 2009; Bansal, 2008; Deltas *et al.*, 2013) and Doni and Ricchiuti (2013)), and less within a framework of horizontal differentiation Conrad (2005). Alternatively, Gil-Moltó and Varvarigos (2013) examine the case in which environmental consciousness leads consumers to devote resources to reduce pollution (participation in carbon offsetting schemes, donations to NGOs, etc).

In all the aforementioned papers, consumers' involvement is due to *a change in their tastes* that makes environmentally friendly products more highly valued (*hedonic* approach). Our approach is to assume a *change in consumers' behaviour*: an environmentally responsible consumer is one that decides her consumption by taking also account of at least a part of the externality she creates. Thus, pro-environment behaviour is not the result of a "warm-glow" effect that attributes higher utility to certain behaviour; instead, it results from a conscious deviation from strict utility maximisation, in order to partially account for damage the consumer creates without immediately receiving its consequences (we call it *social responsibility* (SR) approach). The major difference between the two approaches is that increases in SR leave the first-best solution unaffected, whereas changes in consumers' tastes impact the ideal outcome. For instance, in the case of SR, full internalisation of the externality simply leaves no role for regulation, whereas according to the hedonic approach, changes in the warm-glow effect that affects consumers' preferences call for constant regulatory intervention (more on this issue later).

3. The Model

3.1. *Production, pollution and consumption*

Assume a monopolist producing Q units of a product X with constant marginal production cost, normalised to 0 for simplicity. In the production process, δ units of harmful pollutants are generated per unit of output. In order to reduce its emissions, the firm invests in end-of-pipe abatement technology, such as filters.[8] Since filters represent fixed costs, the cost function is constant in quantity, but assumed quadratic in abatement:

$$C = kv^2, \quad k \geq 1 \tag{1}$$

where v is the amount of emissions reduction the firm undertakes in order to improve the abating technology. When choosing the level of abatement, the firm generates the following total amount of net emissions:

$$e = \delta Q - v, \quad \delta > 0 \tag{2}$$

To avoid negative net emissions the level of abatement must be restricted to the $[0, \delta Q]$ interval. The total environmental damage that the firm generates takes the form of:

$$D = ze^2, \quad z > 1 \tag{3}$$

where z shows how convex the damage function is. The parameter z may be interpreted as either a technical or a social-preference parameter expressing pollution damage in terms of equivalent reductions of the numeŕaire good.

On the consumption side of the model, assume $n \geq 1$ identical consumers, each having the following utility function:

$$U(q_i) = \alpha q_i - \frac{1}{2}q_i^2 + M \quad \alpha > 0 \tag{4}$$

with $q_i \geq 0$ representing individual consumption of X, $\sum_{i=1}^{n} q_i = Q$, and M being the amount of the numéraire good consumed; hereafter, M is dropped.

---

[8]There are also other options for abating pollution, including in the "cleaner production" method such as "the re-circulation of materials, the use of environmentally friendly materials and the modification of the combustion chamber design"(Frondel *et al.* (2007)).

Social consciousness implies that consumers deviate from strict utility maximisation, adopting a behaviour that is guided by maximisation of the following function:

$$\tilde{U}(q_i;\phi,e)=\begin{cases}(\alpha-\phi e)q_i-\dfrac{1}{2}q_i^2, & \text{if } e>0\\ U(q_i), & \text{if } e\leq 0\end{cases} \tag{5}$$

where ϕ shows consumers' aversion to pollution. When $\phi=0$, consumers do not care about net emissions generated by the firm and therefore decide their purchase of X by maximising $U(q)$ in (4). For positive values of ϕ, the representative consumer feels responsible for only part of the externality. In order to avoid over-internalisation, we bound ϕ in the $[0,z]$ interval.

After maximising (5) with respect to quantity, substituting e by $\delta Q-v$ from (2), solving for q_i and aggregating, we obtain aggregate demand function for the case of n consumers:

$$Q(p;n,\delta,\phi,v)=\frac{n(\alpha+\phi v)}{\phi n\delta+1}-\frac{n}{\phi n\delta+1}p$$

Without loss of generality, we assume hereafter a single representative consumer. The inverse demand function that emerges from (5) when $n=1$ is:

$$p(q;n,\delta,\phi,v)=\begin{cases}(\alpha+\phi v)-(1+\phi)q, & \text{if } q\geq v\\ \alpha-q, & q\leq v\end{cases} \tag{6}$$

and is represented by the line aAq_2 in Fig. 1, for a given level of abatement, v. The line D_U corresponds to the demand deriving from (4) while the line $D_{\tilde{U}}$ to that deriving from the first part of (5). At point A, net emissions are zero, therefore $\delta q_A=v$.

In our approach, the responsible consumer sacrifices utility in order to contribute to environmental quality (a public good). The sacrifice corresponds to the utility loss due to maximising (5) instead of (4). For instance, at price p_1, strict utility maximisation implies the purchase of q_2 units, but the consumer voluntarily restricts her consumption to q_1, depending on her ϕ, which determines the position of $D_{\tilde{U}}$. The presence of ϕ makes the consumer behave as if a corrective per unit tax equal to BE were imposed on the good, although

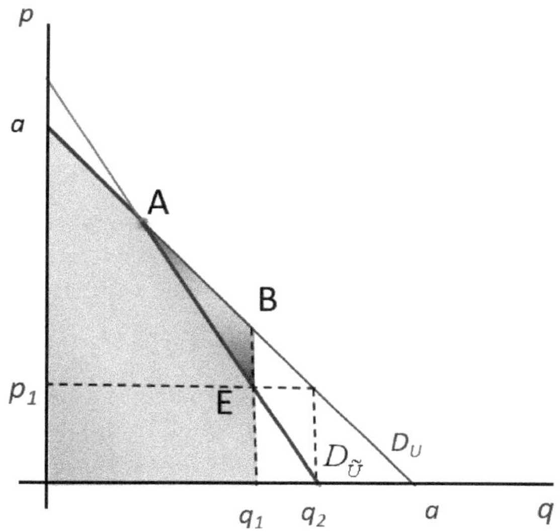

Fig. 1. Social responsibility vs. Hedonic approach.

no tax payment is actually required.[9] Since the quantity restriction q_1, q_2 is not related to a change in the marginal valuation (marginal benefit) function of good X, the total value of the actual purchase is the shaded area $0ABq_1$.

Our *Social Responsibility* (SR) approach differs from *Hedonic* approach models that assume pro-environment action to emanate from *personal satisfaction* considerations. According to those models, the consumer reduces her consumption of X because, once social consciousness makes her see the consequences of such consumption, the good no longer provides her the same utility as before. In those models, total and marginal valuation of X in terms of the numéraire are obtained using $\tilde{U}$ contained in (4). Thus, the line $aAEq_2$ in Fig. 1, not only shows consumer behaviour, but also corresponds to the marginal benefits from each unit consumed. If consumer behaviour is guided by *hedonic* considerations, the total value of the q_1 units is $0aEq_1$.[10] In

[9]The amount BE corresponds exactly to the Pigouvian tax if $\phi = z$.

[10]In most cases, instead of a marginal value reduction due to pollution, hedonic models introduce a "warm-glow" effect from the use of a more environmentally friendly good. In this case, the utility function takes the form $U_H = a + \theta v q_i -$

contrast to this "pleasure-guided" approach, we maintain that social responsibility modifies behaviour without modifying the value of the good.

3.2. *Social welfare and first best*

The Social welfare function consists of consumers' utility from consumption, minus the sum of all costs, namely, environmental damage, production cost (assumed zero) and the cost of abatement, if any:

$$W = u_i - (D + C)$$

The question here is whether consumption utility must be replaced by (4) or (5). According to the discussion surrounding Fig. 1, while consumers' behaviour is described by the demand function aAE, which derives from (6), actual consumer surplus for any given quantity is represented by the area below the line aa, which derives from (4). Hence, while we are using the demand function in (6) in order to determine the quantity at any given price, we use the utility function in (4) in order to determine the value this quantity has for the consumer. The use of (5) in order to compute consumption benefits would imply the inclusion of psychological damage stemming from emissions aversion *per se* on top of the real environmental damage, which is already captured by the D term in the social welfare function.

Substituting (1), (3) and (4) to the social welfare function, we obtain:

$$W = \alpha q - \frac{1}{2}q^2 - z(q - v)^2 - kv^2 \tag{7}$$

We assume that $z \geq \alpha$, implying that the relative importance of the environmental damage is sufficiently high, and set $\alpha = 1$, a mere

---

$(1/2)q_i^2$, where θ is the degree of consciousness, and v an environment-friendly characteristic, here abatement. The corresponding inverse demand is $p = a + \theta v - q_i$, i.e., instead of a negative reaction to emissions, the consumer reacts positively to their restriction (see Lambertini (2017)). Whether the change in consumer behaviour is due to emissions-aversion or a "warm-glow" effect from their reduction, the point is that it is related to changes in personal satisfaction, instead of emanating from a sense of duty that calls for a voluntary deviation from strict utility maximisation.

normalisation. In what follows, we present the first-best solution taking into account all the simplifying assumptions made up to this point, namely that $\delta = 1$, $n = 1$, $a = 1$, and also assuming hereafter $k = 2$.[11] Maximising (7) with respect to abatement and quantity, we obtain:

$$q^* = \frac{z+2}{5z+2}, \quad v^* = \frac{z}{5z+2}$$

where a "*" indicates first-best values. It can be easily verified that $\forall z \geq 1$, $q^* > v^*$, so net emissions are never negative. Substituting the above expressions into (3) and (7), we obtain the first-best level of emissions and social welfare:

$$ne^* = \frac{2}{5z+2}, \quad sw^* = \frac{z+2}{10z+4}$$

Note that the social responsibility approach implies that none of the first-best expressions contains ϕ, thus the maximum achievable level of welfare is independent of consumer consciousness, since the regulator is able to directly control both, consumption and abatement.

All three lines in Figure 2 represent the maximum attainable welfare as a function of the social consciousness parameter ϕ and have been drawn for $\alpha = \delta = 1$ and $k = z = 2$. The cyan horizontal line shows the first best attainable welfare according to the Social Responsibility (SR) approach, where the first-best is independent of ϕ. The magenta line corresponds to first-best welfare if one uses (5) instead of (4), into (7). The decreasing shape of the magenta line shows that as consumers' environmental concerns increase, a regulator in control of both crucial variables is able to generate lower welfare. This is due to the fact that when social consciousness emanates from *hedonic* considerations, the consumption of good X, besides pollution damages, creates also an additional (psychological) burden which increases with consumers' environmental sensitivity. While in some cases consumer behavior may indeed stem from hedonic considerations, we believe that such cases do not truly correspond to

[11] This value has been chosen to avoid corner solutions when the tax is based on output, as well as to always have 2nd order conditions satisfied. Unless for very small values of k–significantly less than 1, changes is k produce no qualitative results.

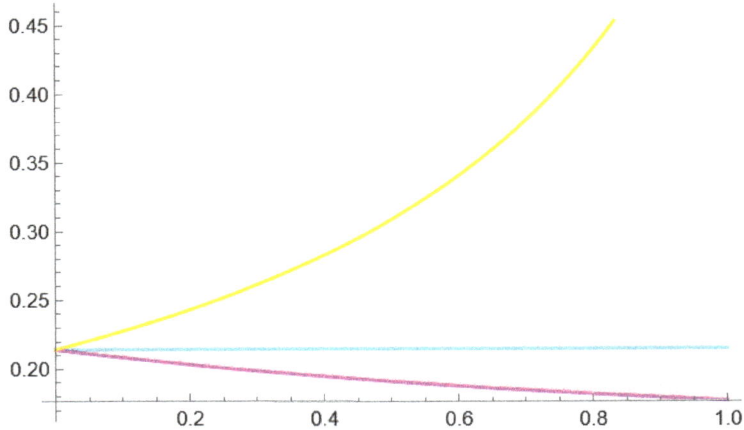

Fig. 2. First best social welfare cases.

SR.[12] Finally, the yellow line shows again first-best welfare under a different types of hedonic considerations, this time assuming that the consumer derives pleasure from consuming goods of higher environmental quality (lower emissions); as a result, first-best welfare *rises* with ϕ. Again, we consider this approach as incompatible with SR in the sense of social duty.[13]

4. Time-consistent Regulator Game

In order to allow for tax base comparisons, we adopt a four-stage game where at the first stage the regulator chooses a tax base (either on emissions or on output), followed by the monopolist who chooses abatement at the second stage. At the third stage, the regulator decides the tax rate and at the final stage the monopolist chooses output. After that, consumers purchase the amount of X they wish,

[12]The horizontal axis in Figure 2 is limited to $[0, 1]$ since beyond $\phi = 1.0$ the magenta line includes negative net emissions.

[13]The difference between SR hedonic approaches is also important when one considers the government's effort to increase consumers' environmental sensitivity. According to SR, the government must invest in order to convince consumers *to change their behavior*, whereas hedonic approaches require investments aiming to *change consumers' preferences*.

and profits and social welfare are determined; we proceed by backwards induction.

Our game structure is almost similar to that in Petrakis *et al.* (2001) and Poyago-Theotoky and Teerasuwannajak (2002) with the addition of a first stage where the tax base is announced. The addition of the tax base choice stage raises the question of whether the regulator, who may not have the power to commit to a tax rate, has the power to commit to a base. Recall, however, that when the emissions-to-output ratio is given, both bases produce the same output and welfare: the choice of tax base matters only to the extent that it affects abatement. Thus, once abatement is undertaken, the regulator has no incentive to renege on its tax base announcement, unlike his announcement on tax rate.[14]

The firm's profit functions in case of output and emissions tax are respectively:

$$\Pi = (p - t)Q - C, \quad \Pi = pQ - te - C$$

By substituting (1), (2) and (6) to these profit functions we obtain:

$$\begin{aligned} \Pi_O &= [(1 + \phi v) - (1 + \phi)q - t]q - 2v^2 \\ \Pi_E &= [(1 + \phi v) - (1 + \phi)q]q - t(q - v) - 2v^2 \end{aligned} \tag{8}$$

where the subscripts denote the output or emissions tax case. Maximisation of either Π_O or Π_E yields the same optimal output expression, namely:

$$q_{3i} = \frac{1 - t + v\phi}{2 + 2\phi}, \quad i = O, \mathrm{E} \tag{9}$$

The first digit of the subscript denotes the game stage (3rd), while the second, the tax regime (O for output and E for emissions tax). Note that for given abatement and tax rate, the output decision is the

[14]Since the regulator is indifferent, an ε reputation cost for reneging on his promise suffices to establish credibility in his first-stage tax base announcement. Note also that while for a given abatement, the choice of tax base does not affect total welfare, it may affect its distribution between surplus and profit. Distributional issues lie outside the chapter's scope since they require modifying the social welfare function in order to weigh profits and consumer surplus differently.

same under the two tax regimes.[15] Quantity is obviously increasing in abatement and decreasing in the tax rate. A bit less obvious but straightforward is to show that when output and net emissions are non-negative, third-stage quantity is decreasing in ϕ, as expected.

At the second stage, the social planner maximises (7) taking the quantity of the firm as given, to obtain:

$$t_{2i} = \frac{-2vz(\phi+2) + (v-2)\phi + 2z - 1}{2z+1}, \quad i = O, E \tag{10}$$

For a *given* abatement level, as long as $\delta = 1$ the regulator's optimal tax rate is the same, independently of the tax base upon which it applies.[16] Hence, the regulator has no incentive to change an already announced tax base. It can be easily shown that the optimal tax rate is decreasing in the abatement level.

4.1. *Subgame perfect Nash equilibrium*

At the second stage, the firm substitutes t and q given by their expression in (9) and (10), respectively, into (8) and maximises with respect to abatement. We limit The thus obtained expressions hold only if at the resulting equilibrium net emissions are non-negative:

Lemma 1. *The abatement in the interior solution equilibrium, under output and emissions tax, is respectively:*

$$\begin{aligned} v_O &= \frac{z(1+\phi)}{2z(-z\phi+z+2)+1} \\ v_E &= \frac{4z(z+1)-1-2\phi}{24z(z+1)+4-2\phi} \end{aligned} \tag{11}$$

Proof. The derivation of the v_O and v_E expressions is straightforward. First substitute (9) and (10) to (8) and then take the first derivative of it. □

[15] The perfect equality is due to the fact that we have assumed a one-to-one relation between output and emissions ($\delta = 1$). If $\delta \neq 1$, in the case of emissions tax, the tax coefficient in the above expression must be multiplied by δ.

[16] For $\delta \neq 1$, the output tax must be multiplied by δ.

The abatement levels in Lemma 1 only hold for interior solutions, yet there are two types of corner solutions that may prevail. First, for a given tax type and SR level, the abatement computed in Lemma 1 may not be higher than actual emissions. Since we assumed $\delta = 1$, if abatement is greater than output, net emissions must be considered equal to zero. Second and most important, corner solutions may occur because we rule out subsidies.[17] Thus, for any v_i value, $i = O, E$, computed by Lemma 1 to hold, it must be that when inserted into (10) the resulting tax rate is non-negative. When this is not the case, the firm must modify its decision away from the rule described in Lemma 1. In the Appendix, it is shown that

Lemma 2. *A necessary and sufficient condition for interior solution in the case of output and emissions tax is $\phi_O \geq 0$ and $\phi_E \geq 0$, respectively, with*

$$\phi_O = \frac{(2z^2 + 3z + 2) - (1 + 2z)\sqrt{4 + z^2}}{2z} \tag{12}$$

and

$$\phi_E = \frac{7}{4} + z(6 + z) - \frac{1}{4}(1 + 2z)\sqrt{81 + 4z(11 + z)} \tag{13}$$

with $\phi_O < \phi_E$.

Hereafter, the analysis is limited in interior solutions, i.e., we only consider values of $\phi \in [0, \phi_i]$.

Proposition 1. (*i*) *If the announced tax is on output,* (*a*) $\forall \phi \leq \phi_O$ *abatement is monotonically increasing in ϕ;* (*b*) *there exists a value of $\phi = \phi^* \in [0, \phi_O]$*

$$\phi^* \equiv \frac{z - 1}{z + 2} \tag{14}$$

such that the market produces the first-best level of abatement ($v_O = v^*$), while for $\phi > (<) \phi^*$ market abatement is above (below) v^*.[18]

---

[17]While output subsidies are not unthinkable, emissions subsidies represent a politically unpalatable measure.

[18]In the main text, we usually refer to $\phi_O > \phi^*$ as the *over-abatement* effect.

(ii) *If the announced tax is on emissions, for all* $\phi \in [0, \phi_E]$ *abatement is monotonically* ***decreasing*** *in* ϕ *and* $v_E < v^*$.

It is remarkable that, while with an output tax increases in environmental consciousness result in higher abatement (as expected), the opposite holds true with an emissions tax: as ϕ increases, the firm abates less.[19] At any tax rate, more aware consumers internalise a larger part of the externality by demanding a lower quantity at any given price (social responsibility–SR–effect). Hence, increases in ϕ cause optimal tax rates to fall.

When the tax base is on output, tax rate reductions boost output,[20] thus allowing for a reduction in the per-unit-of-output cost of abatement,[21] which in turn induces higher abatement (output effect). This output effect works in the same direction with the SR effect and reinforces it. On the other hand, the reduction of the emissions tax due to an increase in ϕ makes emissions less costly and tends to reduce abatement. This effect dominates the SR effect, therefore an increase in ϕ leads to lower abatement.

Figure 3 illustrates the content of Proposition 1. It displays abatement under an output tax (cyan line) and emissions tax (magenta line), as functions of social consciousness, assuming $k = z = 2$, and $\delta = n = 1$. The horizontal brown line represents the abatement level at the first-best solution. The gray-dotted line shows the point where the output tax becomes zero (ϕ_O) and the black-dashed line displays the level of environmental consciousness where the emissions tax becomes zero (ϕ_E). This colour code–brown for first-best, cyan for output tax, and magenta for emissions tax–as well as the aforementioned set of specific values for the exogenous parameters are maintained in all subsequent figures. Like all first-best values, first-best abatement is independent of ϕ. The cyan line representing v_O is monotonically increasing, eventually reaching and exceeding v^*. On the contrary, the magenta line (v_E) is decreasing and lies everywhere

[19]A similar result for the case where the regulator can commit to a tax rate is also shown in CPS.

[20]Even if the output tax rate is positive, a tax rate *reduction* corresponds to quantity subsidisation.

[21]Recall that end-of-pipe abatement represents a fixed cost with respect to output.

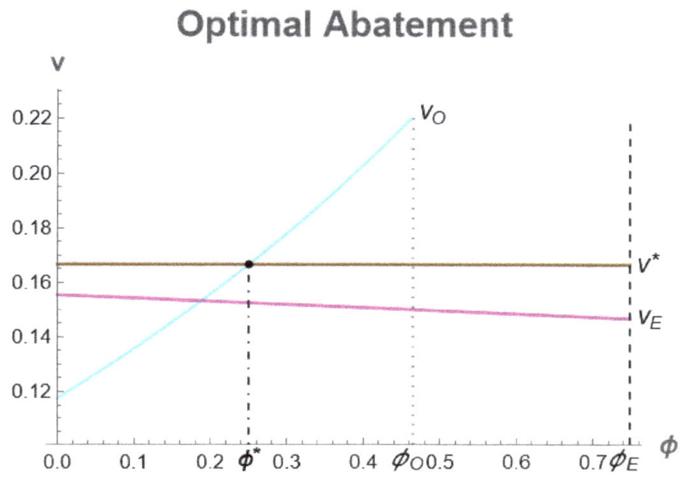

Fig. 3. Equilibrium abatement.

below the brown line. For SR increases on the admissible levels of ϕ, abatement reductions are moderate because the monopolist knows that higher abatement leads ceteris paribus to a lower emissions-tax rate. Moreover, the over-provision of environmental quality, even beyond the first-best level, leads to a substantial reduction in the tax rate, thus the output tax becomes zero at a lower level of SR compared to the emissions tax ($\phi_O < \phi_E$). This is a consequence related to the *over-abatement effect.*

Turning to quantities, we substitute optimal abatement from Lemma 1, as well as the resulting optimal tax rates (see the Appendix) into (9). We obtain the optimal quantity under each type of tax as:

$$
\begin{aligned}
q_O &= \frac{2z+1}{2z(-z\phi+z+2)+1} \\
q_E &= 1-\frac{5z(2z+1)}{12z(z+1)-\phi+2}
\end{aligned}
\tag{15}
$$

One can easily verify (see the Appendix) that when the tax base is output, higher environmental consciousness leads to higher quantity in equilibrium, whereas when the tax is on emissions, the equilibrium quantity decreases in ϕ. This happens because, *ceteris paribus*, higher values of ϕ reduce demand, but while this reduction is compensated by increased abatement in the case of output tax, the lower abatement in case of emissions tax depresses the demand curve further down.

The evolution of net emissions as ϕ increases is not obvious since under either tax base, quantity and abatement move in the same direction, both increasing in the case of output tax, and decreasing in the case of emissions tax. Therefore, it depends on the relative magnitude of the abatement and the output. The following proposition clears this issue. Let $ne_i = ne_i(\phi; z),\ i = O, E$, describe net-emissions in the interior solution equilibrium under the corresponding tax base, and an accent denote derivative with respect to ϕ. Then:

Proposition 2. (*i*) *When the tax is on output, $ne_O' < 0$, with $ne_O(0) > ne^*$ and $ne_O(\phi_O) < ne^*$, i.e., net emissions decrease monotonically with ϕ, starting from a level above that of first-best when SR is zero and ending at a level below it, as ϕ approaches its highest allowed value; at the SR level $\phi = \phi^*$ (see equation* 14) *net emissions are equal to their first-best level.*

(ii) *When the tax is on emissions, $ne_E' > 0$, with $ne_E(0) > ne^*$, i.e., net emissions increase monotonically with ϕ and are always above their first-best level.*

(iii) *For relatively low (high) levels of SR, $ne_O > (<) ne_E$.*

The content of the proposition can be seen in Figure 7, contained in the next section. In the absence of environmental consciousness, an emissions tax yields a cleaner environment than an output tax. However, as ϕ increases, emissions keep increasing under the optimal emissions tax while they are drastically reduced under the optimal output tax. As a result, in a jurisdiction with relatively developed SR, a VA using output taxation initiates lower emissions compared to a VA on emissions taxation. A VA using emissions taxation is superior only when SR is very low. Also, for even moderate levels of SR, the VA using output taxation results in net emissions that are even lower than those at first-best.[22] It is remarkable that this

[22] They may even become zero if the VA includes output subsidies for high environmental performance. Such a complete environmental clean-up is impossible under an emissions tax, which leaves emissions higher than their first-best level for any level of ϕ.

excellent environmental performance of an output tax without regulator's commitment is not the result of a reduction in the quantity of the regulated good, but on a sharp increase in abatement, resulting from increases in SR. The cost of such performance is paid in terms of the numéraire good, i.e., by withdrawing too many resources from the rest of the economy.

Equilibrium social welfare under each tax base is obtained by substituting (11) and (13) into (7). The resulting expressions are relegated to the Appendix, since they are fairly complex and provide no immediate intuition. At this point we simply denote them as $sw_i(\phi; z)$, $i = O, E$, the equilibrium welfare under each tax base.

Lemma 3. (*i*) *Under an output tax,* $\forall \phi \leq (\geq) \phi^*$, $sw_O' \geq (\leq) 0$, *with* $sw_O(\phi^*) = sw^*$.

(ii) *Under an emissions tax, the welfare function is monotonically decreasing in* ϕ; *an emissions tax never achieves first-best welfare, i.e.,* $\forall \phi$, $sw_E < sw^*$

Figure 4 shows the evolution of social welfare with increases in SR when an output or emissions tax is in effect (cyan and magenta line, respectively). As explained earlier, increases in ϕ cause reductions of the optimal tax rate due to *ceteris paribus* lower consumption. Reductions in the emissions tax rate make emissions cheaper,

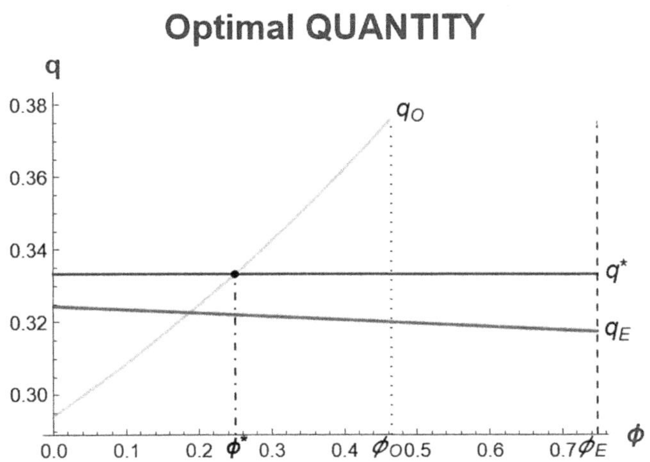

Fig. 4. Equilibrium quantity.

resulting in lower abatement and higher net emissions, which leads in turn to further reductions in consumption. As a result, increases in SR lead society to situations with more pollution and lower consumption; despite abatement-cost savings, total welfare decreases as ϕ increases. On the other hand, reductions in the output tax rate act as output boosting subsidies, countering the initial quantity reduction along with increases in abatement, finally resulting in net-emissions reduction. However, the total cost of abatement also increases and for $\phi > \phi^*$ attains sub-optimally high levels. This implies lower-than-optimal consumption of the numéraire good, causing total welfare to decrease with ϕ when SR reaches levels above ϕ^*. The following proposition formally compare welfare under output and emissions taxes.

Proposition 3. *For all $z \geq 2$, there exist two critical values of ϕ, $\phi_1 < \phi_2$, such that $sw_O(\phi_i) = sw_E(\phi_i)$, $i = 1, 2$. For values of ϕ within (outside) the (ϕ_1, ϕ_2) interval, $sw_O > (<) sw_E$.*[23]

Proposition 3 determines the optimal choice of base at the first stage and therefore provides the overall equilibrium of the game.[24] Its main message is that the level of SR influences the optimal choice of tax base: for low and high levels of SR the emissions tax is more efficient, but there is an intermediate range of SR at which the output tax provides higher welfare.

By using the appropriate tax base and rate, the regulator aims to correct two distortions, a too high level of emissions and a too low level of output, due to market power. In the absence of SR, the emissions tax is more efficient in reducing emissions. This advantage is gradually lost as ϕ increases since net emissions are continuously decreasing under an output tax and continuously increasing under an emissions tax. At the same time, when the tax base is output, increases in ϕ result in higher output, which helps the regulator deal with the monopoly distortion, while under an emissions tax output

[23]The $z \geq 2$ assumption avoids special cases where $\phi_1 < 0$. The exact expressions of the critical values are shown in the Appendix.

[24]Provided that the regulator can commit to a tax base at the first stage, an assumption that has been justified even if tax rate commitment is impossible.

is decreasing in ϕ. Hence, the output tax takes full advantage from increases in SR, whereas such increases reduce the welfare-enhancing power of the emissions tax.

However, for SR levels above ϕ^* the the prospect of more favourable taxation induces the monopolist to over-abate, in the sense of engaging in socially wasteful abatement in order to obtain even higher tax rate reductions (or even subsidies, when allowed). Since the excessive abatement decision cannot be reversed at the moment the tax rate is decided, the regulator has no other choice but to focus on correcting for market power. To illustrate this point, let us allow for a moment output subsidies, which implies levels of SR beyond ϕ_O, and consider that ϕ is so high as to induce zero net emissions. Now, the only choice of the regulator is to target the optimal quantity, i.e., the one at which marginal benefit equals marginal production cost (here, zero). Such a solution would have been optimal in the absence of environmental externality, but not in our context, where the true marginal cost of the good is positive and equal to environmental damage. As SR increases this distortion becomes increasingly serious, leading to welfare levels well below those that could be obtained using an emissions tax.

Since high levels of SR require negative tax rates to be applied on either base, both tax types cease to be valid policy instruments if no subsidies are allowed. If one sees time-consistent taxation as a kind of VA, this implies that no such agreement can be fully efficient in jurisdictions with high SR, unless it provides stimulus in terms of subsidies. Proposition 3 shows that a VA o tax rates without use of subsidies is viable for a wider range of SR if it applies on emissions, since $\phi_E > \phi_O$.

While we do not have a formal proof, extensive numerical simulations corroborate a result illustrated in Fig. 5, namely that, when the regulator is not aware of the exact level of SR, choosing mistakenly emissions instead of output as base produces less damage than the opposite; in other words, offering a menu of emissions tax rates is a safer choice for a regulator who possesses imperfect information.

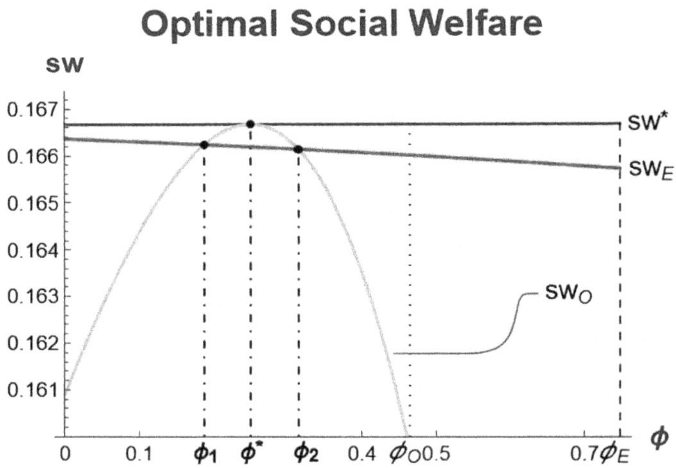

Fig. 5. Social welfare.

5. Change in the Order of Moves: Comparisons

In this section, we compare the equilibrium with no commitment (time-consistent policy) to the equilibrium in case the regulator is able to commit to a tax rate from the outset. The latter has been extensively studied by Constantatos *et al.* (2021), so the analysis in this section consists of comparing the results from the previous section to those contained in that paper. We refer to the commitment model as model C and its equilibrium variables are indicated by a hat (ˆ); whenever it is needed for the comparisons, we refer to time-consistent model analyzed in the previous sections as model N (no commitment). As earlier, the discussion is limited to interior solutions in the optimal choice of the tax rate, nevertheless, in order to enhance comparability *we allow for output, but not emissions-, subsidies.*[25]

[25]The argument in Constantatos *et al.* (2021) is that while output subsidies can be eventually admissible by politicians and the public – especially if one considers time-consistent taxation as a form of VA – emissions subsidies are not acceptable. Note, however, that allowing for any type of subsidy would not affect our previous analysis; we ruled them out up to this point in order to avoid corner solutions that might appear in the N, but not in the C model.

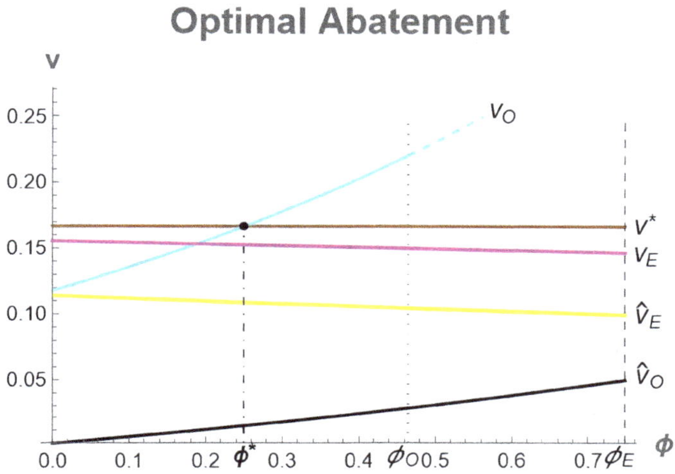

Fig. 6. Abatement comparison.

Allowing for regulator's commitment eliminates the monopolist's motivation to affect the tax rate and therefore reduces its incentive for abatement (see Petrakis *et al.* (2001)). Thus, it is easy to show that while for each tax base the evolution of abatement as function of ϕ exhibits similar pattern in models N and C, $v_i > \hat{v}_i$, $i = O, E$, i.e., in the C model the regulator's commitment lowers abatement independently of the tax base in use. The situation is depicted in Fig. 6 where three new colours are added to our basic colour code and remain in use for all the following figures: a black (yellow) line indicates the equilibrium value of a variable under output (emissions) tax in the C model and is contrasted to the cyan (magenta) line that still indicates the corresponding value in the N model. Note finally that the cyan v_O line now extends beyond ϕ_O since we allow for output subsidies; we do not show the entire line to avoid affecting the figures scale.[26] Due to the absence of the tax rate affecting incentive in model C, the black line lies everywhere below the cyan line, and the same holds true for the yellow compared to the magenta line.

[26]All the figures in CPS have been drawn for $k = 1$, $n = 1$, $\delta = 1$, $\alpha = 1$ and $z = 3/2$. In order to obtain compatibility with our previous figures, we have reproduced the CPS figures assuming $k = 2$ and $z = 2$.

Since abatement under an emissions tax in the N model is always lower than first-best abatement, the incentive reduction caused by a mandatory regulation exacerbates under-abatement. Hence, for any level of social consciousness, the emissions tax yields abatement closer to its first-best level in the absence of regulator's commitment.[27] A similar conclusion does not necessarily hold true for the output tax. As shown in Proposition 1, for some levels of SR, the time-consistent regulator may cause over-abatement, and in such cases, the incentive reduction due to regulator's commitment may bring abatement closer to its socially optimal level. While commitment causes equilibrium abatement to increase monotonically with ϕ – exactly as in the N model – it is shown in CPS that abatement never exceeds its first-best level, which is reached only when consumers fully endogenise the externality their consumption creates. Under regulator's inability to commit, on the other hand, abatement reaches its first-best level at relatively low levels of SR, thus leading to over-abatement in a wide range of ϕ values. For instance, at $\phi = .4$ in Fig. 6, while consumers internalise only 20% of the externality they create,[28] there is already substantial over-abatement.

Turning to net emissions, we see that the emissions tax in the C model (yellow line) produces systematically lower than first-best emissions, not because of over-abatement, but because of a too high reduction in output (see CPS). As consumers become more conscious, the quantity reduction in the N model is less pronounced compared to that in the C model, because of the firm's additional abatement incentive, leading to monotonically increasing net emissions that are always above their first-best level. Thus, the impact of increases in ϕ on net emissions is qualitatively very different in the two models when an emissions tax is in use.

Since for any tax base the N-model equilibrium involves higher abatement, it must also involve higher quantity of the polluting good, therefore the comparison of the performance of each tax base with and without commitment cannot be predicted from the outset. Simple inspection of Fig. 7 shows that for any tax base, the evolution of net emissions as a function of social consciousness are markedly

[27]This is also shown in Petrakis *et al.* (2001), but only for $\phi = 0$.
[28]Recall that the maximum value of $\phi = z = 2$ on this figure.

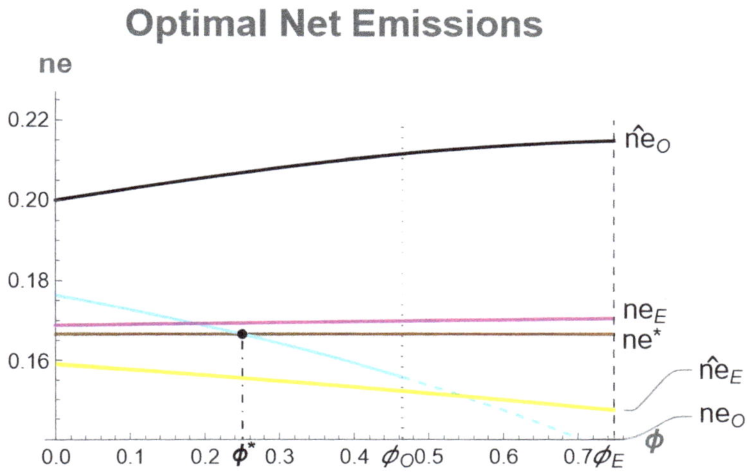

Fig. 7. Net emissions comparison.

different according to whether the regulator is able or not to commit to a tax rate.

The emissions tax produces cleaner environment when the regulator commits to a tax rate. While the time-consistent regulator induces higher abatement, he also induces higher output, yielding overall more pollution. As shown in CPS the *emissions tax* under regulator's commitment produces such a sharp quantity reduction that total net emissions fall below their first-best level for any level of SR (see the yellow line in Fig. 7); in the N model, net emissions are always higher than their first-best level.

Proposition 2 in this chapter states that under an *output tax*, net emissions in the N model decrease rapidly as social consciousness increases, and while at $\phi = 0$ they start from a level above that of first-best, they soon go below it. No such response is observed in the C model, where under an output tax, net emissions are always above their first-best level, initially *increasing* (due to lower tax rate) but eventually decreasing with social consciousness, reaching their first-best level only when consumers become fully responsible.[29] The already identified incentive to affect the tax rate of an uncommitted

[29] See Constantatos *et al.* (2021). The decreasing part of the black curve is not shown in Fig. 7 since it occurs for $\phi > \phi_E$.

regulator and the resulting tendency of the output tax to quickly produce over-abatement in the N model are responsible for the drastic effect that increases in SR have in reducing pollution. Absent this incentive, there is never over-abatement and net emissions never fall below their first-best level. Turning to equilibrium social welfare, we can prove the following proposition.

Proposition 4. *When the tax is on output there is a critical level of SR, call it* ϕ_{sw}*, such that* $\forall\phi \in [0, \phi_{sw}]$, $sw_O > \hat{sw}_O$*, while* $\forall\phi \in [\phi_{sw}, \phi_E]$, $sw_O < \hat{sw}_O$*. When the tax is on emissions,* $\forall\phi \in [0, \phi_E]$, $sw_E > \hat{sw}_E$*, i.e., welfare is always higher in the absence of regulator's commitment.*

The content of Proposition 4 is illustrated in Fig. 8.[30]

It is shown that the social welfare resulting from a VA (magenta line) is always higher than that of the mandatory regulation (yellow line), meaning that when it comes to choosing between offering a VA or using mandatory taxation (i.e., whether committing or not to an emissions tax), by choosing the latter, society enjoys more welfare. The intuition behind this result is straightforward. The time

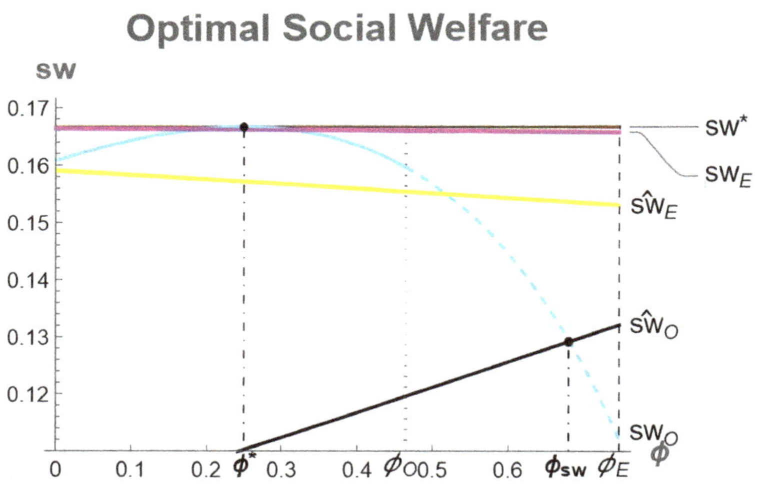

Fig. 8. Social welfare comparison.

[30]Fig. 5 shows clearly that the emissions-tax social welfare in Model N and the first-best case do not coincide as well as the decreasing tendency of the former.

consistent social planner provides motivation to the firms in order to invest more in abating technology. Since there is no exaggeration in abatement investment (see Fig. 5) the resulting social welfare is greater than the one generated by a committed regulator. When it comes to the output tax, there is no clear verdict in favour of a time-consistent schedule, unless negative tax rates are excluded. For sufficiently high levels of SR (above ϕ_{sw}), committing to a tax rate, if feasible, may be welfare superior. The problem with VA allowing the choice of output-tax rate is that they make the firm too eager to provide abatement in exchange of tax rate reductions. For sufficiently high levels of SR, such that the optimal policy calls for subsidies, and if the latter are allowed, the tendency for excessive abatement tendency is even stronger. While this creates a "happy outcome" with high output and very low emissions in the market in question, this outcome is obtained at the expense of withdrawing too many resources from the rest of the economy; the resulting welfare is thus decreasing in ϕ. Such tendency for over-abatement is not created under mandatory regulation with *a priori* commitment to a given tax rate. As a result, mandatory taxation is in tune with increases in SR, yielding higher welfare as the latter increases.

6. Conclusions

In this chapter, we focus on several issues, assuming that (a) consumers are socially responsible and (b) the regulator can adjust the tax rate after observing abatement. Following the work in CPS, we base our analysis on a social responsibility concept that relates environmental consciousness to various degrees of internalisation of the environmental externality. This concept is different than the usual *ad hoc* assumption of preference for green products.

First, we find that increases in SR lower the abatement incentive under an emissions tax, while the opposite holds true for an output tax: as consumers become more responsible, the firm has an always higher abatement incentive.

Second, social welfare under an emissions tax is decreasing everywhere as SR increases. The behaviour of social welfare as a function of SR is more complex under an output tax: social welfare increases with SR up to a point, but curbs down sharply, afterwards.

When at its peak, welfare under an output tax reaches its first-best level, whereas an emissions tax is under no level of SR able to reach first-best welfare. The reason behind the initially harmonious working between output tax and SR is the same which is responsible for the cacophony between these two variables at higher levels of SR: the strong increases in abatement incentive that the output tax produces as SR increases. While for low levels of SR the increases in abatement incentive are beneficial, beyond the point where abatement reaches its first-best level such increases lead to over-abatement, i.e., levels where the marginal abatement cost exceeds the corresponding marginal benefit.

Third, we show that while for low and high levels of SR a time-consistent *emissions tax* is welfare superior to a time-consistent output tax, there is a middle range of SR parameter values for which the *output tax* performs better. This result is related to the evolution of the abatement incentive following increases in SR, discussed in the previous paragraph.

Fourth, we compare the welfare performance of each tax base between the cases where the regulator is, or is not committed to an initial tax rate announcement. For the emissions tax, it is clear that for any SR level, non-commitment is superior, which corresponds to an extension of the similar result in Petrakis *et al.* (2001) and Poyago-Theotoky and Teerasuwannajak (2002), where SR is zero. However, with an output tax, commitment may be superior for high levels of SR. At those levels, the potential of SR to fuel over-abatement makes a time-consistent tax schedule inferior to mandatory imposition of a given tax rate. While increases in SR lead under an output tax to higher abatement levels, the tax-manipulation incentive present when the regulator is unable to commit may easily over-shoot abatement to levels that are uneconomically high.

In terms of policy, our work shows that generally, a tax menu approach (VA) performs better than mandatory regulation, at least when SR is low or moderate, and if the VA is adopted, a tax on emissions is a safer solution than a tax on output. While the latter may outperform the former for some middle-low range of SR values, it may produce very bad results when SR is very low, or high. With low SR levels, the output tax does not create sufficient abatement incentives while for higher tax levels it may induce "over-abatement."

Various extensions of this work are possible. First, we limited the analysis to levels of SR that lead to interior solutions. When no such subsidies are allowed there may be levels of SR for which corner solutions occur, with properties other than the aforementioned results; we are currently working on this issue. Also, the analysis must be extended to cases where the abatement investment reduces pollution per unit of output, a topic that features in our research agenda.

Appendix A. Proofs

Movement of the Quantity expressions. When the tax base is output, higher environmental consciousness leads to higher quantity in equilibrium, whereas when the tax is on emissions, equilibrium quantity is decreasing in ϕ.

Proof. The derivative of $q_O = \frac{1+2z}{1+2z(-z\phi+z+2)}$ is: $\frac{\partial q_O}{\partial \phi} = \frac{2z^2(1+2z)}{[1+2z(-z\phi+z+2)]^2}$ which is positive $\forall \phi,\ z$. Therefore q_O increases in ϕ. The derivative of $q_E = 1 - \frac{5z(2z+1)}{12z(z+1)-\phi+2}$ is: $\frac{\partial q_E}{\partial \phi} = -\frac{[5z(2z+1)]}{[12z(z+1)-\phi+2]^2}$ which is positive $\forall \phi,\ z$. Therefore q_E decreases in ϕ. □

Expressions for tax rate and social welfare functions

Tax Rates:

$$t_O = \frac{2z^2(\phi-1) - z(\phi-3)\phi + 2\phi + 1}{2z(z(\phi-1)-2)-1}$$

$$t_E = \frac{-4z(z+6)\phi + 4z(4z-1) + 2\phi^2 - 7\phi - 4}{24z(z+1) - 2\phi + 4}$$

Social welfare functions:

$$sw_O = \frac{2z\{z[-z(\phi-1)(\phi+3) - 2\phi(\phi+2) + 4] + 3\} + 1}{2(2z(-z\phi+z+2)+1)^2}$$

$$sw_E = \frac{56z^4 + 212z^3 - 16\left(z^2+z+1\right)\phi + 218z^2 + 87z - 6\phi^2 + 6}{4[-12z(z+1)+\phi-2]^2}$$

Proof of Lemma 2

Proof. The expressions ϕ_O and ϕ_E arise when we set the output and emissions tax in equilibrium equal to zero. First, in order to find ϕ_O, we set $t_O = 0$: $-z\phi^2 + (2z^2 + 3z + 2)\phi - 2z^2 + 1 = 0$ with the discriminant being: $\Delta = (1 + 2z)^2(4 + z^2)$. Therefore: $\phi_{1,2} = \frac{(2z^2+3z+2)\pm(1+2z)\sqrt{4+z^2}}{2z}$.

In order to avoid over-internalisation of the externality $\phi \leq z$. Therefore, here we will check which of these values satisfy this condition. First we check, $\frac{(2z^2+3z+2)+(1+2z)\sqrt{4+z^2}}{2z} \leq z \Leftrightarrow 3z^2 + 2 \leq -(1 + 2z)\sqrt{4 + z^2}$ which is not true. However when instead of the plus sign root we check the negative one, ϕ_2, we have: $3z^2 + 2 < (1 + 2z)\sqrt{4 + z^2} \Leftrightarrow 16z^4 + 16z^3 + 8z^2 + 4z \geq 0$, which is true, therefore $\phi_O = \frac{(2z^2+3z+2)-(1+2z)\sqrt{4+z^2}}{2z}$.

In the case of the emissions tax: $t_E = \frac{-4z(z+6)\phi+4z(4z-1)+2\phi^2-7\phi-4}{24z(z+1)-2\phi+4}$, the denominator is always positive. It is a decreasing function in ϕ and therefore for $\phi = 0 \rightarrow 24z(z + 1) + 4 > 0$ and for $\phi = z \rightarrow 24z(z + 1) - 2z + 4 = 24z^2 + 22z + 4 > 0$.

Focusing on the numerator:
$2\phi^2 - [7 + 4z(z + 6)]\phi + 4z(4z - 1) - 4 = 0$.

The discriminant of this polynomial is: $\Delta = 81 + 368z + 504z^2 + 192z^3 + 16z^4$ with the solutions of the polynomial being: $\phi_{1,2} = \frac{7+4z(z+6)\pm\sqrt{\Delta}}{4}$ which are both positive since the coefficient of ϕ^2 and the constant term are positive and by Vieta's formula we know that $P = \phi_1 \cdot \phi_2 = \frac{c}{\alpha} > 0$, where c is the constant term and α coefficient of ϕ^2.

We will now check under which circumstances these values are $< z$. Suppose, $\frac{7+4z(z+6)-\sqrt{81+368z+504z^2+192z^3+16z^4}}{4} \leq z$. After some manipulation, we obtain $32z^3 + 48z^2 + 88z + 32 \geq 0$, which is true without the equality. Therefore, $\phi_1 < z$.

We next check ϕ_2. Suppose $\frac{7+4z(z+6)+\sqrt{81+368z+504z^2+192z^3+16z^4}}{4} \leq z$, this yields $\sqrt{81 + 368z + 504z^2 + 192z^3 + 16z^4} \leq -7 - 4z^2 - 20z$, which cannot be true. Therefore, $\phi_2 > z$, meaning that $t_E \geq 0 \ \forall \ 0 \leq \phi \leq \phi_1, \ z > 1$ and thus we set $\phi_E = \frac{7+4z(z+6)-\sqrt{81+368z+504z^2+192z^3+16z^4}}{4}$.

Due to the complexity of the calculations, we use *Mathematica* software to prove that $\phi_O < \phi_E$. □

Proof of Proposition 1

Proof. The derivative of $v_O = \frac{z(1+\phi)}{2z(-z\phi+z+2)+1}$ is given by $\frac{\partial v_O}{\partial \phi} = \frac{z[2z(-z\phi+z+2)+1]-(-2z^2)(z+z\phi)}{[2z(-z\phi+z+2)+1]^2}$.

Since the denominator is always positive, we focus on the numerator and expand it to obtain: $4z^3 + 4z^2 + z$, which is positive $\forall z > 1$, meaning that v_O is monotonically increasing.

In what follows we determine the value of ϕ at which v_O is equal to v^*. After some manipulation, we obtain this value, given by: $\phi^* = \frac{z-1}{z+2}$.

Next, we show that $\phi^* < \phi_O$. Suppose, that it is not true, i.e., $\phi^* \geq \phi_O$. Then $\frac{z-1}{z+2} \geq \frac{2z^2+3z+2-(1+2z)\sqrt{4+z^2}}{2z} \Leftrightarrow 2z^3 + 5z^2 + 10z + 4 \leq (z+2)(1+2z)\sqrt{4+z^2}$, and upon squaring both parts and simplifying, we obtain $-16z^4 - 16z^3 - 4z^2 \geq 0$ which cannot true. By contradiction, it holds that $\phi^* < \phi_O$.

Since the first-best case is independent of ϕ and v_O increases in ϕ, for $\phi < \phi^*$, $v_O < v^*$ and for $\phi > \phi^*$, $v_O > v^*$. Finally, we can establish that the derivative $\frac{\partial v_E}{\partial \phi} = -\frac{5(2z-1)^2}{2[12z(z+1)+2-\phi]^2} < 0, \forall \phi \in [0, z], z > 1$.

Therefore, v_E decreases in ϕ. □

Proof of Proposition 2

Proof. $ne_O = \frac{1+z-z\phi}{1+2z(2+z-z\phi)}$.

We examine $\frac{\partial ne_O}{\partial \phi} = \frac{-z[1+2z(2+z-z\phi)]-(-2z^2)(1+z-z\phi)}{[1+2z(2+z-z\phi)]^2}$.

Since the denominator is always positive, we focus on the numerator. Let $N_1 = -z[1 + 2z(2 + z - z\phi)]$ and $N_2 = 2z^2(1 + z - z\phi)$, so that $N_1 + N_2 = -z - 2z^2$ which is negative $\forall\ z > 1$. Therefore, ne_O is a downward sloping function of ϕ. We next check whether $ne_O(0) = \frac{1+z}{1+2z(2+z)}$ is greater than the first-best case. Suppose $ne_O(0) > ne^*$, which after substituting and manipulating becomes $z(z-1) > 0$, so that either $z > 1$ or $z < 0$.

By construction, $z > 1$. Therefore, $ne_O(0) > ne^*$. Moreover, we know that $ne_O(\phi^*) = ne^*$ and since $\phi^* < \phi_O$ and $ne'_O < 0$ then $ne_O(\phi_O) < ne^*$.

Turning to the emissions tax, we have: $ne_E = \frac{10z+5}{24z(z+1)-2\phi+4}$, and we obtain $\frac{\partial ne_E}{\partial \phi} = \frac{5(2z+1)}{2[12z(z+1)-\phi+2]^2} > 0$, $\forall z > 1$.

Next, suppose $ne_E(0) > ne^*$ which, following after some manipulation becomes $2 - 3z + 2z^2 > 0$, which is always positive.

Now suppose, $ne_O(0) > ne_E(0)$, which upon following the relevant substitutions and some algebra, becomes $1 + 2z + 2z^2 - 4z3 < 0$.

Let $f(z) = 1 + 2z + 2z^2 - 4z^3$ with $f'(z) = 2 + 4z - 12z^2$. This equation has two solutions, a positive and a negative: The positive one is $\frac{1+\sqrt{7}}{6} \approx 0.607625$ and since $z > 1$, it follows that $f(z)$ is downward sloping. At $z = 1 \rightarrow f(1) = 1$ and at $z = 1.15 \rightarrow f(1.15) = -0.1325$. Therefore, by Bolzano's Theorem, there is a $\tau \in (1, 1.15)$ such that $f(\tau) = 0$. For $1 < z < \tau$, $ne_O(0) < ne_E(0)$ and for $z > \tau$, $ne_O(0) > ne_E(0)$. We keep the latter condition since the former generates uninteresting cases. □

Proof of Lemma 3

Proof. $sw_O = \frac{2z\{z[-z(\phi-1)(\phi+3)-2\phi(\phi+2)+4]+3\}+1}{2(2z(-z\phi+z+2)+1)^2}$. We want to evaluate the sign of $\frac{\partial sw_O}{\partial \phi}$, which can be expressed as

$$\frac{\partial sw_O}{\partial \phi} = \frac{[-4z^2 - 2z^3 - (4z^2 + 2z^3)\phi][2z(-z\phi + z + 2) + 1] + 2z^2}{[2z(-z\phi + z + 2) + 1]^3}$$

The denominator is positive for $\phi < \frac{2z^2+4z+1}{2z^2}$ and since, from the proof of Proposition 1, $\phi < \phi_E < \frac{2z^2+4z+1}{2z^2}$, we focus on the numerator. Let $N_1 = [-4z^2 - 2z^3 - (4z^2 + 2z^3)\phi][2z(-z\phi + z + 2) + 1]$ and $N_2 = 2z^2[1 + 6z + 8z^2 + 6z^3 - (8z^2 + 4z^3)\phi - (4z^2 + 2z^3)\phi^2]$, so that, with some algebraic manipulation, we obtain $N_1 + N_2 = -2z^2(2z+1)^2[2\phi + (\phi - 1)z + 1]$. It then follows that the sign of $\frac{\partial sw_O}{\partial \phi}$ is positive iff $\phi < \frac{z-1}{z+2} (= \phi^*)$.

Hence for $\phi < (>)\phi^*$, sw_O increases (decreases) in ϕ. Therefore, sw_O peaks at $\phi^* = \frac{z-1}{z+2}$ and reaches the first best since both v_O, q_O (see later) reach the first-best at ϕ^*.

In a similar manner we evaluate the derivative of

$$sw_E = \frac{56z^4 + 212z^3 - 16\left(z^2 + z + 1\right)\phi + 218z^2 + 87z - 6\phi^2 + 6}{[-24z(z+1) + 2\phi - 4]^2}$$

given by

$$\frac{\partial sw_E}{\partial \phi} = \frac{[-16(z^2+z+1)][-24z(z+1)+2\phi-4]^2 - 4[-24z(z+1)+2\phi-4](\cdot)}{[-24z(z+1)+2\phi-4]^4}$$

where in $(\cdot)$ we have $56z^4 + 212z^3 - 16\left(z^2 + z + 1\right)\phi + 218z^2 + 87z - 6\phi^2 + 6$. Let $N_1 = [-16(z^2+z+1)][-24z(z+1)+2\phi-4]^2$ and $N_2 = -4[-24z(z+1)+2\phi-4][56z^4 + 212z^3 - 16\left(z^2+z+1\right)\phi + 218z^2 + 87z - 6\phi^2 + 6]$ which leads to $N_1 + N_2 = 2[-12z(z+1)+\phi-2]$ $\{20(1+2z)^2[2+z(-3+2z)+4\phi]$.

Therefore,

$$\begin{aligned}\frac{\partial sw_E}{\partial \phi} &= \frac{2[-12z(z+1)+\phi-2]\{20(1+2z)^2[2+z(-3+2z)+4\phi]}{[-24z(z+1)+2\phi-4]^4} \\ &= \frac{5(1+2z)^2[2+z(-3+2z)+4\phi]}{2[-12z(z+1)+\phi-2]^3}\end{aligned}$$

which is negative because the denominator is negative $\forall\ z > 1$. The numerator is positive because $[2 + z(-3+2z) + 4\phi$ is an increasing function of ϕ and at $\phi = 0$ the expressions become $2 - 3z + 2z^2$, which is positive (the discriminator is negative and therefore the sign of the expressions is dictated by the sign of the coefficient of z^2), meaning that $\frac{\partial sw_E}{\partial \phi} < 0$.

Since sw_E is a decreasing function of ϕ, it suffices to show that $sw_E(0) < sw^*$. Evaluating this latter inequality and simplifying yields $2(1+2z)[2+z(-3+2z)]^2 > 0$.

Thus, $sw_E < sw^*, \forall \phi, z > 1$. □

Proof of Proposition 3

Proof. Let $sw_O - sw_E = \frac{N_1+N_2}{2[2z(-z\phi+z+2)+1]^2[-24z(z+1)+2\phi-4]^2}$, where $N_1 = [1+6z+8z^2+6z^3-(8z^2+4z^3)\phi-(4z^2+2z^3)\phi^2][-24z(z+1)+2\phi-4]^2$, $N_2 = -2[56z^4 + 212z^3 - 16\left(z^2+z+1\right)\phi + 218z^2 +$

$87z - 6\phi^2 + 6][2z(-z\phi + z + 2) + 1]^2$. After some tedious algebraic manipulation, we obtain:

$$\begin{aligned} N_1 + N_2 = & -2(2z+1)\{2z[2z^2(\phi-1) + 7z\phi + z - (\phi-3)\phi + 1] \\ & + 2\phi + 1\}\{z[28z^3(\phi-1) + z^2(66\phi-2) \\ & + z(6\phi^2 + 50\phi + 26) - 2\phi(2\phi+5) - 1] - 4\phi - 2\} \end{aligned}$$

Next, we examine the signs of the individual expressions in curly brackets. Let $P_1 = 2z\left[2z^2(\phi-1) + 7z\phi + z - (\phi-3)\phi + 1\right] + 2\phi + 1$ and $P_2 = z[28z^3(\phi-1) + z^2(66\phi-2) + z\left(6\phi^2 + 50\phi + 26\right) - 2\phi\,(2\phi+5) - 1] - 4\phi - 2$. P_1 has two solutions:

$$\phi_{1,2} = \frac{1 + 3z + 7z^2 + 2z^3 \pm \sqrt{1 + 8z + 27z^2 + 50z^3 + 53z^4 + 28z^5 + 4z^6}}{2z}$$

which should be within the $[0, z]$ interval. It is easy though tedious to show that $\phi_1 < z$ and $\phi_2 > z$.

Next we check whether $\phi_1 < 0$. To verify that, consider the constant term of P_1 in order to see under which cases it is positive. Let, $f(z) = 1 + 2z + 2z^2 - 4z^3$ and $f'(z) = 2 + 4z - 12z^2 = 2(1 + 2z - 6z^2)$. The discriminant of $f'(z) = 0$ is 28 and the roots are:

$$z_{1,2} = \begin{cases} \dfrac{1+\sqrt{7}}{4} \approx 0.6 \\ \dfrac{1-\sqrt{7}}{4} \end{cases}$$

Since the coefficient of z^2 is negative, for $z > 1$, $f'(z) < 0$ meaning that $f(z)$ is downward sloping. $f(1) = 1$ and $f(1.14) = -0.046976$, therefore there is a $\mu \in [1, 1.14]$ such that $f(z) < 0\ \forall z > \mu$. Since we consider $z > 2$, we have that $\phi_1 > 0\ \forall z > 2$. Thus,

$$\phi_1 = \frac{1 + 3z + 7z^2 + 2z^3 - \sqrt{1 + 8z + 27z^2 + 50z^3 + 53z^4 + 28z^5 + 4z^6}}{2z}$$

Therefore, $P_1 > 0$ for $\phi \in [\phi_1, z]$ and $P_1 < 0$ for $\phi \in [0, \phi_1]$.

We now focus on P_2. It has two roots, a negative and a positive one, the latter being:

$$\phi_3 = \frac{(2+5z-25z^2-33z^3-14z^4)}{2z(-2+3z)} + \frac{\sqrt{4+12z-67z^2-272z^3+75z^4+1410z^5+1957z^6+924z^7+196z^8}}{2z(-2+3z)}$$

For $\phi_3 < z$ it must hold that $-8z-8z^2+94z^3+80z^4-88z^5-152z^6-168z^7 < 0$, which is true for $z > 1$. Thus, $P_2 > 0$ for $\phi \in [\phi_3, z]$ and $P_2 < 0$ for $\phi \in [0, \phi_3]$. Note that in the main text we named ϕ_3 as ϕ_2.

To conclude, $sw_O - sw_E > 0 \; \forall \phi \in (\phi_1, \phi_2)$ and $sw_O - sw_E < 0 \; \forall \phi \in [0, \phi_1) \cup (\phi_2, z]$. Due to the complexity in the calculations, we use *Mathematica* software to show that ϕ_1, $\phi_2 < \phi_E$ as well as to show that $\phi_1 < \phi_2$. □

Proof of Proposition 4

Proof. Here we examine the derivative of $s\hat{w}_E$

$$\frac{\partial s\hat{w}_E}{\partial \phi} = \frac{4\phi[32+72z+\phi(8+5\phi)] - 2(8+10\phi)(28+14z+\phi^2)}{4[32+72z+\phi(8+5\phi)]^2}$$

Let $N_1 = 4\phi[32+72z+\phi(8+5\phi)]$ and $N_2 = -2(8+10\phi)(28+14z+\phi^2)$, so that, after some manipulation we obtain, $N_1 + N_2 = 8[2\phi^2 + (z - 54)\phi - (28z+56)]$.

$N_1 + N_2 = 0$ has two roots, a positive and a negative. The positive one is $\phi = 28$. Therefore, for $\phi \in [0, 28]$, $s\hat{w}_E$ is downward sloping. For $\phi > 28$, $s\hat{w}_E$ increases in ϕ.

Since we consider $z > 2$, in order to avoid uninteresting cases, we focus on $28 > \phi_E$, so that $\frac{\partial s\hat{w}_E}{\partial \phi} < 0, \forall \phi \in [0, \phi_E]$, $z > 1$.

Next, we compare sw_E and $s\hat{w}_E$. Since both functions decrease monotonically, if they intersect in the interval $[0, \phi_E]$, the difference $sw_E - s\hat{w}_E$ will be positive for some values of ϕ and negative otherwise. We can show that $sw_E(0) - s\hat{w}_E(0) > 0$.

Ignoring corner solutions and using the expressions for sw_E and $s\hat{w}_E$, to explore the relative positioning of the two curves, we substitute $\phi = \frac{z+1}{z}$. The reason we do not substitute ϕ with ϕ_E is that the resulting expressions are very complex. Following tedious manipulation we find that

$$sw_E\left(\frac{z+1}{z}\right) - \hat{sw}_E\left(\frac{z+1}{z}\right) > 0, \quad \forall\phi \in \left[0, \frac{z+1}{z}\right]$$

Finally, we check the relative positioning of sw_O and $\hat{sw}_O$. From, $\frac{\partial \hat{sw}_O}{\partial \phi} = \frac{-4[2z(\phi-4)+4\phi]}{[8+z(\phi-4)^2+2\phi^2]^2}$, it is evident that for $\phi < \frac{4z}{z+2}$, $\hat{sw}_O$ increases, while for $\phi > \frac{4z}{z+2}$, it decreases in ϕ.

It is relatively straightforward to show that the maximum of $\hat{sw}_O$ lies within the allowed bounds of ϕ, in particular $\frac{4z}{z+2} \leq \frac{z+1}{z}$ and since we consider $z > 2$, this condition is satisfied.

Therefore, $\hat{sw}_O$ increases in ϕ for $\phi > \frac{4z}{z+2}$, $z > 2$. For $\phi > \phi^*$, sw_O decreases, whereas $\hat{sw}_O$ increases and furthermore $sw_O(\phi^*) > \hat{sw}_O(\phi^*)$ $\forall z > 2$.

Next, we compare the social welfare functions at $\frac{z+1}{z}$: $sw_O(\frac{z+1}{z}) = \frac{-3-12z-12z^2}{2(1+2z)^2} = -\frac{3}{2} < 0$ and $\hat{sw}_O\left(\frac{z+1}{z}\right) = \frac{4z^2}{2+5z+4z^2+9z^3} > 0$.

Thus, by Bolzano's Theorem there is a $\phi_{sw} \in (0, \phi_c)$ such that $sw_O(\phi_{sw}) = \hat{sw}_O(\phi_{sw})$ and $sw_O > (<)\hat{sw}_O$ for $\phi < (>)\phi_{sw}$. Notice also that it is the case that $\phi_{sw} < \phi_E$, but due to the complexity of the calculations, we use *Mathematica* software to show that this is the case. □

References

Aoyama, N. and Silva, E. C. (2022). Abatement innovation in a Cournot oligopoly: Emission versus output tax incentives, *The Japanese Economic Review* **73**(2), 325–350.

Arora, S. and Cason, T. N. (1995). An experiment in voluntary environmental regulation: Participation in EPAs 33/50 program, *Journal of Environmental Economics and Management* **28**(3), 271–286.

Bansal, S. (2008). Choice and design of regulatory instruments in the presence of green consumers, *Resource and Energy Economics* **30**(3), 345–368.

Bansal, S. and Gangopadhyay, S. (2003). Tax/subsidy policies in the presence of environmentally aware consumers, *Journal of Environmental Economics and Management* **45**(2), 333–355.

Brouhle, K. and Khanna, M. (2007). Information and the provision of quality differentiated products, *Economic Inquiry* **45**(2), 377–394.

Conrad, K. (2005). Price competition and product differentiation when consumers care for the environment, *Environmental and Resource Economics* **31**, 1–19.

Constantatos, C., Pargianas, C. and Sartzetakis, E. S. (2021). Green consumers and environmental policy, *Journal of Public Economic Theory* **23**(1), 105–140.

Cremer, H. and Gahvari, F. (2001). Second-best taxation of emissions and polluting goods, *Journal of Public Economics* **80**(2), 169–197.

Delmas, M. A. and Montes-Sancho, M. J. (2010). Voluntary agreements to improve environmental quality: Symbolic and substantive cooperation, *Strategic Management Journal* **31**(6), 575–601.

Deltas, G., Harrington, D. R. and Khanna, M. (2013). Oligopolies with (somewhat) environmentally conscious consumers: Market equilibrium and regulatory intervention, *Journal of Economics & Management Strategy* **22**(3), 640–667.

Doni, N. and Ricchiuti, G. (2013). Market equilibrium in the presence of green consumers and responsible firms: A comparative statics analysis, *Resource and Energy Economics* **35**(3), 380–395.

Frondel, M., Horbach, J. and Rennings, K. (2007). End-of-pipe or cleaner production? an empirical comparison of environmental innovation decisions across oecd countries, *Business Strategy and the Environment* **16**(8), 571–584.

Fullerton, D., Hong, I. and Metcalf, G. E. (2001). A tax on output of the polluting industry is not a tax on pollution: The importance of hitting the target, in C. Carraro and G. E. Metcalf. (Eds.), *Behavioral and Distributional Effects of Environmental Policy*, pp. 13–44, University of Chicago Press, Chicago and London.

García-Gallego, A. and Georgantzís, N. (2009). Market effects of changes in consumers' social responsibility, *Journal of Economics & Management Strategy* **18**(1), 235–262.

Gil-Moltó, M. J. and Varvarigos, D. (2013). Emission taxes and the adoption of cleaner technologies: The case of environmentally conscious consumers, *Resource and Energy Economics* **35**(4), 486–504.

Lambertini, L. (2017). Green innovation and market power, *Annual Review of Resource Economics* **9**, 231–252.

Lyon, T. P. and Maxwell, J. W. (2003). Self-regulation, taxation and public voluntary environmental agreements, *Journal of Public Economics* **87**(7–8), 1453–1486.

Nyborg, K., Howarth, R. B. and Brekke, K. A. (2006). Green consumers and public policy: On socially contingent moral motivation, *Resource and Energy Economics* **28**(4), 351–366.

Petrakis, E., Sartzetakis, E. S. and Xepapadeas, A. (2005). Environmental information provision as a public policy instrument, *Contributions in Economic Analysis & Policy* **4**(1), 1–31.

Petrakis, E., Xepapadeas, A. *et al.* (2001). To commit or not to commit: Environmental policy in imperfectly competitive markets, *Typescript, Department of Economics, University of Crete*, https://ideas.repec.org/p/crt/wpaper/0110.html.

Poyago-Theotoky, J. A. (2007). The organization of R&D and environmental policy, *Journal of Economic Behavior & Organization* **62**(1), 63–75.

Poyago-Theotoky, J. and Teerasuwannajak, K. (2002). The timing of environmental policy: A note on the role of product differentiation, *Journal of Regulatory Economics* **21**(3), 305–316.

Requate, T. (2005). Timing and commitment of environmental policy, adoption of new technology, and repercussions on R&D, *Environmental and Resource Economics* **31**(2), 175–199.

Sartzetakis, E. S., Xepapadeas, A. and Petrakis, E. (2012). The role of information provision as a policy instrument to supplement environmental taxes, *Environmental and Resource Economics* **52**, 347–368.

Schmutzler, A. and Goulder, L. H. (1997). The choice between emission taxes and output taxes under imperfect monitoring, *Journal of Environmental Economics and Management* **32**(1), 51–64.

Segerson, K. and Miceli, T. J. (1998). Voluntary environmental agreements: Good or bad news for environmental protection? *Journal of Environmental Economics and Management* **36**(2), 109–130.

https://doi.org/10.1142/9789819816033_0007

Chapter 7

On Green R&D Organisation and Environmental Regulation: Cooperation vs. Non-Cooperation

Marie-Laure Cabon-Dhersin[*,‡] **and Natacha Raffin**[†,§]

[*] *Université Rouen Normandie, LERN, Rouen, France*
[†] *ENS Paris Saclay, CEPS, Gif-sur-Yvette, France*
[‡] *marie-laure.cabon-dhersin@univ-rouen.fr*
[§] *natacha.raffin@ens-paris-saclay.fr*

In this chapter, we compare taxes and standards as environmental policies in a duopoly model where production generates pollution. To lower their emissions, firms invest in upstream green R&D (in the presence of technological spillovers) either cooperatively or non-cooperatively, and then compete in quantities. The outcomes of the two policies are identical when firms do not cooperate in R&D; R&D cooperation under taxes always improves social welfare by increasing both abatement efforts and consumer surplus. Conversely, R&D cooperation under standards pushes firms to reduce production, which is detrimental to consumers though better for the environment and more profitable for firms.

Keywords: Emission tax, Environmental standards, Green R&D spillovers, R&D cooperation vs. competition.

1. Introduction

Governments in developed countries face escalating social pressure to enhance environmental protection, typically involving measures to mitigate industrial emissions. Among the array of pollution control tools, economists identify two primary sets of environmental policy instruments (Requate, 2005). The first set, including taxes, subsidies or tradable permits, leads to emission reduction through pricing, allowing firms to freely decide on their pollution levels. In contrast, the second and more prevalent set involves direct regulation of polluting emissions through environmental standards and caps on firms' emissions. Faced with these binding environmental policies, firms are driven to develop green R&D programs, cooperatively or not.

Some studies in the economic literature have compared the two types of environmental policy instruments, examining the price vs. quantity duality, as evidenced in surveys by Requate (2005) and Hepburn (2006). While many of them emphasise the advantages of environmental taxes in encouraging firms to invest in abatement technologies compared to other instruments Requate and Unold (2003), a competitive oligopoly model, as presented by Montero (2002), suggests that emission standards may offer greater incentives than permits. Taking a closer look at regulators' ability to commit to environmental policy, Moner-Colonques and Rubio (2015, 2016) compare the performance of an emission standard with an emission tax in a competitive R&D framework. Their findings indicate that (i) when the government can commit to its environmental policy before firms' R&D decisions, both policy instruments are equivalent, (ii) when the government cannot commit, the tax performs better in terms of innovation and social welfare. Cabon-Dhersin and Raffin (2024) expand these comparisons to cooperative R&D strategic behaviours although they do not compare the effectiveness of cooperation over non-cooperation.

In this chapter, our objective is to contribute to those existing comparisons by specifically examining the organisational structures of R&D among firms. An important question is how the (non-)cooperative nature of green R&D may influence the effectiveness of environmental policies. Following Moner-Colonques and Rubio (2015, 2016) and Cabon-Dhersin and Raffin (2024), we focus on the two most widely applied instruments: an emission standard (a command-and-control instrument) and an emission tax (a market-based instrument). Therefore, we compare their environmental and economic performances based on whether firms adopt cooperative strategies in R&D or not.

A substantial body of economic literature on innovation emphasises the positive effects of R&D cooperation among competing firms on incentives for R&D investment and on social welfare.[1] The mechanism underlying the benefits of R&D cooperation is based on the existence of technological spillovers generated by R&D activities and the imperfect appropriability of their returns. Spillovers tend to discourage firms from investing in R&D because some of the knowledge generated is appropriated by their rivals Arrow (1962). By adopting R&D cooperation strategies, firms internalise the effects of spillovers on aggregate profits, whereas R&D rivals only consider the competitive impact of R&D flows on their respective costs. A seminal result, established by d'Aspremont and Jacquemin (1988), indicates that above a certain spillover threshold, cooperative R&D investments yield a higher total surplus than non-cooperative R&D. Furthermore, R&D investments increase with the level of spillovers when firms cooperate but decrease when they do not. Numerous theoretical and empirical contributions have confirmed the positive impact of horizontal R&D cooperation for both firms and consumers. Therefore, in many jurisdictions, in response to a consumer welfare standard, competition authorities do not prohibit these horizontal agreements in the presence of substantial technological spillovers (e.g., Article 85 of the EEC treaty, Article 101(3) of the Treaty on the functioning of the European Union for categories of research and development agreements, the Act on Mining and Manufacturing Industry Technology Research Association in Japan, or the National Cooperative Research Act in the USA).

In this study, we investigate whether the positive impact of R&D cooperation persists when the two types of environmental policies under examination are implemented. In other words, does R&D cooperation continue to foster green innovation and social welfare

[1] See Marinucci (2012) for a review of the literature on R&D cooperation.

when environmental policies such as a tax or an emission standard are enforced, as opposed to independent R&D? Another critical aspect is to determine which environmental policy instrument (tax vs. standard) is more effective in reducing polluting emissions and achieving desirable economic performances (innovation, consumer surplus, and social welfare), depending on whether firms engage in R&D cooperation or not. These questions are particularly relevant as the European Commission is currently revising its guidelines on horizontal cooperation agreements, proposing a new chapter on sustainability agreements.[2]

Recent studies have also offered partial insights, particularly in cases where the environmental policy instrument is a tax. However, the combination of green R&D cooperation and environmental standards has not been thoroughly examined. When focusing solely on an environmental tax policy, the model proposed by Chiou and Hu (2001) offers a comparison of various forms of cooperation with R&D competition, albeit without endogenising the tax. They demonstrate that green R&D cooperation when spillovers are sufficiently high maximises R&D efforts and social welfare but minimises emissions. Conversely, the endogenisation of cooperative choices is addressed by Ouchida and Goto (2016b) in a framework where the emission tax is set by a non-committed regulator. Their results confirm those previously obtained by Poyago-Theotoky (2007): In the context of an environmental research joint venture (ERJV), cartelisation is welfare-improving when emissions are highly damaging, provided that R&D is sufficiently inefficient. However, when firms' R&D investments are influenced by the emission tax rate determined by the regulator, who acts as the first mover, the results become more straightforward: green R&D cartelisation is always socially desirable (Ouchida and Goto (2016a, 2022)).

Our contribution builds upon existing works while we address the joint issues of determining the most suitable environmental policy instrument and evaluating the effectiveness of R&D cooperation in

[2]See the European Commission-Press Release "Antitrust: Commission adopts new Horizontal Block Exemption Regulations and Horizontal Guidelines", https://ec.europa.eu/commission/presscorner/detail/en/IP_23_2990.

the provision of end-of-pipe technologies. We provide a theoretical model based on a multi-stage game. In the first stage, the regulator optimally sets the level of the tax or the standard. We presume that environmental policies are credible – the regulator is able to commit to its policy – as they might be driven by international environmental agreements for instance. Then, in stage 2, the firms invest cooperatively or non-cooperatively in green R&D, before competing in quantities at stage 3. This framework allows us to identify the optimal strategic behaviour of the firms for a given environmental policy instrument and the optimal policy instrument depending on whether the firms cooperate or not in green R&D.

We find that R&D cooperation enhances economic performance (green R&D, consumer surplus, and social welfare) when a tax is implemented. These findings align consistently with the conclusions drawn from the previously cited literature. However, when an emission standard is adopted, the advantages of cooperation over independent R&D may disappear, especially for low spillovers and inefficient R&D. When a standard is implemented, cooperation in R&D can lead firms to reduce their production through an anti-competitive effect. More precisely, the R&D cartel acts as a production cartel aiming to reduce green innovation, output, and increase prices, to the detriment of consumer welfare. This result supports the view of critics of R&D cooperation that less competition necessarily leads to less R&D (Scott (2008)). Moreover, if we compare the performance of R&D cooperation under the two instruments, the outcomes are socially more favourable under the tax because of higher R&D efforts and higher consumer surplus. One interesting observation though is that under an emission standard, since the R&D cartel reduces production, the overall level of pollution is lower: a tax therefore has lower environmental efficiency than the standard. Finally, when firms conduct R&D independently, we replicate the results obtained elsewhere that the tax and the standard both lead to the same outcomes at equilibrium, for any levels of spillovers.

The remaining part of the chapter is structured as follows. Section 2 introduces the model. Section 3 examines the emission tax policy (ETP) and the R&D strategic behaviour of the firms (cooperative vs. non-cooperative). In Section 4, we apply the same reasoning while we assess an emission standard policy (ESP). Section 5 compares the results obtained for an ESP and an ETP. Finally, Section 6 concludes.

2. The Model

In this chapter, we consider a duopoly where two identical competing firms, i, j, produce a homogeneous good with the same polluting production technology. Demand is described by a simple linear function: $P(Q) = a - Q$, where Q is the total level of production, $Q \leq a$. Firm i's output is denoted q_i, such that $Q = q_i + q_j$.

The production process in both firms is environmentally degrading such that each unit of output generates exactly one unit of pollution. However, the firms can reduce their emissions by investing in green end-of-pipe technologies, z. Moreover, we consider the presence of green R&D spillovers in that the firms benefit from their rival's pollution mitigation efforts in a proportion $\beta \in (0, 1]$, at no cost. The parameter β is exogenously given and is not affected by the firms' R&D behaviour. Therefore, by investing in green R&D, firm i can reduce its gross polluting emissions by between $z_i + \beta z_j$ and $z_i + z_j$. Accordingly, firm i's net emissions can be expressed as:

$$e_i = e(q_i, z_i) = q_i - z_i - \beta z_j \tag{1}$$

We assume that the R&D cost function is quadratic, leading to diminishing returns on R&D investments. Firm i's cost function is additively separable and given by $C(q_i; z_i) = cq_i + \gamma {z_i}^2/2$. In this setup, the marginal cost of production is constant and equal to c with $a > c > 0$. In addition, γ is usually interpreted as a measure of R&D efficiency, with firm i having to spend an amount $\gamma z_i^2/2$ to reduce their emissions by z_i. In what follows, we investigate the effectiveness of two environmental policies in two different scenarios h:

- In the first scenario ($h = nc$), the firms do not cooperate in R&D and compete during the production stage;
- In the second scenario ($h = c$), the firms coordinate their green R&D investments to maximise the sum of their profits although they compete during the production stage.[3]

[3]This approach, referred to as an R&D cartel, is well-documented in the literature on R&D cooperation. Our analysis also covers the case in which $\beta = 1$,

Given the net emissions of each firm, the total level of emissions is $E^h = \sum_i^j e^h(q_i^h, z_i^h)\ \forall\, h = \{nc, c\}$. The environmental damage is given by the function $D(E^h) = d(E^h)^2/2$, which is assumed to be quadratic, with $d > 0$ being the slope of the marginal environmental damage curve, i.e., the severity of the damage. Finally, to protect the environment, governments implement environmental policies to which they commit *ex ante*. Two instruments are separately considered in the following: a per unit tax on emissions and an emission standard. When the regulator enforces an Emission Tax Policy (ETP), the game has three stages: In stage 1, the regulator sets the level of the emission tax so as to maximise social welfare. In stage 2, the firms invest, non-cooperatively or cooperatively, in green R&D; and in stage 3, the firms compete in quantities. When the regulator implements an Emission Standard Policy (ESP), the game has only two stages: outputs are determined once the regulator has set the emission standard (stage 1) and the firms have adopted, non-cooperatively or cooperatively, their R&D efforts (stage 2).

We solve the multi-stage game by backward induction and obtain the equilibrium outcomes for the two environmental policy tools (ETP and ESP) and the two types of R&D behaviour (non-cooperative and cooperative).

3. Green R&D under an Emission Tax Policy (ETP)

When the regulator adopts an emission tax policy, it imposes a per-unit tax, denoted as τ, on each unit of polluting production (q), where $\tau > 0$ represents the environmental tax. In an effort to alleviate the impact of the tax, firms invest in green R&D expenditures (z). Consequently, the tax is applied exclusively to the net emissions, reflecting the emissions after accounting for the environmentally friendly innovations resulting from the green R&D activities (τe). Moreover, firms either coordinate or not their R&D activities while competing in production.

In the last stage of the game, no matter whether the firms cooperate in R&D or not, and using equation (1), firm i chooses the level

that is when firms form a cartelised Research Joint Venture (RJV) whereby they coordinate their R&D efforts and share all the resulting knowledge.

of output q_i that maximises its profits below, taking its' rival's R&D efforts as given, $\forall i, j$:

$$\pi_i(q_i, z_i) = (a - Q)q_i - cq_i - \gamma z_i^2/2 - \tau(q_i - z_i - \beta z_j) \tag{2}$$

By symmetry and the First-Order Condition (FOC) w.r.t. q_i, a firm's equilibrium output under an ETP is:

$$q(\tau) = \frac{A - \tau}{3} \tag{3}$$

where $A = a - c > 0$ and A is a measure of market size. Obviously, this individual equilibrium output depends negatively on the stringency of the tax. Hence, we can re-write a firm's profits, $\forall i, j$, as:

$$\pi_i(\tau, z_i) = q(\tau)^2 + \tau(z_i + \beta z_j) - \gamma z_i^2/2 \tag{4}$$

Let us now turn to the second stage of the game and compute the equilibrium outcomes in the non-cooperative and cooperative green R&D sub-games. If the firms compete during the green R&D stage, they simultaneously choose their levels of R&D spending, taking the R&D spillovers from their competitor as given. If, on the contrary, they choose to cooperate, they maximise the sum of their profits: $\Pi = \sum_i^j \pi_i(\tau, z_i)$. Then, symmetrically and taking the ETP as given, we obtain the individual equilibrium green R&D efforts in each scenario h:

$$\begin{cases} z^{nc}(\tau) = \dfrac{\tau}{\gamma} \\ z^{c}(\tau) = (1 + \beta)\dfrac{\tau}{\gamma} \end{cases} \tag{5}$$

These equilibrium levels of green R&D investment consistently rise in response to higher tax rates, resulting in a decrease in polluting emissions. It is important to observe that within the context of R&D cooperation, incentives for investing in green R&D grow with the degree of spillover. This contrasts with situations where firms do not cooperate. In fact, in line with the economic literature on R&D, coordination ensures that the issue of free-riding is internalised. From equation (1) and for a given ETP, we can deduce individual polluting emissions in each scenario:

$$\begin{cases} e^{nc}(\tau) = \dfrac{A}{3} - \dfrac{3(1+\beta)+\gamma}{3\gamma}\tau \\ e^{c}(\tau) = \dfrac{A}{3} - \dfrac{3(1+\beta)^2+\gamma}{3\gamma}\tau \end{cases} \tag{6}$$

As expected, emissions decline with the strengthening of the environmental constraint. In addition, under R&D cooperation, emissions are lower than under R&D competition by an amount equal to $\frac{\beta(1+\beta)}{\gamma}\tau$ for the same given tax rate. This implies that the extent of spillover becomes a determining factor – the higher the spillover rate, the less pollution occurs when firms engage in R&D cooperation, resulting in a wider gap in emissions between the two scenarios.

Using equations (5) and (6), we can alternatively express the equilibrium R&D effort as a function of emissions in each scenario:

$$\begin{cases} z^{nc}(e) = \dfrac{A-3e}{3(1+\beta)+\gamma} \\ z^{c}(e) = (1+\beta)\dfrac{A-3e}{3(1+\beta)^2+\gamma} \end{cases} \tag{7}$$

where $z^{nc}(e)$ and $z^{c}(e)$ are positive for $A-3e>0$. From these equations, we can confirm our earlier claim that R&D is consistently greater in the cooperative scenario compared to the non-cooperative one, for all values of γ and β:

$$z^{c}(e) - z^{nc}(e) = \frac{\beta\gamma}{(3(1+\beta)^2+\gamma)(3(1+\beta)+\gamma)}(A-3e) > 0 \tag{8}$$

From this differential, we can also deduce that cooperation promotes production, for a given level of emissions (see equation (1)): $q^{c}(e) - q^{nc}(e) > 0$.

Turning to the first stage of the game, the regulator sets the welfare-optimal environmental tax rate based on how firms will respond to it. Social welfare (SW) is defined as the sum of consumer surplus (CS), firms' profits (PS) and tax revenues minus the environmental damage:

$$SW^h = \underbrace{\frac{(Q^h)^2}{2}}_{\text{CS}} + \underbrace{(\pi_i^h + \pi_j^h)}_{\text{PS}} + \underbrace{\tau E^h}_{\text{Tax revenue}} - \underbrace{D(E^h)}_{\text{Environmental damage}}$$
$$h = \{nc, c\} \tag{9}$$

Hence, using equations (3), (5) and (9), the social welfare, for a given ETP, can be written, in each scenario h, as follows:

$$\begin{cases} SW^{nc}(\tau) = 2\left(A\left(\frac{A-\tau}{3}\right) - \left(\frac{A-\tau}{3}\right)^2 - \frac{\tau^2}{2\gamma} \right. \\ \qquad \left. -d\left(\frac{A-\tau}{3} - (1+\beta)\frac{\tau}{\gamma}\right)^2\right) \\ SW^{c}(\tau) = 2\left(A\left(\frac{A-\tau}{3}\right) - \left(\frac{A-\tau}{3}\right)^2 - (1+\beta)^2\frac{(\tau)^2}{2\gamma} \right. \\ \qquad \left. -d\left(\frac{A-\tau}{3} - (1+\beta)^2\frac{\tau}{\gamma}\right)^2\right) \end{cases} \tag{10}$$

Equilibrium environmental taxes are obtained from the FOCs with respect to τ:[4]

$$\begin{cases} \tau^{*,nc} = 2\gamma\frac{2d(3(1+\beta)+\gamma)-\gamma}{X}A \\ \tau^{*,c} = \gamma\frac{2d(3(1+\beta)^2+\gamma)-\gamma}{Y}A \end{cases} \tag{11}$$

with $X = 2d(3(1+\beta)+\gamma)^2 + \gamma(9+2\gamma) > 0$ and $Y = 2d(3(1+\beta)^2 + \gamma)^2 + \gamma(9(1+\beta)^2 + 2\gamma) > 0$. Using equations (11) into (3), (5) and

[4]The second-order condition for welfare maximisation always holds, i.e., $\frac{\partial^2 SW}{\partial \tau^2} < 0$. Notice that Ouchida and Goto (2016a) provides a clear comparison of the two equilibrium tax rates. From their Corollary 1 (p. 327), one knows that when there is no product differentiation – i.e., $\theta = 1$ in their setting – and $d > 1$, the non-cooperative tax rate is always higher with respect to cooperative one.

(10), we derive equilibrium green R&D efforts, outputs and social welfares (see Table A.1). A natural question to address is which of the two scenarios (cooperation or non-cooperation) generates more R&D and how the equilibrium ETPs compare. As demonstrated by Ouchida and Goto (2016a) when there is no product differentiation, we first present some comparisons in the following lemma:

Lemma 1. *Under an ETP,* $\forall d \geq 1$, $\gamma > 0$ *and* $\beta \in (0, 1]$,

(1) $z^{*,c} > z^{*,nc}$,
(2) $CS^{*,c} = 2\,(q^{*,c})^2 > 2\,(q^{*,nc})^2 = CS^{*,nc}$,
(3) $SW^{*,c} > SW^{*,nc}$.

The better welfare performance of R&D cooperation stems mainly from the larger consumer surplus when firms cooperate. According to equation (3), output demonstrates an inverse relationship with the tax. Since the tax is lower under R&D cooperation, as demonstrated by Ouchida and Goto (2016a), production levels exceed those of the non-cooperative scenario, thereby benefitting consumers. Let's remind the reader that when spillovers are internalised within a R&D cooperation agreement, this leads to a stronger response from firms to a tax policy, prompting them to increase their green R&D efforts more than in a non-cooperative scenario. Consequently, the regulator has less incentive to tax firms to stimulate R&D expenditures. However, the heightened production levels lead to increased emissions. For technological spillover levels sufficiently high (>0.5), the increase in R&D efforts could more than offset the joint increase in production and resulting emissions, ultimately reducing net polluting emissions: $e^{*,c} < e^{*,nc}$ (see Fig. 1). Despite, the additional costs incurred by firms to finance R&D expenditure, the overall damage is mitigated and the consumer surplus is higher, resulting in a larger welfare. Conversely, in configurations characterised by low spillovers, it is conceivable that net emissions within the cooperative R&D framework surpass those in the non-cooperative scenario: $e^{*,c} > e^{*,nc}$ (see also Fig. 1). Therefore, the superior welfare performance of R&D cooperation primarily arises from its more substantial positive impact on consumer surplus, notwithstanding a comparatively poorer environmental performance – entailing a higher damage.

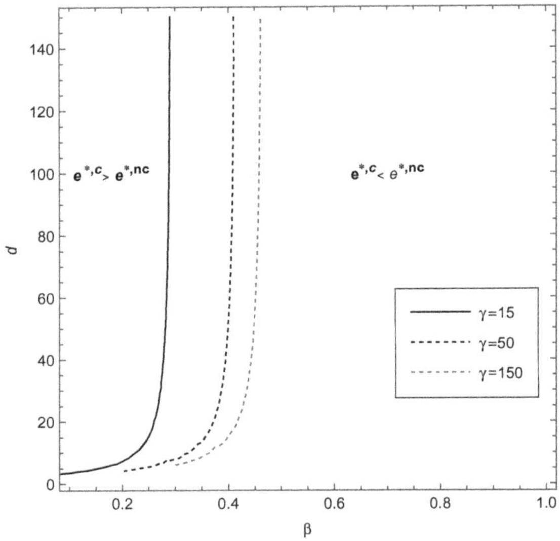

Fig. 1. Emissions difference under ETP when the firms cooperate or not in green R&D.

4. Green R&D under an Emission Standard Policy (ESP)

Under the Emission Standard Policy, the regulator enforces a limit on polluting emissions induced by firms production, $\bar{e}$. Therefore, by investing in green R&D, firm i may produce more ($q_i > \bar{e}$) though net emissions must satisfy the environmental constraint, $\bar{e} = q_i - z_i - \beta z_j$. Notice that to comply with the emission standard, firms benefit, at least partially, from the green R&D effort of their rival.

Different from the ETP, the firms may still opt for a cooperative or non-cooperative green R&D effort, but as an ESP is implemented, the production competition stage vanishes. Indeed, everything goes as if the firms simultaneously choose their levels of production and R&D investment, since polluting is limited. Essentially, per-firm outputs are predetermined by the emission cap and the R&D efforts selected by the firms (with variables under the ESP denoted by a superscript line): $\bar{q}_i = \bar{e} + \bar{z}_i + \beta\bar{z}_j$. Let us directly jump to stage 2 of the game, where firms adopt their green R&D investments. When the two firms do not cooperate in green R&D, they maximise their respective profits, taking the emission standard $\bar{e}$ as given. The optimisation program for firm i is, for all i, j:

$$\begin{cases} \max_{\bar{z}_i} \ \bar{\pi}_i^{nc} = (A - \bar{Q})\bar{q}_i - \dfrac{\gamma \bar{z}_i^2}{2} \\ \text{s.t. } \bar{q}_i = \bar{e} + \bar{z}_i + \beta \bar{z}_j \end{cases} \tag{12}$$

In the case where the firms coordinate their R&D efforts, they choose the level of green investment that maximises their joint profit under the two individual constraints defined by the ESP. The program for firm i becomes, $\forall i, j$:

$$\begin{cases} \max_{\bar{z}_i} & \sum \bar{\pi}_i^c = (A - \bar{Q})(\bar{q}_i + \bar{q}_j) - \dfrac{\gamma \bar{z}_i^2}{2} - \dfrac{\gamma \bar{z}_j^2}{2} \\ \text{s.t.} & \bar{q}_i = \bar{e} + \bar{z}_i + \beta \bar{z}_j \\ & \bar{q}_j = \bar{e} + \bar{z}_j + \beta \bar{z}_i \end{cases} \tag{13}$$

Then, by symmetry, the equilibrium levels of green R&D in each scenario can be expressed as a function of the emission standard only:

$$\begin{cases} \bar{z}^{nc}(\bar{e}) = \dfrac{A - 3\bar{e}}{3(1+\beta) + \gamma} \\ \bar{z}^{c}(\bar{e}) = (1+\beta)\dfrac{(A - 4\bar{e})}{4(1+\beta)^2 + \gamma} \end{cases} \tag{14}$$

As expected, these equilibrium green R&D efforts increase with the stringency of the environmental policy: firms tend to increase their R&D efforts when governments tighten their emission standards. Notice that in the non-cooperative scenario, the similarity between equations (7) and (14) implies that, for a given environmental objective $e = \bar{e}$, equilibrium R&D efforts are consistent regardless of the instrument used, ETP or ESP. Moreover, like in Section 3, outcomes of cooperative and non-cooperative R&D strategies can also be compared for a given emission cap. In particular, using equation (14), we obtain:

$$\bar{z}^{c}(\bar{e}) - \bar{z}^{nc}(\bar{e}) = -\frac{((1+\beta)^2 - \beta\gamma)A + (1+4\beta)\gamma\bar{e}}{(4(1+\beta)^2 + \gamma)(3(1+\beta) + \gamma)} \tag{15}$$

Contrary to the usual results in the literature on R&D cooperation, we find that green R&D efforts in the non-cooperative scenario can be higher than those in the cooperative scenario even when spillovers are high, provided the abatement technology is very efficient (γ is low). For larger values of γ however, we obtain the "expected" result that for sufficiently large spillovers, R&D investments are higher when firms cooperate and increase with the level of spillover, whereas under non-cooperative R&D they decrease (d'Aspremont and Jacquemin, 1988; Kamien *et al.*, 1992).

Taking the firms' R&D choices as given, we can now deduce the equilibrium outputs in each scenario:

$$\begin{cases} \bar{q}^{nc}(\bar{e}) = \dfrac{(1+\beta)A + \gamma\bar{e}}{3(1+\beta)+\gamma} \\ \bar{q}^{c}(\bar{e}) = \dfrac{(1+\beta)^2 A + \gamma\bar{e}}{4(1+\beta)^2+\gamma} \end{cases} \tag{16}$$

Like under an ETP, as the emission cap becomes more binding, per-firm outputs diminish, regardless the firms R&D strategic behaviour. For a given ESP, we can highlight a positive and linear relationship between the production and R&D differentials:

$$\bar{q}^{c}(\bar{e}) - \bar{q}^{nc}(\bar{e}) = (1+\beta)\left(\bar{z}^{c}(\bar{e}) - \bar{z}^{nc}(\bar{e})\right)$$

Because green R&D expenditure might be lower when the firms cooperate, it implies that levels of production might also be lower (in particular for low values of β and γ). R&D cooperation pushes the firms to reduce production and their R&D effort. The cartel solution is even reached when spillovers are null.

Finally, at the first stage of the game, the government maximises the social welfare function by determining the emission standard, taking as given the equilibrium green R&D efforts of the two firms previously obtained. In the absence of environmental taxation, social welfare is now defined as follows:

$$S\bar{W}^h = \frac{(\bar{Q}^h)^2}{2} + (\bar{\pi}_i^h + \bar{\pi}_j^h) - D(\bar{\mathrm{E}}^h), \quad h = \{nc, c\} \tag{17}$$

Then, using equations (14) and (16), the social welfare function can be expressed, in each scenario h, as a function of the emission standard only:

$$\begin{cases} \bar{SW}^{nc}(\bar{e}) = 2\left(A\left(\frac{(1+\beta)A+\gamma\bar{e}}{3(1+\beta)+\gamma}\right) - \left(\frac{(1+\beta)A+\gamma\bar{e}}{3(1+\beta)+\gamma}\right)^2 \right. \\ \qquad\qquad \left. -\frac{\gamma}{2}\left(\frac{A-3\bar{e}}{(3(1+\beta)+\gamma)}\right)^2 - d\bar{e}^2\right) \\ \bar{SW}^{c}(\bar{e}) = 2\left(A\left(\frac{(1+\beta)^2A+\gamma\bar{e}}{4(1+\beta)^2+\gamma}\right) - \left(\frac{(1+\beta)^2A+\gamma\bar{e}}{4(1+\beta)^2+\gamma}\right)^2 \right. \\ \qquad\qquad \left. -\frac{\gamma}{2}\left(\frac{(1+\beta)(A-4\bar{e})}{4(1+\beta)^2+\gamma}\right)^2 - d\bar{e}^2\right) \end{cases} \tag{18}$$

Equilibrium ESP in both cases can be deduced from the FOCs w.r.t. $\bar{e}$:

$$\begin{cases} \bar{e}^{*,nc} = \gamma\frac{((4+\beta)+\gamma)}{X}A \\ \bar{e}^{*,c} = \gamma\frac{(6(1+\beta)^2+\gamma)}{W}A \end{cases} \tag{19}$$

with $W = 2d(4(1+\beta)^2+\gamma)^2 + 2\gamma(8(1+\beta)^2+\gamma) > 0$. Figure 2 depicts the emissions difference under an ESP, depending on whether the firms coordinate their R&D efforts or not. It clearly appears that cooperation induces lower emissions for most relevant parameters configurations while this is not true only when both the severity of the damage is huge and R&D is very inefficient. As shown in the following lemma, this is mainly due to lower production levels as the firms adopt a cartel-like behaviour under an ESP. Using equation (19) into equations (14), (16) and (18), we obtain the SPNE levels of green R&D, production and social welfare (see Table A.2).

The lemma below provides broad insights into the ranking of economic outcomes in the cooperative and non-cooperative scenario under an equilibrium ESP.

Lemma 2. *Under an ESP,* $\forall d \geq 1$ *and* $\beta \in (0, 1]$,

- *for* $\gamma < 4$, $\bar{z}^{*,c} < \bar{z}^{*,nc}$, $\bar{CS}^{*,c} < \bar{CS}^{*,nc}$ *and* $\bar{SW}^{*,c} < \bar{SW}^{*,nc}$,
- *for* $\gamma \geq 4$,
  (a) $\bar{z}^{*,c} \gtreqless \bar{z}^{*,nc}$ *when* $d \gtreqless d_{\bar{z}}(\beta, \gamma)$;

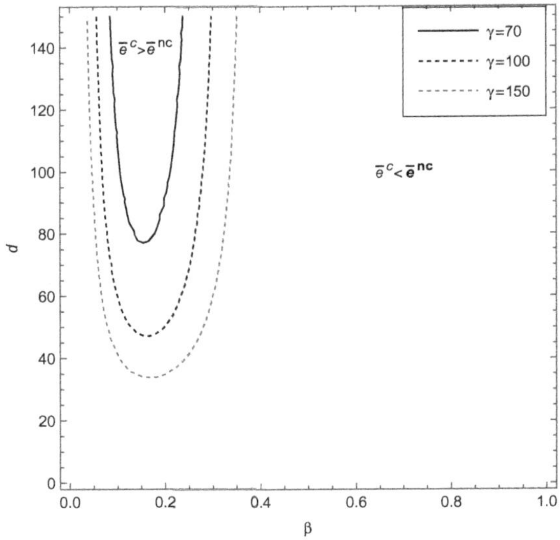

Fig. 2. Emissions difference under ESP when the firms cooperate or not in green R&D.

(b) $\bar{CS}^{*,c} \gtreqqless \bar{CS}^{*,nc}$ *when* $d \gtreqqless d_{\bar{CS}}(\beta,\gamma)$;

(c) $S\bar{W}^{*,c} \lesseqqgtr S\bar{W}^{*,nc}$ *when* $d \lesseqqgtr d_{S\bar{W}}(\beta,\gamma)$;

with $d_{\mathcal{X}}(\beta,\gamma)$ *defined in Appendix* B.

Proof. See the proof in Appendix B. □

Under an ESP, the comparative performance of the two scenarios crucially hinges upon the efficiency of green R&D refer to equation (15): When R&D is efficient ($\gamma < 4$), whatever the parameter values for β and d, non-coordinated innovation results in higher green R&D efforts and further larger consumer surplus and social welfare (see Fig. 3(a)). When R&D is inefficient ($\gamma \geq 4$), there exists a threshold $d(\beta,\gamma)$ that delineates Region A, where cooperative outcomes are more socially desirable, from Region B, where non-cooperation performs globally better (see Figs. 3(b) and 3(c)). In Region A, firms trigger more innovation efforts which lead to increased production levels and a tightening of environmental regulations. Consequently, welfare is higher in the cooperative scenario. It is true all the more that spillovers are sufficiently high, consistent with the literature on R&D cooperation. However, at low spillover

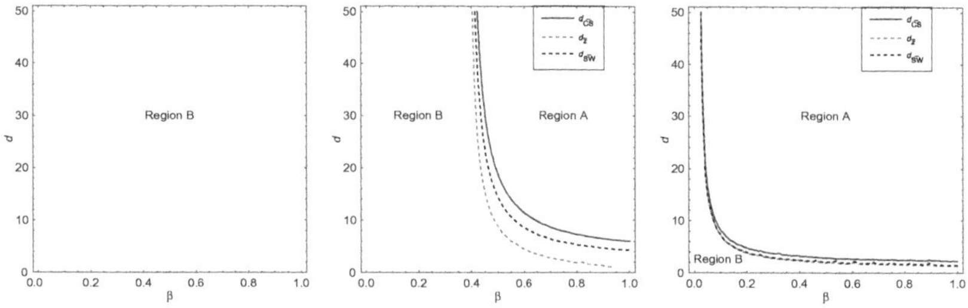

(a) $\gamma = 2$ (b) $\gamma = 5$ (c) $\gamma = 70$

Fig. 3. Non-cooperation vs. cooperation under ESP.

levels, to circumvent the environmental constraint in the cooperative scenario, the firms choose reduce production instead of investing in R&D, irrespective of the efficiency of the green technology. The decline in production is offset by a rise in prices, adversely affecting consumer surplus. As a consequence, cooperative social welfare becomes lower than the non-cooperative one (Region B).

5. ETP versus ESP

In this final section, we compare the two environmental policy instruments when firms cooperate in R&D and when they do not.

5.1. *Non-cooperation in R&D*

Let us first establish the similarity of the two policy instruments when firms do not cooperate in green R&D.

Lemma 3. *For all* $\beta \in (0,1], \gamma > 0$ *and* $d \geq 1$, $e^{*,nc} = \bar{e}^{*,nc}$.

Proof. From equations (6), (19) and equilibrium outcomes given in Table A.1, it is straightforward that equilibrium individual emissions are identical under ETP and ESP. □

Then, using Lemma 3, we can assess different economic outcomes.

Proposition 1. *In the non-cooperative R&D scenario, for all* $\beta \in (0,1], \gamma > 0$ *and* $d \geq 1$:

- $z^{*,nc} = \bar{z}^{*,nc}$,
- $CS^{*,nc} = \tilde{CS}^{*,nc}$,

- $SW^{*,nc} = \bar{SW}^{*,nc}$,
- $\bar{\pi}^{*,nc} > \pi^{*,nc}$.

Proof. From Tables A.1 and A.2, we can see that innovation, consumer surplus (deduced from equilibrium per-firm outputs) and social welfare are identical. Finally, from the definition of profits, we deduce:

$$\bar{\pi}^{*,nc} - \pi^{*,nc} = \tau^{*,nc}\left(q^{*,nc} - (1+\beta)z^{*,nc}\right) = \tau^{*,nc}e^{*,nc} > 0 \qquad \square$$

These results have partially been reported in the literature (see Moner-Colonques and Rubio (2015, 2016)). However, in our setup, it is obtained in a duopoly game rather than a monopoly, and in the presence of R&D spillovers. In this context, the similarity between the two types of instruments is driven by the binding target on emissions given by equation (1). At the R&D/production stage, the firms compete in the same way under the two instruments. As an ETP is enforced, the tax burden disappears: the cost of taxation associated with an additional unit of polluting production is precisely offset by a reduction in taxation resulting from an additional unit of the firm's R&D effort. Then, the firms' only consideration when choosing their R&D investments is the trade-off between the direct cost of R&D and its benefit in terms of increased production. This is the same trade-off as under an ESP. The competition conditions are therefore exactly the same way whether the policy instrument is an emission tax or an emission standard. Consequently, the regulator designs the optimal environmental policy based on a similar objective function, irrespective of the nature of the policy instrument. Therefore, the emission standard adopted by the regulator is consistent with individual equilibrium emissions levels induced by the ETP. In addition, the economic performances – innovation, consumer surplus and social welfare – are similar. Notice however that, as far as profits are concerned, the similarity does not hold any-more due to the tax burden on firms.

5.2. *Cooperation in R&D*

Let us now compare emissions according to the policy instrument when the firms coordinate their green R&D efforts:

Lemma 4. *For all* $\beta \in (0,1], \gamma > 0$ *and* $d \geq 1$, $e^{*,c} > \bar{e}^{*,c}$.

Proof. From equations (6) and (11), individual equilibrium emissions generated under an ETP can be deduced:

$$e^{*,c} = \gamma \frac{(4(1+\beta)^2 + \gamma)}{Y} A$$

Then, using equation (19), the difference in emission levels between the two policy instruments when firms cooperate in R&D is given by the following expression:

$$e^{*,c} - \bar{e}^{*,c} = \frac{A\gamma}{YW}(1+\beta)^2(2d(1+\beta)^2 + \gamma)(10(1+\beta)^2 + 3\gamma) > 0$$

□

The two policy instruments perform differently from an environmental point of view when the firms cooperate in R&D, contrary to what happens when they choose their R&D efforts separately (see Lemma 3). More precisely, under an ESP, the firms emit less than they would under an ETP, mainly because they produce less. The following proposition help us to further describe the key mechanisms at stake:

Proposition 2. *In the cooperative R&D scenario, for all* $\beta \in (0,1], \gamma > 0$ *and* $d \geq 1$:

- $z^{*,c} > \bar{z}^{*,c}$,
- $CS^{*,c} > \bar{CS}^{*,c}$,
- $SW^{*,c} > \bar{SW}^{*,c}$,
- $\bar{\pi}^{*,c} > \pi^{*,c}$.

Proof. See the proof in Appendix C. □

Proposition 2 shows that when the firms cooperate in green R&D, an ETP outperforms an ESP except as far as profits are concerned. First of all and like in the articles by Ouchida and Goto (2016a,b) and Cabon-Dhersin and Raffin (2024) among others, a tax always drives the firms to increase their cooperative efforts of R&D – with respect to the non-cooperative scenario – meanwhile this is not necessarily the case when the government uses environmental standards. As an ETP provides the right incentives for firms to trigger greater efforts of R&D when they cooperate, it means that cooperative R&D investments under an ETP are higher than under an ESP. But surprisingly this R&D difference between ETP and ESP is linear and increasing with the difference in emissions as shown by Cabon-Dhersin and Raffin (2024). As soon as emissions are higher under an ETP although R&D efforts are larger, it involves that an other emission-driver variable plays a key role. In particular, the larger production levels under an ETP offset the green R&D efforts and thus entail higher polluting emissions.

Indeed, in the setup considered here, the ETP offers firms an additional degree of freedom. Under an ETP, the firms choose their R&D expenditures and their levels of production separately (which allows them to endogenise the level of emissions). If the firms choose their R&D efforts cooperatively, it turns out that production levels are (still) chosen competitively. Under an ESP, on the other hand, the firms simultaneously choose their levels of production and R&D investment, since polluting emissions are constrained. As a result, when the firms coordinate their green R&D efforts, this amounts to them choosing levels of production that maximise the sum of profits. Eventually, the firms tend towards a cartel formation so that when they cooperate in R&D, they emit less than they would under an ETP, mainly because they produce less: $\bar{e}^{*,c} < \bar{e}^{*,nc}$ for relevant parameters values and $\bar{e}^{*,c} < e^{*,c}$. Consequently, both production and R&D investment are lower under an ESP, further reducing consumer surplus. Although polluting emissions are lower under an ESP, social welfare remains higher under an ETP: either $SW^{*,c} > SW^{*,nc} = S\bar{W}^{*,nc} > S\bar{W}^{*,c}$ for low γ and/or low spillover degrees; or $SW^{*,c} > S\bar{W}^{*,c} > SW^{*,nc} = S\bar{W}^{*,nc}$ for sufficiently high values of γ and high spillover degrees (see Figure 3).

Finally, profits under an equilibrium ETP are always lower compared with an equilibrium ESP. Cooperation under ESP entails cartel behaviours featured by a reduced production level and higher prices, which both allow for higher profits. At the same time, despite larger production and R&D levels, the firms suffer from the burden tax as well as convex R&D costs that are squeezing profits under an ETP.

6. Conclusion

In this chapter, we have demonstrated that coordinated efforts in green R&D consistently foster innovation and yield a greater consumer surplus compared to R&D competition, provided that a tax is implemented. Conversely, this expected positive impact of R&D cooperation does not always hold true when an emission standard is in place. It is also crucial to highlight that when firms engage in cooperative R&D, the tax outperforms the emission standard in terms of fostering innovation, enhancing consumer surplus, and contributing to overall social welfare. However, an optimal emission standard policy proves to be more environmentally beneficial. This is so because this policy instrument leads to a reduced level of production and subsequent lower emission levels. Consequently, our findings underscore significant distinctions between the two regulatory instruments when firms collaborate in green R&D.

In terms of public policy recommendations, regulators are confronted with a trade-off. They must choose between adopting an ESP if their primary concern is environmental protection or an ETP if their focus is predominantly on economic considerations, even though the latter may have adverse effects on firms' profitability. In Cabon-Dhersin and Raffin (2024), a deeper analysis is offered when the regulator's selection of the instrument becomes endogenous. They show that an ETP is a better choice when firms cooperate in green R&D, albeit with a focus solely on economic performance.

Appendix A. Equilibrium results

Table A.1. Equilibrium outcomes under ETP.

	Non-cooperative R&D	Cooperative R&D
q	$\frac{2d(1+\beta)(3(1+\beta)+\gamma)+\gamma(3+\gamma)}{X}A$	$\frac{(2d(1+\beta)^2+\gamma)(3(1+\beta)^2+\gamma)}{Y}A$
z	$\frac{2d(3(1+\beta)+\gamma)-\gamma}{X}A$	$(1+\beta)\frac{2d(3(1+\beta)^2+\gamma)-\gamma}{Y}A$
E	$2\gamma\frac{4+\beta+\gamma}{X}A$	$2\gamma\frac{4(1+\beta)^2+\gamma}{Y}A$
SW	$\frac{2d\left(4(1+\beta)^2+\gamma(2\beta+1)\right)+4\gamma+\gamma^2}{X}A^2$	$\frac{(2d(1+\beta)^2+\gamma)\left(4(1+\beta)^2+\gamma\right)}{Y}A^2$

$X = 2d(3(1+\beta)+\gamma)^2+\gamma(9+2\gamma), \quad Y = 2d(3(1+\beta)^2+\gamma)^2+\gamma(9(1+\beta)^2+2\gamma)$

Table A.2. Equilibrium outcomes under ESP.

	Non-cooperative R&D	Cooperative R&D
q	$\frac{2d(1+\beta)(3(1+\beta)+\gamma)+\gamma(3+\gamma)}{X}A$	$\frac{(2d(1+\beta)^2+\gamma)(4(1+\beta)^2+\gamma)}{W}A$
z	$\frac{2d(3(1+\beta)+\gamma)-\gamma}{X}A$	$(1+\beta)\frac{2d(4(1+\beta)^2+\gamma)-2\gamma}{W}A$
E	$2\gamma\frac{4+\beta+\gamma}{X}A$	$2\gamma\frac{(6(1+\beta)^2+\gamma)}{W}A$
SW	$\frac{2d\left(4(1+\beta)^2+\gamma(2\beta+1)\right)+4\gamma+\gamma^2}{X}A^2$	$\frac{(2d(1+\beta)^2+\gamma)\left(6(1+\beta)^2+\gamma\right)}{W}A^2$

$X=2d(3(1+\beta)+\gamma)^2+\gamma(9+2\gamma)$, $W=2d(4(1+\beta)^2+\gamma)^2+2\gamma(8(1+\beta)^2+\gamma)$

Appendix B. Proof of Lemma 2

Let us define $\mathcal{X}^{*,h}=\{\bar{z}^{*,h},\bar{CS}^{*,h},\bar{SW}^{*,h}\}\ \forall h=\{nc,c\}$. Using equilibrium outcomes in Table A.2, the difference $\mathcal{X}^{*,nc}-\mathcal{X}^{*,c}$ can be expressed as a polynomial in d of degree 2. When $\gamma<4$, it is easy to see that $\mathcal{X}^{*,nc}-\mathcal{X}^{*,c}>0$ always. For $\gamma\geq 4$ and $\forall\,\beta\in(0,1]$, the unique positive root solution of this polynomial in d is given by:

$$d_{\mathcal{X}}(\beta,\gamma)=\frac{N_{\mathcal{X}}}{\beta\gamma-(1+\beta)^2}\quad\text{with } N_{\mathcal{X}}>0$$

Indeed, we also have $N_{\bar{z}}=\frac{2(1+\beta)^3(7-8\beta)\gamma+(1+\beta)(9+4\beta(1-2\beta)\gamma^2+\gamma^3-\sqrt{\Delta_{\bar{z}}}}{4(3(1+\beta)+\gamma)(4(1+\beta)^2+\gamma)}$, with $\Delta_{\bar{z}}=\gamma^2(4(1+\beta)^6(5+8\beta)^2+4(1+\beta)^4(25+4\beta(3+2\beta(-33+8\beta)))\gamma+(1+\beta)^2(45+4\beta(19+4\beta(-9+2\beta)(3+2\beta)))\gamma^2+2(1+\beta)(1+4\beta)(5+4\beta+8\beta^2)\gamma^3+(1+4\beta)^2\gamma^4)$; $N_{\bar{SC}}=\frac{24(1+\beta)^4\gamma+4(1+\beta)^2(3+2\beta(1+\beta))\gamma^2+(1+2\beta^2)\gamma^3+\sqrt{\Delta_{\bar{SC}}}}{(4(1+\beta)(3+3\beta+\gamma)(4(1+\beta)^2+\gamma)}$, with $\Delta_{\bar{SC}}=(\gamma^4(4(1+\beta)^4(1+16\beta(3+\beta(13+\beta(6+\beta))))+4(1+\beta)^2(1+2\beta(15+4\beta(17+5\beta(3+\beta))))\gamma+(1+4\beta(1+3\beta)(5+\beta(7+3\beta)))\gamma^2)))>0$; and $N_{\bar{SW}}=\frac{10(1+\beta)^4\gamma+(1+\beta)^2(3+2\beta(1+\beta))\gamma^2-\beta\gamma^3+2\sqrt{\Delta_{\bar{SW}}}}{20(1+\beta)^4+6(1+\beta)^2(1+2\beta)\gamma+2\beta\gamma^2}$, with $\Delta_{\bar{SW}}=\beta^2(1+\beta)^2\gamma^4((1+\beta)^2(24+\beta(6+\beta))+(10+\beta(13+6\beta))\gamma+\gamma^2))$.

By the definition of $d_{\mathcal{X}}(\beta,\gamma)$, it is obvious that it admits a vertical asymptote when $\beta\to\hat{\beta}$ such that $\hat{\beta}\gamma-(1+\hat{\beta})^2\to 0$. To determine the value of $\hat{\beta}$, let us define the second degree polynomial $\mathcal{P}(\hat{\beta})$ and the corresponding discriminant $\Delta_{\hat{\beta}} = \gamma(\gamma - 4) \geq 0$ since $\gamma \geq 4$ by assumption. When $\gamma = 4$, $\hat{\beta} = 1$. When $\gamma > 4$, two roots of the Polynomial exist, but only one belongs to $(0, 1)$: $\hat{\beta} = \frac{(\gamma-2)-\sqrt{\Delta_{\hat{\beta}}}}{2}$. Then, we can define $d_{\mathcal{X}}(\beta, \gamma) \equiv \{d \geq 1 | \mathcal{X}^{*,nc} - \mathcal{X}^{*,c} = 0, \gamma \geq 4\}$ such that for $d \gtreqless d_{\mathcal{X}}$, $\mathcal{X}^{*,nc} - \mathcal{X}^{*,c} \lesseqgtr 0$.

Appendix C. Proof of Proposition 2

Using Lemma 4 and equations (7) and (14), we can express the difference between $z^{*,c}$ and $\bar{z}^{*,c}$ as follows:

$$z^{*,c} - \bar{z}^{*,c} = \frac{12d(1+\beta)^4 + (1+7d)(1+\beta)^2\gamma + (1+d)\gamma^2}{(1+\beta)(10(1+\beta)^2 + 3\gamma)} \times (e^{*,c} - \bar{e}^{*,c}) > 0$$

In addition, from equation (1), the difference between $q^{*,c}$ and $\bar{q}^{*,c}$ can be expressed:

$$q^{*,c} - \bar{q}^{*,c} = (e^{*,c} - \bar{e}^{*,c}) + (1+\beta)(z^{*,c} - \bar{z}^{*,c}) > 0$$

We deduce that:

$$CS^{*,c} - \bar{CS}^{*,c} = \frac{1}{2}((2q^{*,c})^2 - (2\bar{q}^{*,c})^2) > 0$$

and

$$SW^{*,c} - \bar{SW}^{*,c} = \left(\frac{2d(1+\beta)^2 + \gamma}{\gamma} A\right)(e^{*,c} - \bar{e}^{*,c}) > 0$$

Then we derive the profits difference $(\pi^{*,c} - \bar{\pi}^{*,c})$ from the equilibrium social welfares:

$$\begin{cases} SW^{*,c} = 2(q^{*,c})^2 + 2\pi^{*,c} + 2\tau^{*,c}e^{*,c} - 2d(e^{*,c})^2 \\ \bar{SW}^{*,c} = 2(\bar{q}^{*,c})^2 + 2\bar{\pi}^{*,c} - 2d(\bar{e}^{*,c})^2 \end{cases}$$

Hence, we obtain the equilibrium profits difference:

$$\bar{\pi}^{*,c} - \pi^{*,c} = \underbrace{\left((q^{*,c})^2 - (\bar{q}^{*,c})^2\right) - \left(\frac{2d(1+\beta)^2+\gamma}{2\gamma}A\right)(e^{*,c} - \bar{e}^{*,c})}_{\text{Term } A}$$

$$+ \underbrace{d((\bar{e}^{*,c})^2 - (e^{*,c})^2) + \tau^{*,c}e^{*,c}}_{\text{Term } B}$$

$$\text{Term } A > 0 \Leftrightarrow \frac{2(q^{*,c})^2}{(2d(1+\beta)^2+\gamma)A} - \frac{e^{*,c}}{\gamma} > \frac{2(\bar{q}^{*,c})^2}{(2d(1+\beta)^2+\gamma)A} - \frac{\bar{e}^{*,c}}{\gamma}$$

Using the equilibrium values of $e^{*,c}$ and $\bar{e}^{*,c}$, we can rewrite the inequality above as follows:

$$q^{*,c}\frac{3(1+\beta)^2+\gamma}{Y} - \frac{(4(1+\beta)^2+\gamma)A}{Y}$$
$$> \bar{q}^{*,c}\frac{4(1+\beta)^2+\gamma}{W} - \frac{(6(1+\beta)^2+\gamma)A}{W}$$

Since $W > Y$, Term $A > 0$ iff $q^{*,c}(3(1+\beta)^2+\gamma) > \bar{q}^{*,c}(4(1+\beta)^2+\gamma) \Leftrightarrow (3(1+\beta)^2+\gamma)^2 W > (4(1+\beta)^2+\gamma)^2 Y \Leftrightarrow \gamma(1+\beta)^2(10(1+\beta)^2 - 4 + 7\gamma) > 0$.

$$\text{Term } B > 0 \Leftrightarrow \tau^{*,c}e^{*,c} > d((e^{*,c})^2 - (\bar{e}^{*,c})^2)$$
$$\Leftrightarrow e^{*,c}(\tau^{*,c} - de^{*,c}) > -d(\bar{e}^{*,c})^2)$$

We have that $\tau^{*,c} - de^{*,c} = \frac{\gamma}{Y}(2d(1+\beta)^2 + d\gamma - \gamma)A > 0$, $\forall d \geq 1$. Hence, Term $B > 0$ and we deduce $\bar{\pi}^{*,c} - \pi^{*,c} > 0$, $\forall \gamma > 0$, $d \geq 1$ and $\beta \in (0, 1]$.

References

Arrow, K. (1962). Economic welfare and the allocation of resources for invention, in *The Rate and Direction of Inventive Activity: Economic and Social Factors*, pp. 609–626, Princeton University Press, Princeton, New Jersey, US.

Cabon-Dhersin, M.-L. and Raffin, N. (2024). Cooperation in green R&D and environmental policies: Tax or standard, *Journal of Regulatory Economics* **66**, 205–237.

Chiou, J.-R. and Hu, J.-L. (2001). Environmental research joint ventures under emission taxes, *Environmental and Resource Economics* **20**(2), 129–146.

d'Aspremont, C. and Jacquemin, A. (1988). Cooperative and noncooperative R&D in duopoly with spillovers, *The American Economic Review* **78**(5), 1133–1137.

Hepburn, C. (2006). Regulation by prices, quantities, or both: A review of instrument choice, *Oxford Review of Economic Policy* **22**(2), 226–247.

Kamien, M. I., Muller, E. and Zang, I. (1992). Research joint ventures and R&D cartels, *The American Economic Review* **82**(5), 1293–1306.

Marinucci, M. (2012). A primer on R&D cooperation among firms, *Bank of Italy Occasional Paper* No. 130.

Moner-Colonques, R. and Rubio, S. J. (2015). The timing of environmental policy in a duopolistic market, *Economía Agraria y Recursos Naturales-Agricultural and Resource Economics* **15**(1), 11–40.

Moner-Colonques, R. and Rubio, S. J. (2016). The strategic use of innovation to influence environmental policy: Taxes versus standards, *The B.E. Journal of Economic Analysis & Policy* **16**(2), 973–1000.

Montero, J.-P. (2002). Permits, standards, and technology innovation, *Journal of Environmental Economics and Management* **44**(1), 23–44.

Ouchida, Y. and Goto, D. (2016a). Cournot duopoly and environmental R&D under regulator's precommitment to an emissions tax, *Applied Economics Letters* **23**(5), 324–331.

Ouchida, Y. and Goto, D. (2016b). Environmental research joint ventures and time-consistent emission tax: Endogenous choice of R&D formation, *Economic Modelling* **55**, 179–188.

Ouchida, Y. and Goto, D. (2022). Strategic non-use of the government's precommitment ability for emissions taxation: Environmental R&D formation in a Cournot duopoly, *Australian Economic Papers* **61**(1), 181–206.

Poyago-Theotoky, J. A. (2007). The organization of R&D and environmental policy, *Journal of Economic Behavior & Organization* **62**(1), 63–75.

Requate, T. (2005). Dynamic incentives by environmental policy instruments—a survey, *Ecological Economics* **54**(2–3), 175–195.

Requate, T. and Unold, W. (2003). On the incentives of environmental policy to adopt advanced abatement technology: Will the true ranking please stand up? *European Economic Review* **47**(1), 125–146.

Scott, J. T. (2008). The national cooperative research and production act, *Issues in Competition Law and Policy* **2**, 1297.

https://doi.org/10.1142/9789819816033_0008

Chapter 8

Environmental Regulation with and without Commitment under Long Term Investments

Jean-Philippe Nicolaï
University of Grenoble, Grenoble INP – Génie Industriel, France
jean-philippe.nicolai@grenoble-inp.fr

This chapter analyses the effect of the government's commitment on the value of emission taxes when firms take long-term investment decisions and perceive a degree of market power in their respective output markets. In the commitment case, the government announces a long-run tax on emissions, and firms decide upon their investment levels. In the case without commitment, the regulator announces a tax level that it is free to modify once firms have made their investments. This chapter illustrates the interactions between firms' decisions and the regulator's choice, stressing the role of the strategic effects of investments. The chapter shows that when strategic effects lead firms to reduce investments, the optimal tax under commitment is higher than the no-commitment tax. Otherwise, the tax under commitment may be higher or lower than the tax without commitment.

Keywords: Emission tax, Strategic "green" investment, Committed regulator, Non committed regulator.

1. Introduction

Climate change is likely the most pressing issue challenging human society throughout the world. While addressing climate change requires implementing environmental regulations worldwide, these regulations are also conditioned on the renewal of polluting production processes. Substantial investments are required over long periods in many industrial sectors that emit large amounts of pollutants. For example, the average lifetimes of generators can exceed 30 years. Moreover, these types of investments also typically induce sunk costs. Thus, once firms have made these investments, they cannot modify them. The issue of commitment arises because environmental regulations and investment decisions are sequential.

Environmentally-friendly investments consist for instance in new plants as well as new industrial machines, which both emit less pollution. Such investments reduce the emission rate and consequently lower the effective marginal cost of production (the sum of the marginal cost of production and the tax). However, environmental regulation ordinarily covers oligopolistic sectors such as steel, cement and electricity. Hence, environmentally friendly investment alters competition among firms modifying the marginal costs and in turn the strategies of firms. While deciding the level of environmentally friendly investment, firms take into account these strategic effects, i.e., how investment alters rivals' reaction. Such strategic effects lead to a non-optimal level of investment.

This chapter examines the interactions between firms' decisions and the regulator's choice by stressing the role of the strategic effects of investments. In the context of firms making irreversible investment decisions and imperfect competition, the chapter aims to determine whether a regulator who modifies the tax on emissions after firms have invested implements more lenient or more stringent regulations, which is a crucial issue for redistributive matters. More lenient regulations ordinarily induce a decrease in the regulator's revenue and an increase in consumer surplus. It is also important to determine whether compliance costs increase or decrease with a change in regulation to determine how firms' profitability is affected.

The chapter compares two different scenarios under which environmental policies are implemented, i.e., under commitment and without commitment. The differences in these scenarios relate to the regulator's behaviour. Under commitment, the regulator commits herself ex ante to a certain level of tax. Without commitment regulation, the regulator first announces the level of the tax, and firms invest for the long term, but the regulator may decide to change the level of taxation after investments have been made. As we focus on unexpected policy changes, we first assume that firms are myopic and do not consider the possibility of changing the regulation. We relax latter this assumption. In addition, this chapter considers differentiated goods. Moreover, it is assumed that the regulator has no direct investment policy instruments at her disposal (neither command-and-control instruments nor subsidies for investment) and only uses an emission tax. The regulator maximises its social welfare function while accounting for environmental damage.

To determine whether a time-inconsistent regulator implements more lenient or more stringent regulations, we compare the tax without commitment and the tax under commitment. We show that when strategic effects lead firms to reduce investments, the optimal tax under commitment is higher than the no-commitment tax. Otherwise, the tax under commitment may be higher or lower than the tax without commitment. However, when firms are also strategic towards the regulator there is an additional effect which pushes the regulator to decrease the tax under commitment. Indeed, when firms are strategic towards the regulator, they over-invest in order to decrease the level of tax. Therefore, under commitment the regulator corrects the two distortions on the level of investment: both coming from strategic behaviours, one relative to the other firms and the second one relative to the regulator.

This chapter contributes to the literature that compares commitment and no-commitment environmental regulation. Since Laffont and Tirole (1996) demonstrated that no-commitment environmental regulation is socially preferable, an ongoing debate has been engaged regarding the advantages of an environmental regulator moving first (Requate (2005) surveys this debate). Numerous papers have discussed this comparison but the following remarks emphasise the contribution of this chapter.

First, most papers have studied the impact of commitment to environmental regulations under technology adoption and perfect competition in the product market (Laffont and Tirole, 1996; Requate and Unold, 2001, 2003; Amacher and Malik, 2002; Petrakis and Xepapadeas, 1999; Golombek *et al.*, 2010). These papers assume that a sector innovates and sells a clean technology to firms. Firms decide whether they adopt or not this new technology. Said differently, the literature has mainly focused on technology adoption and not on irreversible investments, as we do. Technology adoption and irreversible investment do not involve the same actors and these two contexts are not comparable. Second, quite all the papers of this strand of literature have analysed the role of commitment from a social welfare perspective – except for Golombek *et al.* (2010). To our best knowledge, the latter is the only paper that compares the commitment and no-commitment tax, in the context of technology adoption. They show that the comparison between the two taxes depends on the value of the subsidies to innovate.

Three papers analyse the role of commitment focusing on irreversible investment and imperfect competition. Gersbach and Glazer (1999) focus on the implementation of pollution permits and assume that firms are price-makers in the market for permits. Gersbach and Glazer (1999) show, that the regulator may have incentive to modify policies after firms have made irreversible investments. They propose a mechanism of permit allocation that prevents the regulator from being time-inconsistent. Our concern is different. While they analyse how to prevent the regulator to be time-inconsistent, we determine whether a time-inconsistent regulator implements a more lenient or a more stringent regulation once firms have invested. Our chapter is then complementary to Gersbach and Glazer (1999); Petrakis *et al.* (2001) and Puller (2006) analyse the introduction of a tax and a standard, respectively, considering a quadratic environmental damage function. They show that ex-post regulation may be preferable. However, in this chapter, linear damages are assumed.

The remainder of the chapter is structured as follows. Section 2 presents the modelling assumptions. In Section 3, the regulations with commitment and without commitment are described and compared. In Section 4, firms are assumed to be strategic towards the regulator. Section 5 concludes.

2. A Simple Model of Environmental Regulation and Investment

2.1. *The set-up*

We assume that n firms produce differentiated goods and consumers choose among these n goods. All firms have the same constant marginal cost, denoted as c. Let p_i and q_i be the price and production, respectively, of firm i. The relation between p_i and q_i is given by $\frac{\partial p_i}{\partial q_i} < 0$. Moreover, $S(q_1, q_2, \ldots, q_n)$ denotes the gross surplus from consuming n goods in quantities denoted as q_1, q_2, ..., and q_n. By definition, the marginal gross surplus is given by $\frac{\partial S}{\partial q_i} = p_i$.

Production involves pollution. Let α_i be the emission rate associated with the production technology of firm i. Thus, one unit of product generates α_i units of pollution. However, assume that irreversible investment alters the production process and lowers the emission rate: $\alpha_i(y_i) = \overline{\alpha} - y_i$, where $\overline{\alpha}$ is the initial emission rate and y_i constitutes the irreversible investment of firm i. The cost of irreversible investment is denoted by $C(y_i)$ with $C' > 0$. Notably, we employ a two-stage game to model irreversible investment (building a cleaner plant). As Tirole explains (1988, chapter 5), this two-stage game formalises the assumption that investment decisions are generally made prior to price or production decisions. In other words, investment decisions are long- or medium-run choices, whereas prices and production decisions are fairly flexible.

The regulator implements an emission tax to curb pollution. Let E be total emissions, and let τ be the level of the tax. First, we focus on a single sector and then relax this assumption in Section 4. We consider a linear damage function, and the marginal damage is denoted by λ. There is no shadow cost of public funds. This chapter addresses two externalities (market power and emissions). Therefore, we consider a social welfare function, which we assume is defined as follows:

$$W = CS + \Sigma_1^n \pi_i - \lambda E + \tau E \tag{1}$$

where π denotes firm profits, CS represents the net consumer surplus, λE is environmental damage and $E\tau$ the tax revenue. The net consumer surplus corresponds to the gross surplus minus the expenses and profits equal sales minus costs. Hence, the net consumer surplus plus the profits are equal to the gross surplus minus the firms' costs.

With commitment and without commitment, the two different types of regulations considered in this chapter, are denoted by C and NC, respectively. Each type of regulation is defined by a specific sequence of decisions. Under commitment, the regulator commits to the level of tax. This commitment allows firms to plan their long-term investments by considering the future emission tax decided by the regulator. Regulation with commitment is thus characterised by the following timing:

- **Stage 1:** The regulator sets the tax τ^C and announces it.
- **Stage 2:** Firms make investment choices.
- **Stage 3:** Firms choose production levels.

In the case without commitment, firms invest in the long term, trusting what the regulator has announced in stage 1. We assume then that firms are myopic.

The timing of regulation without commitment is as follows:

- **Stage 1:** The regulator sets the tax τ_1^{NC} and announces it.
- **Stage 2:** Firms make investment choices.
- **Stage 3:** After firms have invested, the regulator may decide to modify the tax by announcing τ_3^{NC}.
- **Stage 4:** Firms choose production levels.

Because firms are myopic relative to the regulator, firms' investment and production decisions are the same in the two timings. Moreover, if $\tau_1^{NC} \neq \tau_3^{NC}$, the regulator is time-inconsistent.

To highlight the role of strategic effects in optimal environmental regulation, we first examine how investment might alter competition. First, we focus on the last stage of each scenario.

Firm i's profits are equal to:

$$\pi_i = (p_i - c)q_i - \tau(\overline{\alpha} - y_i)q_i - C(y_i) \tag{2}$$

Firm i sells its product, pays its production costs and emission taxes and also bears an investment cost.

PRODUCTION STAGE. Optimal production decisions satisfy the following:

$$p_i + q_i \frac{\partial p_i}{\partial q_i} = c + (\bar{\alpha} - y_i)\tau \tag{3}$$

INVESTMENT STAGE. The optimal investment satisfies:

$$q_i \Sigma_{j=1}^{n-1} \underbrace{\frac{\partial p_i}{\partial q_j}}_{-} \underbrace{\frac{\partial q_j}{\partial y_i}}_{+/-} + q_i \tau = C'(y_i) \tag{4}$$

Investment decisions clearly depend on production but are also based on the strategic effects of investment.

Consider for a moment the case of perfect competition in which firms are price-takers in the market for products. Thus, firms do not consider how investment modifies competition because they take product prices as exogenous. Thus, the variation in firm i's revenue relative to an increase of irreversible investment is null under perfect competition, i.e., $\Sigma_{j=1}^{n-1} \frac{\partial p_i}{\partial q_j} \frac{\partial q_j}{\partial y_i} = 0$.[1]

If the marginal revenue due to investment is negative ($\Sigma_{j=1}^{n-1} \frac{\partial p_i}{\partial q_j} \frac{\partial q_j}{\partial y_i} < 0$), then strategic effects lead firms to reduce investments relative to perfect competition. Otherwise, the strategic effects lead firms to increase their investments relative to perfect competition.

Let us discuss the sign of the strategic effects. When firms invest, they decrease the effective marginal cost of production and thereby increase their own production. The effect on the rival's best response depends on whether the productions are strategic substitutes or complements. For instance, if demand is linear, quantities are then strategic substitutes, i.e., $\frac{\partial q_j}{\partial q_i} < 0$. In such a case, the marginal revenue due to investment is positive. When demand is nonlinear, the situation may become more complex. Notice that the sign of strategic effects is straightforward if and only if demand is linear.

[1]It should also be noted that if firms do not behave strategically, they do not consider the strategic interactions in the market for products and $\Sigma_{j=1}^{n-1} \frac{\partial p_i}{\partial q_j} \frac{\partial q_j}{\partial y_i} = 0$. This issue may then be formulated as a comparison involving an open loop and a closed loop. See Vives (1999).

3. With and without Commitment

This section compares commitment and no-commitment taxation and solves for the resulting investment decisions, tax and welfare levels. The pollution is equal to $E = \Sigma_{i=1}^{n}(\bar{\alpha} - y_i)q_i$. We then rewrite welfare as a function of the equilibrium production quantities, which are denoted by q_i, and the following investments:

$$W(\tau, y_1, \ldots, y_n) = S(q_1, q_2, \ldots, q_n) - \Sigma_{i=1}^{n}\left(q_i^* c + C(y_i)\right) - \lambda\left[\Sigma_1^n(\bar{\alpha} - y_i)q_i^*\right] \quad (5)$$

The equilibrium production quantities clearly depend on the tax.

In the commitment case, the regulator fixes the tax prior to firms making their investments and then reduces three distortions: environmental damage, under-production and under-investment. In the case without commitment, the regulator reduces two distortions: environmental damage and under-production. We start by analysing the case without commitment.

THE THIRD STAGE OF TIMING WITHOUT COMMITMENT. In the case without commitment, the optimal tax satisfies the following equation:

$$\frac{\partial W^{NC}}{\partial \tau_3} = \Sigma_{i=1}^{n}\left(\frac{\partial S}{\partial q_i} - \lambda\alpha y_i - c\right)\frac{\partial q_i}{\partial \tau_3} = 0 \quad (6)$$

By definition $\frac{\partial S}{\partial q_i} = p_i$, thus we rewrite equation (6) as follows:

$$\frac{\partial W^{NC}(\tau_3, y^C)}{\partial \tau_3} = \Sigma_{i=1}^{n}\left(p_i - \lambda\alpha y^C - c\right)\frac{\partial q_i}{\partial \tau_3} = 0 \quad (7)$$

From equation (3), we know that $p_i = c + (\bar{\alpha} - y_i)\tau_3 - q_i\frac{\partial p_i}{\partial q_i}$. Thus, equation (7) may be rewritten as follows:

$$\frac{\partial W^{NC}}{\partial \tau_3} = \Sigma_{i=1}^{n}\left((\tau_3 - \lambda)(\bar{\alpha} - y_i) - q_i\frac{\partial p_i}{\partial q_i}\right)\frac{\partial q_i}{\partial \tau_3} = 0 \quad (8)$$

Next, we deduce the optimal emission tax, which is given by:

$$\tau_3^{NC} = \lambda + \frac{\Sigma_{i=1}^{n} q_i \frac{\partial p_i}{\partial q_i}\frac{\partial q_i}{\partial \tau_3}}{\Sigma_{i=1}^{n}(\bar{\alpha} - y_i)\frac{\partial q_i}{\partial \tau_3}} \quad (9)$$

Since $\frac{\partial p_i}{\partial q_i} < 0$ and $\frac{\partial q_i}{\partial \tau} < 0$, the no-commitment tax is lower than the marginal damage, i.e., $\tau_3^{NC} < \lambda$. This result is well known in the literature since Barnett (1980). On one hand, the regulator reduces pollution and, on the other hand, it increases production and reduces under-production.

The second stage has already been analysed. Since firms are myopic, the investment stage can be analysed independently. We focus now on the first stage.

THE FIRST STAGE OF TIMING WITHOUT COMMITMENT. The regulator in the no-commitment case maximises welfare by fixing the tax. The optimal emission tax is given by:

$$\begin{aligned}\frac{\partial W^{NC}(\tau_1,\tau_3,y)}{\partial \tau_1} &= \frac{\partial W(\tau,y)}{\partial q_i}\left(\frac{\partial q_i}{\partial \tau_1}+\frac{\partial q_i}{\partial y_i}\frac{\partial y_i}{\partial \sigma_1}+\frac{\partial q_i}{\partial \tau_3}\frac{\partial \tau_3}{\partial \tau_1}\right)\\ &\quad+\frac{\partial W}{\partial y_i}\frac{\partial y_i}{\partial \tau_1}+\frac{\partial W}{\partial \tau_3}\frac{\partial \tau_3}{\partial \tau_1}=0 \qquad (10)\end{aligned}$$

The following lemma determines whether the regulator fixes at the third stage a level of emission tax different or not from the level before the investment decisions.

Lemma 1. *The regulator has incentive to modify the emission tax once firms have invested.*

Proof. The optimal tax is defined such that,

$$\tau_3^{NC}(y^{NC}) = argmax W(\tau, y^{NC})$$

We conclude then that,

$$W^{NC}(\tau_1^{NC}, y^{NC}) \leq W^{NC}(\tau_3^{NC}(y^{NC}), y^{NC}) \qquad \square$$

The regulator has incentive to change the emission tax after firms have invested. Thus the regulator is time-inconsistent. Let first present the case under commitment and latter we will compare τ_1^{NC} and τ_3^{NC}.

THE FIRST STAGE OF TIMING UNDER COMMITMENT. The regulator in the commitment case maximises welfare by fixing the tax. The optimal emission tax is given by:

$$\frac{\partial W^{C}(\tau,y)}{\partial \tau} = \frac{\partial W(\tau,y)}{\partial q_i}\left(\frac{\partial q_i}{\partial \tau}+\frac{\partial q_i}{\partial y_i}\frac{\partial y_i}{\partial \tau}\right)+\frac{\partial W}{\partial y_i}\frac{\partial y_i}{\partial \tau}=0 \qquad (11)$$

To determine whether an inconsistent regulator implements more lenient or more stringent regulations, we compare the tax without commitment and the tax under commitment. In so doing, we focus on the sign of $\frac{\partial W^C(\tau,y)}{\partial \tau}|_{\tau^C=\tau_3^{NC}}$. If it is positive, it means that the tax under commitment is higher than the tax without commitment. Otherwise, the tax under commitment is lower than the tax without commitment.

Equation (11) may be divided into two parts: (i) the effect of the tax on output, and (ii) the effect of the tax on investment. When the regulator implements the no-commitment tax in the commitment case, the first part of equation (11) is null. Indeed, the no-commitment tax is such that $\frac{\partial W}{\partial q_i}\frac{\partial q_i}{\partial \tau} = 0$. However, because $\frac{\partial q_i}{\partial \tau}$ is obviously non-null, we deduce that it implies that $\frac{\partial W}{\partial q_i} = 0$.

Let us then focus on the effects of a variation in investment on welfare.

$$\frac{\partial W(\tau,y)}{\partial y} = \Sigma_1^n \left(\frac{\partial S}{\partial q_i} - \lambda\alpha_i - c\right)\frac{\partial q_i}{\partial y} + \lambda\Sigma_1^n q_n^* - nC'(y) = 0 \quad (12)$$

By using the envelope theorem and fixing the tax at the no-commitment tax level after investment, equation (12) may be rewritten as:

$$\left.\frac{\partial W}{\partial y}\right|_{\tau^C=\tau_3^{NC}} = \lambda q_i - C'(y) \quad (13)$$

We then deduce that,

$$\left.\frac{\partial W^C(\tau,y)}{\partial \tau}\right|_{\tau^C=\tau_3^{NC}} = \lambda q_i - C'(y) \quad (14)$$

Plugging in equation (4), the previous equation may be rewritten as follows:

$$\left.\frac{\partial W^C(\tau,y)}{\partial \tau}\right|_{\tau^C=\tau_3^{NC}} = \underbrace{\left(\lambda - \tau_3^{NC}\right)}_{(+)} q_i - \underbrace{\Sigma_{j=1}^{n-1}\frac{\partial p_i}{\partial q_j}\frac{\partial q_j}{\partial y_i}}_{(+/-)} \quad (15)$$

The following proposition compares the two optimal taxes.

Proposition 1. *The relative magnitudes of the tax under commitment and the tax without commitment depends on the strategic effects*:

(i) *If strategic effects lead firms to reduce investments* ($\Sigma_{j=1}^{n-1}\frac{\partial p_i}{\partial q_j}\frac{\partial q_j}{\partial y_i} < 0$), *then the tax under commitment is higher than the tax without commitment.*

(ii) *If strategic effects lead firms to increase investments* ($\Sigma_{j=1}^{n-1}\frac{\partial p_i}{\partial q_j}\frac{\partial q_j}{\partial y_i} > 0$), *then the tax under commitment may be higher or lower than the tax without commitment.*

Two effects are at stake. First, the regulator has incentive to increase the tax because the no-commitment tax leads to under-investment. Second, strategic effects encourage firms to invest in ways that are sub-optimal. If the strategic effects lead firms to invest less than they would when not behaving strategically, then the two effects are in the same direction, and the tax under commitment is thus higher than the no-commitment tax. However, if the strategic effects lead firms to invest more than they would when not behaving strategically, then the two effects move in opposite directions; either effect can prevail and the tax under commitment may be either higher or lower than the no-commitment tax.

Turning back to the case without commitment, we compare the emission taxes before and after firms invest. The following corollary determines the relationship between the relative magnitudes of tax under commitment and the tax without commitment and the relative magnitudes of the no commitment emission taxes before and after investment.

Corollary 1. *The relative magnitudes of taxes, without commitment, before and after investment are the same as the relative magnitudes of tax under commitment and the tax without commitment.*

Proof. Using the same method as in the proof of Proposition 1 and the envelope theorem, we show that

$$\left.\frac{\partial W^{NC}(\tau_1,\tau_3,y)}{\partial \tau_1}\right|_{\tau_1^{NC}=\tau_3^{NC}} = (\lambda-\tau_3^{NC})q_i - \Sigma_{j=1}^{n-1}\frac{\partial p_i}{\partial q_j}\frac{\partial q_j}{\partial y_i} \tag{16}$$

□

As in the commitment case, if the strategic effects lead firms to invest less than they would when not behaving strategically, then the two effects are in the same direction, and the no-commitment tax before investment (τ_1^{NC}) is thus higher than the no-commitment tax after investment (τ_3^{NC}). Otherwise, the two effects move in opposite directions; either effect can prevail and the no-commitment tax before investment may be either higher or lower than the no-commitment tax after investment.

4. Strategic Firms towards the Regulator

We consider now that firms are strategic and anticipate without commitment that the regulator may modify its environmental policy. Since the timing with commitment is not affected by this assumption, we focus on the case without commitment.

The timing of regulation without commitment is as follows:

- **Stage 1:** The regulator sets the tax τ_1^S and announces it.
- **Stage 2:** Firms make investment choices.
- **Stage 3:** After firms have invested, the regulator may decide to modify the tax by announcing τ_3^S.
- **Stage 4:** Firms choose production levels.

The two last stages are unchanged compared to the case with myopia and on stage 3 the optimal tax is given by:

$$\tau_3^S = \lambda + \frac{\Sigma_{i=1}^n q_i \frac{\partial p_i}{\partial q_i} \frac{\partial q_i}{\partial \tau_3}}{\Sigma_{i=1}^n (\bar{\alpha} - y_i) \frac{\partial q_i}{\partial \tau_3}} \tag{17}$$

The optimal tax decreases with investment and we focus then on the investment stage.

Investment stage. Firm i's profits are equal to:

$$\pi_i = (p_i - c)q_i - \tau(\overline{\alpha} - y_i)q_i - C(y_i) \tag{18}$$

The first-order condition with respect to investment satisfies:

$$q_i \Sigma_{j=1}^{n-1} \frac{\partial p_i}{\partial q_j} \frac{\partial q_j}{\partial y_i} + q_i \tau_3^S - (\overline{\alpha} - y_i) q_i \frac{\partial \tau_3^S}{\partial y_i} = C'(y_i) \tag{19}$$

In such a case, firms invest more than when they are myopic. With respect to the case in Section 2, firms invest also to make the emission tax decrease.

As previously, we compare the tax without commitment and the tax under commitment. The timing under commitment is not affected by relaxing the assumption of myopia. Therefore, we focus on the sign of $\frac{\partial W^C(\tau,y)}{\partial \tau}|_{\tau^C=\tau_3^S}$, which is given by:

$$\left.\frac{\partial W^C(\tau, y)}{\partial \tau}\right|_{\tau^C=\tau_3^S} = \left.\frac{\partial W^C}{\partial y_i}\frac{\partial y_i}{\partial \tau}\right|_{\tau^C=\tau_3^S} = \lambda q_i - C'(y) \tag{20}$$

Plugging in equation (19), the previous equation may be rewritten as follows:

$$\left.\frac{\partial W^C(\tau, y)}{\partial \tau}\right|_{\tau^C=\tau_3^S} = \underbrace{(\lambda - \tau_3^S)}_{(+)} q_i - \underbrace{\Sigma_{j=1}^{n-1}\frac{\partial p_i}{\partial q_j}\frac{\partial q_j}{\partial y_i}}_{(+/-)} + \underbrace{(\overline{\alpha} - y_i)q_i\frac{\partial \tau_3^S}{\partial y_i}}_{(-)} \tag{21}$$

Three effects are now at stake. First, the regulator has incentive to increase the tax because the no-commitment tax leads to under-investment. Second, strategic effects may encourage firms either to over-invest or under-invest. Third, firms are strategic towards the regulator and over-invest in order to make the emission tax decrease. The following proposition compares the two optimal taxes.

Proposition 2. *The likelihood that the tax under commitment is higher than the tax without commitment is lower when firms are strategic towards the regulator relative to the case with myopia.*

Comparing the tax under commitment and the tax without commitment depends on the distortion in the investment level, which comes from the two previous effects and this latter effect that pushes firms to invest more. This effect moves in the same direction as when strategic effects lead firms to increase investments. To conclude, even if the strategic effects lead firms to reduce investments, the tax under commitment may be lower than the tax without commitment.

5. Discussion and Concluding Remarks

This chapter demonstrates the role of imperfect competition in defining taxes on emissions for upcoming periods. Comparing the taxation levels of tax for the two types of regulation (i.e., with and without commitment) depends on whether the strategic effects lead firms to reduce or increase their investments. To conclude, the sign of strategic effects is crucial to determining whether a lack of commitment induces an increase or a decrease in stringency.

The chapter focuses on the implementation of a tax on emissions. If the regulator implements pollution permits, our results are the same under the assumption of myopia. However, relaxing myopia, the main difference is in the case of commitment. If firms are strategic towards the regulator, they may influence the permit price once the regulator has decided the total pollution cap. Therefore, introducing such an assumption may be a promising extension.This chapter has also not considered the existence of reversible abatement technologies. Reversible abatement is defined as a decision to reduce emissions made simultaneously with price or production decisions. As abatement and production decisions are simultaneous, there is no strategic effect. Thus, the introduction of abatement technologies does not alter our results. Moreover, we have assumed that firms compete in quantities. If we consider price competition, our results hold and the comparison between the level of taxes with and without commitment depend on whether the strategic effects push firms to over-invest or to under-invest.

This result is particularly relevant because it allows us to determine which scenario harms the most firms and consumers. Ordinarily, profits decrease as the tax rises. In this case, firms are less harmed under commitment, when the strategic effects lead firms to reduce investment. Indeed, the tax under commitment is then higher than the tax without commitment. However, profits may increase with the introduction of an environmental regulation. This phenomenon results from the characteristics of demand and abatement technologies (see Seade (1985) or Meunier and Nicolai (2014)). If profits increase with environmental regulation, then firms benefit more from the commitment when strategic effects lead firms to increase investments. Nevertheless, the consumer surplus always decreases with the emission tax. Thus, consumers are less affected by the type of regulation that leads to the lowest emission tax.

References

Amacher, G. S. and Malik, A. S. (2002). Pollution taxes when firms choose technologies, *Southern Economic Journal* **68**(4), 891–906.

Barnett, A. H. (1980). The Pigouvian tax rule under monopoly, *American Economic Review* **70**, 1037–1041.

Gersbach, H. and Glazer, A. (1999). Markets and regulatory hold-up problems, *Journal of Environmental Economics and Management* **37**(2), 151–164.

Golombek, R., Greaker, M. and Hoel, M. (2010). Carbon taxes and innovation without commitment, *The B.E. Journal of Economic Analysis & Policy* **10**(1).

Laffont, J. J. and Tirole, J. (1996). Pollution permits and compliance strategies, *Journal of Public Economics* **62**, 85–125.

Meunier, G. and Nicolai, J. P. (2014). Higher costs for higher profits: A general assessment and an application to environmental regulations, Economic working paper, CER-ETH–Center of Economic Research at ETH Zurich, http://www.cer.ethz.ch/research/WP-14-191.pdf.

Petrakis, E. and Xepapadeas, A. (1999). Does government precommitment promote environmental innovation? in E. Petrakis, E. Sartzetakis and A. Xepapadeas. (Eds.), *Environmental regulation and market power*, pp. 145–161, Edward Elgar Publishing, Cheltenham, UK.

Petrakis, E., Xepapadeas, A. *et al.* (2001). To commit or not to commit: Environmental policy in imperfectly competitive markets, *Typescript, Department of Economics, University of Crete*, https://ideas.repec.org/p/crt/wpaper/0110.html.

Puller, S. L. (2006). The strategic use of innovation to influence regulatory standards, *Journal of Environmental Economics and Management* **52**(3), 690–706.

Requate, T. (2005). Dynamic incentives by environmental policy instruments—a survey, *Ecological Economics* **54**(2–3), 175–195.

Requate, T. and Unold, W. (2001). On the incentives created by policy instruments to adopt advanced abatement technology if firms are asymmetric, *Journal of Institutional and Theoretical Economics* **157**(4), 536–554.

Requate, T. and Unold, W. (2003). On the incentives of environmental policy to adopt advanced abatement technology: Will the true ranking please stand up? *European Economic Review* **47**(1), 125–146.

Seade, J. (1985). Profitable cost increases and the shifting of taxation, Working Paper 260, University of Warwick, Warwick Economic Research Papers.

Vives, X. (1999). *Oligopoly Pricing: Old Ideas and New Tools*, MIT Press, Cambridge, Mass., US.

https://doi.org/10.1142/9789819816033_bmatter

Index

R

S

T

V

W

www.ingramcontent.com/pod-product-compliance
Lightning Source LLC
LaVergne TN
LVHW010336220926
848484LV00004BB/906

9789819816026